*Women's Voices on Africa*

# WOMEN'S VOICES ON AFRICA

## A Century of Travel Writings

PATRICIA W. ROMERO
EDITOR

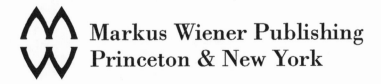 Markus Wiener Publishing
Princeton & New York

© 1992 COPYRIGHT BY PATRICIA W. ROMERO
FOR INFORMATION WRITE TO:
MARKUS WIENER PUBLISHING INC.
114 JEFFERSON ROAD, PRINCETON, NJ 08540

LIBRARY OF CONGRESS CATALOGING-IN-PUBLICATION DATA

WOMEN'S VOICES ON AFRICA:
A CENTURY OF TRAVEL WRITINGS/
PATRICIA W. ROMERO, ED.— (TOPICS IN WORLD HISTORY)
INCLUDES BIBLIOGRAPHICAL REFERENCES AND INDEX.
ISBN 1-55876-047-4 (HC): — ISBN 1-55876-048-2 (PB)
1. AFRICA—DESCRIPTION AND TRAVEL—TO 1900.
2. AFRICA—DESCRIPTION AND TRAVEL 1901-1950
3. WOMEN TRAVELERS—AFRICA-BIOGRAPHY.  4. BRITISH—
AFRICA—BIOGRAPHY.  5. BRITISH—TRAVEL-AFRICA-HISTORY-
19TH CENTURY.  6. TRAVEL IN LITERATURE.
7. ENGLISH PROSE LITERATURE—WOMEN AUTHORS—HISTORY AND CRITICISM.
8. ENGLISH PROSE LITERATURE—19TH CENTURY—HISTORY AND CRITICISM.
I. SERIES
DT11.W67  1992
916.804'4—DC20        90-36228 CIP

THIS BOOK HAS BEEN COMPOSED IN TIMES TYPEFACE

PRINTED IN THE UNITED STATES OF AMERICA BY PRINCETON UNIVERSITY PRESS
ON ACID-FREE PAPER

# DEDICATION

TO MITY CLARKE GANN, my friend and mentor over the years; the liveliest and most generous of women, now entering her eighty-third year of life and just beginning.

# CONTENTS

# ACKNOWLEDGEMENTS

No book ever comes to publication without the input of many behind the scenes contributors. I would like to thank Dr. Robert Baldock of Yale University Press, for putting me on the track of Her Highness, the Princess Marie Louise. To Edward Rodwell, I owe gratitude for bringing Katherine Fannin to my attention and for lending me his original copies of the Kenya *Post*. Again, I turn to Edward Rodwell and his wife, Olivia, for introducing me to the American adventurer, May French Sheldon. Professors B. Marie Perinbam and Robert O. Collins read and commented on the entire manuscript. Rowan Lindley read and criticized the introduction. Thanks to all three of them for their input.

My appreciation also goes to the Towson State University Interlibrary Loan Department for yeoman service in obtaining several original editions of these books for me. During a research trip to England in January, 1989, Professor Richard Rathbone was most encouraging and helpful. In England also Allen Lodge, Rhodes House, Oxford, was most generous with his time and his aid, as was Jean Woods of the Christian Missionary Society Library in London.

I am grateful to Towson State University Faculty Research Committee for release time to prepare parts of this volume. The Faculty Development Committee provided funding that enabled me to stop in England enroute from Africa in 1989. Thanks, too, to my colleagues at the History Seminar for their helpful suggestions and criticisms on an earlier draft of the general introduction.

The publisher is grateful to Africana Publishers for permission to extract from Margery Perham, *African Apprenticeship: An Autobiographical Journey in Southern Africa,* 1974.

Note: some modern spellings differ from those used in the text. The general and section introductions refer to the modern names while the archaic spellings used by the authors at the time they wrote remain in the excerpts from their works. The inconsistencies, too, between spellings that reflect the same places or names are due to the original usage employed by the authors.

# INTRODUCTION

"It is customary to ridicule the traveller who passes rapidly through a country, and then writes his impression of it. The truth is he sees much that is hidden forever from the eyes of the inhabitants. Habit and custom have blinded them. . . ." Olive Shreiner[1]

When westerners think of nineteenth-century Africa, the personalities who usually come to mind are the "great explorers" who "conquered" the "unknown" on the "Dark Continent." Or they recall those who led the wars of conquest that left Europe in control of most of the continent by 1900. The texts included in this book are unusual in that they represent the voices of women—missionaries, colonial wives, and travelers—who, until recently, have rarely been heard.

In the selections that follow we meet an assortment of women. Some, the early travelers especially, come across as haughty, racist, arrogant—or, in the case of the nineteenth-century missionary—maternalistic. All but two of the women reflect various shades of jingoism in their writings on Africa and Africans. Unless we understand these women in context, they tend to present a rather unfavorable impression of themselves and their "Africa." While it is impossible to lump together a group of unassociated and dissimilar women and render judgments as to their individual motivations, one feature seems to characterize all. In their respective relationships with Africa, the women were in the process of forging separate identities for themselves. The missionaries identified with their God and their church. This identity compelled them to share their calling with the African natives. (Jocelyn Murray, whose memoirs are included here, falls in two camps: missionary; and participant-observer during a period of political upheaval in Kenya.)

In traditional European circles, adult female identity was viewed in relation to the husband and his status in society. Most of the western women who were travelers to Africa were either divorced or spinsters. (Rosita Forbes remarried but her second husband allowed the spotlight to continue to focus on her.) Forging an independent identity meant accomplishing something unique and exclusive. While they were different from their female peers, they were recognized in the larger sphere of society for their adventures abroad.

These women were adventurers who relied on colonial civil servants and missionaries for relief and often for supplies. The earlier travelers set

9

off on their personal explorations accompanied only by their African porters, at a time when parts of the African interior were still unknown to European colonizers.

Do women's voices differ from those of men? And, what do women see that men do not? One facet that particularizes the women from their male counterparts is their interest in and commentary on African women they meet along their respective routes. Trivial matters concerning servants seem of special concern to women. In fact, the descriptions of interrelationships with servants in Africa—written home in letters or published in travel accounts—were often injudicious, sometimes ludicrous. When these materials were read in the west, they helped reinforce negative stereotypes of Africans that the missionaries initially created through frequent misunderstandings of African culture.

For women travelers accent was on detail; intensity of individual experiences; empathy for some people; criticisms of others. The *personal* nature of their experiences distinguishes the women from their equally adventuresome male colleagues.

Men travelers in Africa doted on describing their heroic exploits (sometimes with exaggeration) as well as the mountains, lakes, and savannah. Women more often voiced their fears. Women differed from men, too, in that obstacles of every sort were put before them, especially objections of their traveling alone (with the help of the African men, which in itself was regarded as a special obstacle).

The following accounts of Africa and Africans cover a little over a century, spanning the period of early missionary activity in West Africa until the eve of independence. We move with women who are interested in retracing the steps of others (men) who preceded them. We travel with women whose interests are in their own conquests, e.g., conquering the male world of the "Dark Continent." The Africa of one woman is not the Africa of another, thus the selections featured in this volume are as revealing of the women who wrote them as they are of the Africa on which they report.

Anna Martin Hinderer kept a journal and wrote endless (if sometimes lonely) letters back to friends in England. Her letters are typical of those written by scores of other women who accompanied family members to distant outposts of empire. Posted to Nigeria in the year 1853, Hinderer and her husband suffered illness, privation, and even the possibility of danger during the Yoruba Wars, which had a direct impact on their lives. They watched helplessly while people around them succumbed to the "fevers" (mostly malaria), consoling themselves with faith in eventual reconciliation in the next world after the trials of this one had passed. "I have been ill again, from too much exertion on arriving at Abeokuta so soon after the fever at Lagos . . . I thought it impossible to recover, and looked upon myself as passing away from this world." Childless herself, Hinderer "adopted" numbers of African children—loving them as her own and seeming to win the respect of the ever-growing African congregation she and her husband served in Ibaden, a station they founded among the Yoruba people.

Hinderer's early life sheds some light on her missionary zeal in Africa. Orphaned as a child, Anna went to live with a grandfather who regularly took her to Anglican services. She taught Sunday school. Later she became a governess to a middle class family and in 1852, she married German-born David Hinderer. Her husband was from Schorndorf in the kingdom of Wurtemberg. Because Germany was not then united, and there were no German colonies, Protestant German men with an urge to work among the "heathen" traveled to England to join missionary societies. Many, like David Hinderer, later married English women.

The great evangelistic fervor that characterized nineteenth century England and North America spurred religious societies to found foreign missions. The London Missionary Society, run by the Methodist Church, was formed soon after the Church of England's Christian Missionary Society (CMS); and later, the Scottish Missionary Society was founded, to be followed by the Basel Mission. The Catholic Church sent male missionaries to Africa from the sixteenth century on, but failed to convert significant numbers of local peoples away from their traditional beliefs until the mid-nineteenth century, when the French efforts began anew. Soon after the resurgence of Catholic activity, nuns went out to join priests in opening convent schools, especially in western and central Africa. Southern Africa was an area of special interest to Protestant missionaries, and mission stations were opened from the Cape to British Central Africa. In the Shire Highlands of Nyasaland the Scottish missionaries were especially active—prodded in their efforts by the antislavery tracts of Dr. David Livingstone. (Livingstone's wife, Mary, died in central Africa in 1862, briefly mourned by him and otherwise forgotten by history.)

Initially, single women were not accepted for missionary duties in Africa. By the 1880s the rules had changed enough for Marian Goodall to go to Lagos and take over the "Female Institution," which had been founded in 1872 by another German missionary and his English wife. Many of the missionaries were trained as doctors and nurses. Among Protestants, families tended to follow one another to foreign missions. For instance, Katherine Timpson trained as a nurse at Guy's Hospital in London, and married Dr. A. R. Cook. At the end of the nineteenth century the Cooks went to Uganda (which had become a British Protectorate in 1890) as medical missionaries. They were followed in 1900 by his brother, a nephew, and a cousin and his wife. Dr. Cook founded the well-known Mengo Hospital, and Katherine Cook worked to revolutionize maternity care.[2]

A quick run through a few names from the vast archival trove of the CMS suggests that, in the early years of foreign missionary activity, wives were unpaid, almost unnoticed at home, but nevertheless very much involved in teaching or carrying out other activities in the name of the society. Kathleen Barton, niece of a Church of England clergyman, married an engineer who joined the CMS in 1900. Both went to Uganda, where he had the title of missionary but she worked as an unpaid teacher. Barton had been a governess before marriage, as had Elizabeth Forsythe, who went to another East African mission after her marriage. Lady Mary Hilda Clements went to Cairo alone and worked as a missionary. At her marriage she was forced to resign, possibly because her husband was not a missionary.

The missionary societies were long run by men. When women were permitted to go to the mission stations, they reported directly to male supervisors who, in turn, reported back to the church organizations at home. A "Miss Buckle" posted in Antananarivo, Madagascar at the end of last century, wrote letters to various members of the CMS in England but all official reports concerning her (and the mission) were from male clergy.[3]

In 1922, when medical missionary Mary Floyd Cushman signed up for a foreign station, the Congregationalist Church in New England allowed her to go alone. But because Cushman was fifty-two years of age, they required that she pay her own transportation and living costs until the expiration of her first term of appointment. The idea was that, if she survived that first year, the church fathers would provide for her future employment in the field. The doubts expressed concerning her age, however, did not prohibit the Congregationalists from sending the lone Cushman to a remote outpost in Angola. Nevertheless, Cushman's response was exuberant: ". . . after many years my life long desire has its fulfillment."[4]

By the time Jocelyn Murray went to Kenya in the mid–1950s, women may actually have outnumbered men in the mission fields. Murray's memoir notes the changes that occurred between the time she reached Kenya and today (gender roles are the same), but male African clergy have replaced the formerly all-British male clergy in the bureaucratic structure.

Although this volume includes the memoirs of only two actual missionaries, religious communities and missionary stations are mentioned by the assortment of other women travelers we meet as we make our way chronologically from the mid–1800s to the mid–1950s. Intrepid and committed to their religious crusades in the African communities among which they lived and worked, the missionaries were followed by an assortment of women for a variety of reasons.

Florence Ninian von Sass, first mistress to, and later wife of, explorer Sir Samuel Baker, traveled to eastern and central Africa in 1861. She should be recognized as the first European female explorer in Africa. Florence Baker was with her husband when he "discovered" Lake Albert. (History has recorded Sir Samuel Baker alone as official discoverer—failing to take into account that Florence Baker was there, too.)[5] Samuel Baker, however, mentioned his wife in the introduction to his published diary of the trip. His views were those of most men of his time: "I shuddered at the prospect for her, should she be left alone in savage hands at my death; and gladly would I have left her [at home] instead of exposing her to the miseries of Africa." Baker's pleas fell on deaf ears—as did those of the many men who tried to prevent the women who followed her from accomplishing their own adventures in Africa. ". . . I implored her to remain, and that I painted the difficulties and perils still blacker than I supposed they would really be: she was resolved with woman's constancy and devotion to share all the dangers."[6]

Florence Baker was followed nearly thirty years later by Mary Kingsley, commonly regarded as the first woman to travel alone (unaccompanied by a European man) in West Africa. Kingsley made two trips to West Africa: one in 1893 and a second in 1895. She lumped them both together in *Travels in West Africa,* excerpts from which are included here.

To help pay for her trip, Kingsley angled to obtain certain rare species of fish, which she collected and returned to England for scientific study. In this pursuit she followed Livingstone, who engaged in the scientific study of fish from the Nile as well as the Zambezi Rivers. Using the fish as a pretext for her travel with the British colonial officials, and trade as her mode of introduction to local Africans, Kingsley collected ethnographic material, which she wrote up for popular consumption, and later delivered in lecture form to serious audiences at home.

Kingsley's memoirs have been more widely read than her serious ethnographic work, a portion of which is also reproduced in this volume—showing the contrast between the uncritical traveler and the scholar, who was more judgmental of the Africa she knew. "Life in West Africa . . . seems a world apart . . . it is [a] strange mixture of savagery with little patches of civilization on it here and there . . . You feel that at any moment day or night, you have but to stretch your hand and you could lay it on the clammy skin of King death himself."[7]

Ethnography was in an early stage of development as a field when Kingsley journeyed to West Africa. Still, the Royal Geographic Society was closed to female members. A few semi-academic groups with interests in Africa included women among their number. On occasion, these women were invited to present lectures. Alice Werner, an 1880s graduate of Newnham College, Cambridge, who was first a missionary, then an ethnographer in Central Africa, lectured to the Sunday Afternoon Course at the South Place Institute in Finsbury. She was followed on the platform at a later date—both lectured in the 1890s—by Frances Ellen Colenso, whose father had been the first Anglican bishop of Natal in South Africa.

Born and brought up around the Zulu people, Frances Ellen Colenso was intellectually and emotionally absorbed with them from her youth. She never married but lost the man she loved during the Zulu wars; and later wrote a novel about him under a pseudonym. As compensation for the loss of her loved one, Colenso devoted herself to Zulu affairs, including extensive writings, until the end of her life.[8]

These early female students of African ethnography—Werner, Colenso, and Kingsley—were precursors of the women anthropologists who studied with the renowned Bronislaw Malinowski in his London School of Economics seminars in the 1930s. Today the yellowed and faded field notes of Phyllis Kaberry and Margaret Read can be found in Malinowski's archive. Read went to Nyasaland in 1935, perhaps on the advice of Alice Werner at the University of London. Werner had by that time gained an international reputation as a linguist. Kaberry went first to Papua New Guinea, in the 1930s. After World War II she worked among the Bamenda in British Cameroon.[9]

Then, there were the women who began to accompany husbands sent out to govern in Africa. After the Scramble (1884–85), and pacification (mostly completed by 1912), the British recreated aspects of their Indian empire in Africa. Ladies began to appear on the scene. Proper houses were constructed, social clubs opened (always racially segregated), and numbers of Africans were Europeanized into humble servants.

One of the colonial wives to preside over tea in the African empire was Mrs. Bartle Frere, whose husband was Colonial Governor of South Africa in the 1890s. South Africa was different from other parts of Africa. European women had long been on the scene there; and "society" was already fully developed by the time Mrs. Frere ruled Government House in Capetown—her colonial domain. In fact, Lady Lippino Barker traveled around the Cape before joining her husband, a colonial administrator, in Natal back in 1875. Barker's interest was typical of other women travelers: the weather, the scenery, and the people. "We are close alongside of a wharf, and still a capital and faithful copy of a Scotch mist wraps houses, trees and sloping uplands in a fibry fantastic veil, and the cold drizzle seems to curdle the spirits and energies of the few listless Malays and half-caste boys who are lounging about."[10]

Still in the Cape, Lady Barker wrote her impressions of an African chief with whom she and her party met:

> . . . we present our pass and the people in authority satisfy themselves that we are quite in rule. Then the old chief walks quietly in, takes off his soft felt hat and sits himself down in a Windsor arm-chair with grave deliberation. He is uncommonly ugly; but when one remembers that he is nearly seventy years of age, it is astonishing how young he looks. Langalibalele is not a true Kafir at all: he is a Fingor, a half-caste tribe. . . . His wool grows in distinct and separate clumps like hassocks of grass all over his head. . . . In vain he sends commands and entreaties to those dusky ladies [wives] to come and share his solitude. They return for answer that 'they are working for someone else'. . . . Neither he nor his stalwart son would dream for a moment of touching spade to hoe; but if the ladies of the family could only be made to see their duty, an honest penny might be turned. . . .
>
> I gave him a large packet of sugar-plums, which he seized with childish delight and hid away exactly like the big monkeys in the zoo.[11]

Lady Barker, the wife of a respected colonial official, thus introduces "her" South Africa to friends and family back home.

Of the growing numbers of wives who moved into the less settled areas of the continent, Mrs. Flora Shaw Lugard is perhaps the most well-known. Flora Shaw reported to the *Times* from South Africa before she married Frederick Lugard and then joined him to co-rule in northern Nigeria. An ardent supporter of empire, she later wrote *A Tropical Dependency,*[12] which was a history of the western Sudan from a pro-British point of view.

Anne Dundas, a voice we hear from inside the colonial service, went to Tanganyika in the early 1920s as a newlywed. In *Beneath an African Glacier,* Dundas is the first woman to provide an eyewitness account of the controversial ritual of female circumcision.[13] Dundas, too, was a proponent of empire but her views were often tempered with an attempt to understand the people among whom she lived, and whom her husband governed. Her memoir was Dundas' way of forging an identity that removed her from the rank of mere colonial wife.

Some women spoke of Africa in terms of sorrow or out of bereavement. Two vignettes from southern Africa illustrate. Ellen Ryke's husband, Captain Arthur Campbell Ryke, "lost his right arm at the Shangani War while at the guns. . . . Age of my husband, 23 years." Ellen was in England at the time, later joining her young husband in Rhodesia where she "spent the happiest years of my life" surrounded by beauty and with all of her domestic needs provided by African servants.[14] Margaret White's brother, Cecil, a member of the Suffolk Regiment, was killed at Colesberg on 6 January 1900 during the South African (Boer) War. In 1924 White made a pilgrimage to her departed brother's grave, writing back home in somber tones to describe his last resting place.[15]

The sadness that greeted the women above is quite different from the reception white domestic workers received when they reached South Africa. Class lines were heavily drawn in the empire. Women who might have had little or no place in society back home were often quickly elevated in status (or elevated themselves). In South Africa class and racial lines were as distinctly drawn as anywhere. Having African servants for domestic duties was a given; but some white women linked up with emigration societies in England to import domestics who provided a buffer between themselves and their lowly African staff. Housekeepers, cooks, nurses were all desired. But, as a woman writer in South Africa noted: "An emigrated servant very speedily adopts the 'I am as good as you, probably better' tone . . ." and soon after arrival begins looking for a husband who will then provide her with the comforts she was hired to provide.[16] (Katherine Fannin, the Kenyan spy, was involved in contracting with and hiring out white domestics in that colony during the 1930s.)

A unique traveler to southern Africa was butterfly collector Margaret Fountaine. In 1908 and for nearly two years, she traveled with her Indian lover, Khalil, in racially-segregated Kenya, Rhodesia, South Africa, and parts of Portuguese Mozambique, without experiencing any overt hostility. Khalil "passed" as a southern European. Of South Africa Fountaine noted that

> The English people out here had lost much of that insular stiffness which at home often keeps them aloof. Under the delightful climatic conditions of South Africa they seemed to have acquired all the charm and looseness of foreigners. Khalil was treated well on all sides and no one thought anything of my travelling with him, for without a courier (eg chaperon) . . . it would have [been] quite impossible for me to have gone out alone into the bush.[17]

Fountaine was representative of the young and carefree who traveled around Africa from the turn of the century on. The mostly wealthy, and some titled, youths of yesteryears, resemble their latter-day counterparts: the "travelers" of today. The Hon. Susan Hicks Beach sent descriptive accounts of her excursions from Khartoum to Rhodesia back home to her mother, the Viscountess.[18]

The Baroness Karen von Blixen married her Baron in Denmark, then moved to a life of vinegar and honey in Kenya—this period of her life dramatized in *Out of Africa.*[19] Another woman familiar to many is the British-born Beryl Markham, whose life was portrayed in a television production by the BBC. Her autobiography *West With the Night*[20] became a best-seller when reissued in the 1980s. Elspeth Huxley, "a daughter of Kenya" who was "famous with the old settlers," actually spent very little of her life in Africa. Regarded as "the first modern writer on the colony," Huxley retraced her youth in *Flame Trees of Thika,* which was also made into a television series by the BBC.[21]

A novel view of Ethiopia is presented by another Kenyan white woman, Katherine Fannin. In the 1930s Fannin went to the then Italian-occupied country to spy on military operations as fears mounted that, should war break out in Europe, an attack on the British colonies would be forthcoming. A brief excerpt from Fannin's travelogue, which was published in the Sunday *Post,* is included. Her description of Addis Ababa contrasts with that of Rosita Forbes, who visited the capital in 1922, only twenty years after it was founded. For example, in the interim period, tarmac roads, an accomplishment of the Italian occupation, took the place of the horse and wagon tracks Forbes noted in her memoir.

Both women were adventurous and undaunted by danger. Forbes was the first woman to visit the nearly impenetrable Kufra Desert in Libya, whereas Fannin proclaimed that "I was the only English woman to cross the Danikil desert. . . ." Neither Forbes nor Fannin felt the fascination with Ethiopia that was characteristic of Sylvia Pankhurst when she made her first visit to that country following World War II. By then, Sylvia had been the Emperor Haile Selassie's chief propagandist in England for nearly twenty years. Hers was the fantasyland of dreams before her arrival; and Pankhurst's exhilaration at all she saw was without parallel. The quaintness of the peasantry was especially remarkable: "Ethiopian people in their traditional dress, with their donkeys and mules . . . straw umbrellas . . . I was enchanted and bewildered."[22]

Many of the accounts that follow feature women as tourists-travelers who visited various parts of Africa south of the Sahara for the purpose of either writing about their experiences or the pleasure of visiting places they regarded as different and exotic. The exception, however, is the Princess Marie Louise, who made an official visit to the Gold Coast in 1925. Colonial officials welcomed royal visitors. The promise of their presence in a territory gave the officials leverage with the Colonial Office to build roads or carry out other favored projects that might not otherwise have been funded.

So, when H. H. Marie Louise visited the Northern Territories (in today's Ghana), new roads had been freshly laid. What no one took into account was the onset of the rainy season before the tarmac had hardened. As the entourage of lorries (trucks) loaded with the necessities for a royal's travel and the cars carrying various officials made their way over these newly-constructed roads, the rains came with force, washing out the roads from under the royal party traveling on them. Enlightened, accustomed to travel in the Empire, and unusually complacent, the Princess Marie Louise reported on, but did not complain about, the various breakdowns, pauses, and even her own involvement in moving items to and from lorries. But though her mission was official, she frequently projects the image of a curious, atypical, and unroyal tourist.

One of the earliest Victorian women travelers was the American May French Sheldon.[23] Sheldon ventured into areas where only two or three white men had preceded her. She arrived in Zanzibar in 1891, expecting to outfit an expedition to Masailand. Despite intense opposition from colonial officials there, Sheldon prevailed and hired on several carriers. She had connections with men who had traveled with Henry M. Stanley, and used them to secure more porters on the Kenya mainland. Wearing "two pistols at her belt" and carrying an "iron pointed staff," Sheldon set off for Mount Kilimanjaro, where the Masai were thought to be carrying out cattle raids on their neighbors.

At night, Sheldon's table "gleaming with napery and silver, set . . . under the stars" featured her dining alone in an "evening dress and pistols." By day the little band, led by their determined mistress, made their way into the interior. Nearing Masai country, however, her servants rebelled. She is said to have placed one of her pistols at the head porter's temple, threatening to shoot if he turned back. He still refused and Sheldon succumbed to the will of the Africans—unable to go on without them. Later, after Sheldon's wealthy American husband died, she toured West Africa and then retired to England. Unfortunately she never wrote what could have been an exciting (if flamboyant) account of her African travels.

Mary Hall, traveling in Central Africa in the early 1900s, represents the symbol of western white elitism.[24] On one occasion during her travels, Hall arrived at an unspecified spot for lunch. She found the meal under preparation by an African cook, a "boy who had run 17 miles" for that purpose alone. After she ate, Hall noted merely that he had to trudge back home again. "This was but one of the many kindnesses," provided by her English friends. Quoting an early (and male) authority, Hall referred to the three Africas: "North Africa, where men go for their health; South Africa where they go for money; and Central Africa where they go for adventure." She visited all three and indeed chose to adventure in Central Africa. The difference, however, is that she was a woman. Hall was accompanied on her mission by as many as forty African carriers—four men who operated in shifts to carry Mary Hall in her hammock; and the rest to tote her considerable baggage, medical supplies, and food.

In fact, huge amounts of equipment were required for these European and American women travelers—tents, mosquito netting, camp beds, bedding and towels, folding tubs for bathing, and fancy dress for formal dining in mission stations and with colonial officials they encountered during their travels. They had to carry stores of food while they were between stations, including some for the Africans doing the hard work. Some travelers stowed typewriters in their luggage; others, artists' supplies; some had heavy camera equipment. These individual travels represented expeditions that could have outfitted several people but almost always included one lone woman. In the case of the Princess, contingents of followers were required, and thus even more supplies had to be carted, carried by mule or donkey. With Mary Hall, goods were piled on the backs of men who walked, while she rode in the comfort of her hammock.

Travel by hammock, which could accommodate one either sitting or lying in repose, was the mode of human transportation commonly employed by missionaries, colonial officials visiting outposts, explorers, and early travelers in nineteenth and early twentieth century Africa. Princess Marie Louise and others recalled the basket in which they moved from shipboard, to small boat, to land. Many African ports in the early days of colonial empire lacked deep water facilities for docking ships. In that case, a kind of derrick was erected on the ship, to which was attached a large basket. The embarking passengers climbed in the basket, which was then lifted by the derrick, and the passengers were slowly deposited in a homemade and rickety canoe; or placed in a small but more secure boat; then they were taken ashore.

Mary Hall mentions "Hospital Hill" and "Government Hill" in Blantyre, Nyasaland. Europeans, especially the British, made a practice of building their quarters as far from the African settlements as possible. If hilly areas were available, they always built on them. The mortality rate for Europeans was high before the introduction of modern medicine. The current theory was that, by keeping themselves separate from Africans, and as far above sea level as possible, they were less susceptible to illness, especially malaria.

Mary Gaunt, who undertook considerable travel in various parts of Africa, was skeptical of some health measures introduced by British medical authorities. She rejected the idea of screening or using mosquito nets. Hers was the "fresh air theory," which Gaunt brought with her from her native Australia.

Mary Gaunt was born in Australia in the 1860s to a family of travelers. Filled with wanderlust as a child, she and her only sister both experienced traditional marriages at home while their brothers roamed the world. Fate was both unkind and then generous to Gaunt. Her husband died young, leaving her a widow with no children, and a small income. Gaunt cashed in the savings and went to England, where she wrote a novel. The proceeds brought her to Africa in about 1910. Gaunt later traveled to China and the West Indies, writing novels and travel books about her experiences in these areas. Thus, her identity as travel authority was firmly established by the time of her retirement to England.

Gaunt carried her Australian racial prejudices with her to Africa, where they coexisted nicely among the colonials she encountered in her travels. She grew up in a home that contained servants. In the course of her travels she was not timid in issuing orders to her bearers. As she saw it, her success, even survival, depended on the mettle she displayed in keeping her porters in line, and, on at least one occasion, preventing them from deserting her altogether.

Ironically, although H. H. Marie Louise was proud of the symbols and examples of British rule she met in the Gold Coast, Gaunt was the more imperious, noting that, as the white man has "always ruled the blacks; so, I think, he must always rule."

Pseudo-scientific racism, which gave excuse for white to rule over black, lingered among some colonials as long as they were part of the ruling class. The rhetoric died down after World War II. But, as Jocelyn Murray illustrates in her memoir on Kikuyu, whites were still practicing segregation, although by then they had stepped back from the doctrine of Social-Darwinism (which is somewhat evident in Mary Kingsley's lecture before the Sunday Afternoon Study Group).

Mary Gaunt's trip up the Gambia in the 1920s differed little from that experienced on the Niger by Scottish explorer Mungo Park, in the mid-nineteenth century. In fact, some of Gaunt's descriptions of her ride up the Gambia were similar to those of Helen Winteritz, who shipped down the Congo by steamer in the 1980s. The familiar tugs were as much a part of the scene both women encountered nearly fifty years apart, as were the crowds, chickens, goats, and traders.[25]

The American traveler, May Mott-Smith, came from Yankee trader stock. She read the diary of her great-uncle who, with her great grand-father, "were of those sturdy early merchantmen who sailed their ships from Plymouth, Massachusetts. . . ." Born in Hawaii to a family that had acquired its wealth in New England, Mott-Smith (married but later divorced) was related to Lucretia Mott, the well-known Quaker preacher, abolitionist, and early pioneer for women's rights. Charles Mott, a founder of General Motors, was a relative. Mott-Smith had a private income and traveled widely. She was both an artist and a jewelry designer, with Paris among the centers in which her works were exhibited. She wrote travel accounts for the New York *Times,* and *Times of India.* After her African adventures, Mott-Smith journeyed to Afghanistan. One of the most widely traveled of the women included in this volume, she was in Spanish Morocco at the beginning of the rebellion (1924–25), and went down the West African coast to the Congo, determined to follow in the footsteps of the Portuguese sailor, Vasco de Gama. She may have been the only woman to have successfully navigated her way around Africa unaccompanied until modern air and ship transportation made it possible to fly in and out of capital cities throughout the continent. Like Gaunt, Mott-Smith was not intimidated by circumstances, nor by the colonial officials she encountered.

Margery Perham represents the transition between the casual traveler and the modern academic in search of concrete knowledge. Perham's memoir marks a difference in attitudes towards colonialism and the Africans who were its victims. Hawaii-born Mott-Smith and Australian Mary Gaunt both brought their personal experiences with darker colored servants in their cultural baggage to Africa. Perham seems to have been relatively free of paternalism or racial stereotypes.

As the first woman to receive a Rhodes Trust Traveling Fellowship, Perham decided to study "the nature of the coloured problem" and chose to undertake this study by going to the United States, and on to the Pacific including Australia, before she landed in South Africa. In terms of the "coloured problem," South Africa had special appeal in the late 1920s when Perham arrived.

Jocelyn Murray left Kenya after eleven years as a missionary teacher to the Kikuyu. The dramatic change in the times between missionary Anna Hinderer in the mid–nineteenth century and those of Murray is illustrated in what happened to the two women after their departure from the missions. Hinderer died from weakness brought on by the many illnesses she suffered in mid-nineteenth century Nigeria. Murray went to America, where she earned a Ph.D. Her book, *Proclaim the Good News* was appropriately a history of the Christian Missionary Society for whom she worked during "The Emergency" in Kenya.[26] "Kenya," she wrote, "was a divided country. With a large and largely progressive African population it had also a strong and vocal white settler population, with many upper-class members of the House of Lords, baronets, retired officers of the armed services, a considerable portion of former members of the Indian Civil Service—all were found in Kenya." The whites controlled the "land in the so-called White Highlands" and "African rights were confined to 'the Reserves,' areas reserved by the Crown for members of certain ethnic groups. . . . The Kikuyu, among whom witchcraft is of minor importance, traditionally make use of oaths, whereby the suspect affirms his innocence, and by which people band themselves together for mutual purposes. . . ."[27] This brief excerpt from *Proclaim the Good News* provides background for "The Emergency" and Murray's experiences among the Kikuyu, which she wrote especially for this volume.

Only Rosita Forbes traveled with a white male companion. Harold Jones, who joined her in the Ethiopian explorations, was described by Forbes as a "cinema operator." He was much more than that. Jones shared all of the travails that Forbes so notably describes in her memoir.

Each of these women tells us something about Africa that not only distinguishes one area from another, but also, one woman from another. Experiencing comforts and socializing in the European communities they visited, the travelers also bravely ventured into the "unknown." Some showed trepidation; most did not. The "unaccompanied" Mary Hall, traveling around Africa with her African schoolboy interpreters and her considerable staff of carriers, was as heroic in her way as those early male explorers who also were assisted by interpreters, guides, and bearers.

The adventures of ethnologist Mary Kingsley were in many respects equal to those of Richard Francis Burton. Burton was interested in exotic cultures and languages; Kingsley in African culture and trade. Burton is celebrated (and berated) in film and in many books. Kingsley has recently been brought back to mind by way of a new biography. Rosita Forbes, who is merely represented here with the vignette concerning her stay in Ethiopia, actually experienced dramatic and hair-raising adventures in the Kufra desert, and later, in the high Atlas Mountains, where she interviewed a notorious bandit and kidnapper (whose biography she wrote). The mid-1920s, when Forbes journeyed to Ethiopia, represents a rather benign period in her active life.

Katherine Fannin, the spy for Britain, makes her brief debut on the larger stage here in this volume. Jocelyn Murray explains "The Emergency" in Kenya, which she experienced, unperturbed, in the mid-1950s. In the pages that follow, artists connect with writers, and missionaries join ordinary tourists to produce a unique picture of their "Africa"—the experiences of western women on that continent from the mid-nineteenth century into the 1960s.

Patricia W. Romero
Towson State University

1. Olive Shreiner, *Thoughts on South Africa,* London: T. Fisher Unwin Ltd, 1923, 28.
2. Rhodes House Mss. Afr. 5.4. *Guidebook of Miscellaneous Letters,*

372. Carol Summers, "Intimate Colonialism: The Imperial Production of Reproduction in Uganda, 1907–1930." Paper presented at The Atlantic Seminar, Johns Hopkins University, 26 April 1988. Gordon Hewitt, *The Problems of Success: A History of the Christian Missionary Society 1910–1942,* London: Hodde Christian Paperbacks, 1971. Earlier, the Society for the Propagation of the Gospel was founded as an arm of the Anglican church. In the eighteenth century USPG (as it is formally now known) sent German Lutherans to India where it began its missionary activity. For this information I am grateful to the Reverend Guy Hawtin, Baltimore.

3. USPG December 1890–November 1896; CLR 129, Rhodes House.

4. Mary Floyd Cushman, *Missionary Doctor: The Story of Twenty Years in Africa,* New York: Harper & Brothers 1944, *ix.*

5. Florence Ninian von Sass Baker has been ill-served by a poorly produced semi-autobiographical account published in the 1970s. Actually, the book contains excerpts from Baker's diary and from letters that were preserved; these are strung together by a very weak series of explanatory remarks. See Anne Baker, *Morning Star: Florence Baker's diary of the expedition to put down the slave trade on the Nile 1870–1873,* London: Kimder, 1972.

6. Samuel White Baker, *Albert Nyanza Great Basin of the Nile,* London: Sedgwick & Jackson 1962 reprint, 2.

7. Recently an American woman retraced Kingsley's footsteps in West Africa. See Caroline Alexander, *One Dry Season: In the Footsteps of Mary Kingsley.* New York: Knopf, 1989.

8. For Alice Werner and Frances Colenso at the Sunday Afternoon Course see "British Central Africa" in *British Empire Series* II, London: Kegan, Paul, French, Truber & Co., Ltd, 1899, 113–133; 233–258.

9. Phyllis Kaberry, papers concerning the Bamenda Provinces, 1945–46; and Margaret Read, papers concerning the Ngoni of Nyasaland, 1935–69. Malinowski Papers, London School of Economics.

10. Lippino Barker (Lady), "Letters from South Africa" [October 17, 1875] *Eclectic Review* 17:227.

11. Barker, "Letters," 233.

12. Flora Shaw Lugard, *A Tropical Dependency,* New York: Barnes & Noble, 1906.

13. Anne Dundas, *Beneath African Glaciers,* London: H.F.&G Witherby, 1924.

14. Ellen Ryke, "Sketch bidding farewell," Rhodes House Mss. Afr. s.4 *Guidebook of Miscellaneous Letters,* 198–200.
15. Margaret White to Eaton, from Colesberg, South Africa. National Register of Archives, London.
16. E. Cecil, "Female Emigration to South Africa" in *Nineteenth Century London* 51–71:1905. See also Margaret Strobel, "Gender and Race in the Nineteenth- and Twentieth-Century British Empire," in Renate Bridenthal, Claudia Koonz, and Susan Stuard (eds.), *Becoming Visible: Women in European History,* Boston: Little, Brown, 1987.
17. W. F. Cater (ed.), *Love Among the Butterflies: The Travels and Adventures of a Victorian Lady,* London: Collins, 1980. My thanks to Virginia Hamill for providing me with this account.
18. Letters to Viscountess St. Aldwyn from Susan, 1909–1910. PPC/23, National Register of Archives.
19. Isak Dinesen, *Out of Africa,* London: Putnam, 1937.
20. Beryl Markham, *West with the Night,* Boston: Houghton Mifflin, 1942.
21. Elspeth Huxley, *Flame Trees of Thika,* London: Chatlo & Windus, 1957.
22. Patricia W. Romero, *E. Sylvia Pankhurst: Portrait of a Radical,* New Haven: Yale University Press, 1990.
23. The following account comes from Edward Rodwell, "The Way it Was" Sunday *Standard* (Kenya) March 20, 1983. I am grateful to Olivia and Edward Rodwell for calling this column, and thus Sheldon, to my attention while I was recuperating at their home on Matpwa Creek, January 1991.
24. British Central Africa was compelling to Victorian women travelers in the late nineteenth and twentieth centuries. See Jane F. Moir, *A Lady's Memoirs from Central Africa,* Glasgow: James Maclehose & Sons, 1881; Helen Caddick, *A White Woman in Central Africa,* London: T. Fisher Unwin, 1900; Mary Hall, *A Woman's Trek,* London, 1907; Catherine Barnes Stevenson, *Victorian Women Travel Writers in Africa,* Boston: Twayne Publishers, 1982.
25. Helen Winternitz, *East Along the Equator,* New York: Ballantine Books, 1987.
26. Jocelyn Murray, *Proclaim the Good News,* London: Hodde Christian Paperbacks, 1985.
27. Murray, *Proclaim,* 237–39.

# ANNA MARTIN HINDERER*
# (Nigeria, 1853)

Born in 1827 in the Norfolk area, Anna's early childhood was marked with sadness. Her ailing mother died when Anna was five. Soon thereafter, her father sent the little girl to Lowestoft where she lived with her grandfather and an aunt. Early on, Anna found emotional security in religion, writing that she "had a strong desire to become a missionary, to give myself up to some holy work, and I had a firm belief that such a calling would be mine." Fortunately for Anna's dreams, German-born missionary David Hinderer entered her life in 1852. After their arranged marriage, Anna joined her husband in his return to Yoruba country, in today's Nigeria. A single woman, even one of Anna's determination, would not have been considered eligible for missionary work in foreign fields in mid-nineteenth century England. Before her marriage, Anna had extensive training in church-related activities. At the age of fourteen she taught her first Sunday school class—and the children were among the poorest in her diocese, preparation for the African children with whom she would later work.

David Hinderer had gone to the Yoruba country in 1848, just after the Christian Missionary Society (CMS) established a station in Abeokuta, and only a few years after the slave trade had been abolished (although slavery continued as did the trade to the north). His return to England was in connection with a new missionary station Hinderer was commissioned to open in Ibadan. At the time of her marriage, Hinderer "rejoiced at the thought of living and dying for Africa," little realizing, perhaps, how many Europeans did die in that forbidding climate.

During the years she was in Africa, Hinderer kept journals and diaries, and wrote hundreds of letters to friends and relatives back home. Many of her letters and some of her other writings survived and were later edited into the book from which the following selections are taken. Anna was the first woman missionary to provide us with an account of what life was like for Europeans posted in distant lands, living amongst people who had

---

*Richard A. Hone (ed)., *Seventeen Years in the Yoruba Country: Memorials of Anna Hinderer gathered from her Journals and Letters*, London: Seeley, Jackson & Halliday, 1883, 99–106, 130–136, 248–260.

*Church at Ibadan*

never before encountered westerners (whose purpose was to change their society through the introduction of Christianity).

Anna and her husband were in Abeokuta only a few weeks before both were stricken with malaria. They survived, but three members of their original party of ten succumbed to the fevers within a short time. Hinderer left his wife in Abeokuta while he went to Ibadan to open the mission. Within a few months after her arrival in Nigeria, however, Anna was keeping house in Ibadan and had established a school for local children. Islam had penetrated south as far as Ibadan. The Hinderers, therefore, were combating the "evils" of heathenism as well as the forces of Islam as they set about their goal of Christian conversion. In the first selection included here, in mid–1854, Anna has returned to Ibadan after a brief visit to Abeokuta. Her new and western-influenced home has been completed and she is anxious to show it off to the local chief. On arrival, Anna is disappointed to learn that students in her mission school are being kept at home by Muslim fathers who have learned that the price of western education includes Christian conversion. Later, Anna and her husband experience problems with traditional religionists, priests who attempt to thwart their conversion attempts among the mostly animist (but nevertheless faithful) Yoruba. Although Christian faith negates polygyny—a facet of traditional Yoruba culture—Anna and her husband had to accept the many wives of the local chief, otherwise they would not have been able to enjoy his support of their presence in the area.

The evils of slavery in Africa and wars between the Yoruba characterize some of the difficulties Anna describes in the passages that follow. No matter the problems that beset them, Anna turns to the *Bible* for inspiration and often for justification. In the typical conceit of Christian assurance, Anna writes home about a man who is sacrificed to war. He died, she said, expecting to reach "the other world . . . of mystery." Yet, her own faith taught about a similar world of "mystery." The paradox eluded Anna altogether.

Despite war being waged in their vicinity from 1862–65, Anna had no personal fears. She does, however, refer often to the precarious state of her health and that of her husband, David. Anna's letters home during the first two years of the Yoruba Wars describe the hardships they endure. (Unfortunately, few of her letters from 1863–65 have survived.) The Hinderers were stranded in Ibadan during the last years of the war and a rescue mission was organized to take Anna away by stealth. Even her adopted African children did not know she was leaving until after her departure for Lagos. While she was away, rumors of a plot against Anna's life finally convinced her she must return to England. In increasingly poor health by this time, she sailed home in the spring of 1869. David joined her a few months later. In 1870, in her forty-fourth year of life, Anna died, still hoping to return to Nigeria and her mission. She was remembered lovingly by the Yoruba children back home who wrote

> . . . The sons and daughters she had kindly brought up, and cared for in the Gospel, will ever lament her loss; and her good deeds, as books, will ever be read among us. . . . Iya [Anna] is now freed from this world of sin and sorrow for a better one . . . to repay her labours with a crown of glory.

# *Progress of the Work*

"*Ibadan, May 14th.* [1854]—Yesterday I reached my loved Ibadan home, amidst a hearty greeting from the dear boys. Laniyono, who was the most sorrowful when I left, gave a shriek of delight, and sprang into my arms, with his legs round my waist, hanging there to his heart's content, shouting and making the oddest remarks you ever heard; that I was never to go away again, seemed to be a certainty to his mind. But a tinge of bitterness is generally mixed with every cup, so I found here. Two of my boys had been taken away by their parents in my absence: Adelotan is not allowed to appear anywhere, but Abudu came at once to see me. I put my hand on his shoulder, and he burst into a flood of tears. 'O Iya, it is not me, it is not me, it is my father who has done it.' Poor child! I could only soothe and calm him, and bid him be patient. I believe he will soon get leave from his father to come back.

"Our new house, after all the toil in building it promises to possess all the comfort we could expect or desire in this country; it is water-tight! has a good-sized sitting and bed-room, white-washed walls, and a good iron roof; comfortable piazzas, and all very airy, and as cool as anything can be in Africa, which was my principal desire. It is wonderful what my dear husband has achieved in my absence, and now he rejoices to have his wife in it, and so does she to be there. We pray that a rich blessing may be given us with it, and that though we have the comfort of a dwelling, we may never forget that this is not our home, but a tent pitched for the day."

"*May 17th.*—Bale, the head chief, paid us a special visit to-day. He came in great state, with drums and various strange instruments of music, with his host of attendants, singing men and singing women. He marvelled greatly at our house, and could not imagine how it was made. He was quite alarmed to think of mounting the steps; but with my husband pulling, and others pushing, we got him up. I stood at the top to receive him, in his mass of silks and velvets; he very graciously took my hand, and we walked into the room, at the sight of which he gave a great shout and wondered; he then took a fancy to the sofa, and sat there. We admitted upstairs his wives, his eldest son, and a few of his great people, and then were obliged to move away the steps, or the house, strong as it is, must have broken down with the mass of people. We gave him, and those in the room with him, a little refreshment, English bread, biscuits, and a few raisins. They looked at the bedroom, and all the things in both rooms. Bale was extremely amused to see himself in the looking-glass. I took the women by themselves; the washing-stand attracted their attention, so I washed my hands to show them the use of it. My soap was wonderful; and that I wiped

*Anna Martin Hinderer*

my hands after I had washed them, was a thing unheard of. But they took it into their heads to follow my example, and all hands must touch the soap, and go into the water, and there was a fine splashing, and a pretty towel, for the indigo dye comes off their clothes so very much, that I believe the towel will be blue and white for ever. At last we got into a state of composure again, and all being quiet, Mr. Hinderer made a little speech, telling Bale how glad we were to see him, why we built the house, and what brought us to this country."

"*May 22nd.*—A woman of about fifty years of age came to me. I noticed her in church, two or three Sundays before I went away, and again she was there yesterday. She brought with her a fowl, and corn to feed it with, and yams; she put them before me as a present, and said, 'Iya, all my life I have served the devil; he has been my god; but he never gave me peace in my heart. My husband was stolen away by war, the devil did not help me; my children all died, the devil could not help me; but since you white people have come, I have heard the words of the Great God, which we never heard before, and they are sweet to me. I want to hear more, and to walk in the right road, for it has been a wrong road all my life.' She has thrown her husband's images into the water. After our last words, 'God bless you, and give you peace in your heart!' she uttered a most fervent and hearty 'Amen.' As it is the constant practice to take fowls, cowries, and other offerings to their gods, I thought it necessary to tell her we did not desire she should bring a 'full hand' to us: she said she knew it, but begged we would accept her little present, to make her happy. I had a little chintz bag hanging up, with not a handful of cowries in it; she would not have had cowries as a payment on any account, but the bag she could not refuse; such a possession she never thought to have, and she went off with it greatly delighted.

"Now, dear friends, farewell; remember us in our work, our weakness and infirmities, bodily and mental, and may all your love, sympathy, and prayers be returned in tenfold measure in blessings on yourselves."

"*June 22nd.*—We are both in very good health, and both as busy as bees. A day is never long enough for me; a great deal falls to my share, and I can fancy no one more happy than myself in being equal to it in bodily power.

"My dear little boys give me great comfort and satisfaction. I must tell you one story about them. On Sunday week we had studied and talked over the picture of Dorcas. Yesterday evening they came to me for their prayers in my bedroom, and particularly noticed the beautiful figure I have of dear Mrs. Fry, which stands on my dressing-table, and which always seems to say, 'Be ye followers of them who through faith and patience inherit the promises.' They asked me who it was, I told them; and, as far as

I could, of her love to all people, especially the afflicted ones, the prisoner, the slave, &c. They listened attentively till big tears stood in the eyes of one. I then asked if they had ever heard of any one being so kind. One said she was like Dorcas, full of good deeds; another that she was like their own Iya, who could leave her own country and friends and come to them, and love little black boys and girls and people so much. 'No,' I said, 'there was One whose example Mrs. Fry followed, who did far more than either Dorcas or Iya.' A little fellow, the youngest of all, exclaimed, 'It is Jesus, Iya means, who went about always doing good, and then gave His life for all.' Do you now, I thought it was worth while to come to Africa, only to hear this from little lips which, such a short time ago, were taught senseless words over wood, and stone, and charms."

"*July 11th.*—Early this morning the wife of one of our native agents and our young schoolmaster went into the town, to accompany a friend on the road to Ijaye. On their way back they saw a little boy, not three years old, looking cold, starved, and filthy; they went towards the poor little thing, who said, 'Era mi,'— 'Buy me, buy me; I want to go home with you.' On enquiring they found that he was the child of a slave; the mother was sold many months ago, far away; the master of the house where the child was is gone to war, and so what was everybody's charge became nobody's. One man, who did just feed him for a time, got tired of him, and said he had enough to do to feed himself, for he also was a slave; so the poor child was cast out into the street. No one would dare to take him, lest they should be charged with stealing a slave, and for three moons, as the people say, he had been there, night and day; a few days more, and he must have died. All the food he got would be a bit of agidi, or corn, which would be thrown to him by passers by, as you would to a fowl. Olubi talked with the people, but they only said they could not help it, and wondered [why] any one should care about a little slave boy.

"Mr. Hinderer immediately returned with Olubi. Meantime a woman in the yard had washed the child, and shaved his head; he had also been abundantly oiled, and rubbed over with canewood. Mr. Hinderer talked with the people, and at last they said, 'Take him if you like; if he live, he live; if he die, well; no one make palaver with you;' so my husband hired a woman to carry him on her back, and bring him to me; and here he is, a pretty-looking little child, but with a countenance so full of sorrow, and he is a poor miserable skeleton. After a little more washing, I put on him a frock, and wrapped him in a warm cloth, which he seemed thoroughly to enjoy. I took him on my lap, and he seemed quite at home there. We gave him a little food, which he ate most greedily. We must be very careful about his food for some little time, or he would kill himself with eating. He soon fell fast asleep in my arms. As I was watching his sweet sleep, 'Take this child and nurse it for me, and I will give thee thy wages,' seemed to ring in my ears, and we do receive him as a precious little charge. May I be enabled to bring him up for God. He may be a bright and shining light. I wish his poor mother could know he was well taken care of."

"*July 20th.*—The little boy improves in health, but is not very good-tempered. The poor dear child has all the effects of being starved and unkindly treated, and at present all he can think of is eating. The other day I played with him a little, and he condescended to look at me. On my saying, 'I think you like me a little better to-day,' the reply was, 'What will you give me to eat?' This dear child has hardly a mind to appreciate kindness, having only known cruelty and oppression". . . .

July 23rd was a day peculiarly interesting to both missionaries and converts, who for the first time assembled for worship in the church. Months had still to pass before the building could be completed, but they were glad to make use of the bare mud walls, with their grass roof, as the old palm leaf church had been destroyed by the heavy tornadoes. She writes on this subject:

"Now we have the outward walls and we pray God to build up a spiritual house within. Grant that the sons and daughters of Ibadan may become polished corners of the temple! Hear Thou from heaven Thy dwelling-place, and send out Thy grace and Thy blessing!

"It is curious to watch people listening for the first time to the new tidings, a little gentle remark, then an expression of doubt, then such a hearty 'Amen.' ". . . .

"*Nov. 26th.* [1855]—The mail arrived with a most delightful packet of letters. Though fortunate and favoured every mail, I never had such a goodly heap, forty-one letters, or notes! and such boxes and parcels of things for ourselves, the children, and people. How very kind are friends, known and unknown, in dear England. It is very pleasant and refreshing to us to be so kindly remembered and cared for by many, rich and poor, enabling us to give so much pleasure, not only to the little ones, but to chiefs and others, to whom it is necessary to make presents; and these nice things from their white friends' country produce a very kind and friendly feeling in the poor African's heart, and they often say, 'What good kind people they must be in that far country.' I wish the kind givers could see the happy faces and sparkling eyes, when their things are displayed.

"But by this mail came another rich present for Africa, two new missionaries, Mr. Buhler and Mr. Hoch. They appear so fresh, and full of spirit and energy, quite refreshing to us to see, who have been melting away, as it were, in the past three years."

"*Ibadan, Dec. 15th.*—We reached our dear home again, with our friend Mr. Hoch, brought safely through the bush by the good hand of God upon us. We arrived amidst warm greetings and welcomes from many, surprising others greatly by the sight of another white man, when they had been doing their best to get rid of us by their persecution of our young converts. The fire and fury of persecution has raged to a very great extent; our hearts have ached, and still ache, for the sufferings of the little flock. Satan fights because his kingdom is endangered. The country priests fight under their master's banner, because their cruel lies and deceit are being exposed. The second Psalm just describes our state:—'The heathen rage; the people imagine a vain thing; kings set themselves; the rulers take counsel together against the Lord.' Their power of endurance is wonderful. There is, no doubt, something of this in the natural character of the Africans; but that there is something much deeper, is quite evident; even their persecutors ask, 'What is it?' and they think we have some charm in our eye, and they are therefore trying to keep some of them quite out of our sight.

"The story of one young woman is most touching and interesting. She stands with the courage of a dependant child on the love, mercy, and help of a great and gracious God. Her marriage was hastened by her parents, who thought it would prevent her coming to church. Her husband treated her even more cruelly than her parents, which had been hard enough. When told by him, 'You shall never enter white man's house again,' she said, 'Very well; as you wish it, it shall be.' 'Neither shall you go to his church.' To this she replied, 'I cannot and will not submit; it is God's house; I will go.' She was then cruelly beaten with sticks and cutlasses, and stoned, till her body was swelled all over; a rope was tied round her neck, and she was dragged, as an ox to the slaughter, to her father's house. Mr. Hinderer went to beg them to cease their cruelties. He found her lying prostrate before the idols, which had been brought out for her to worship: she was held there by furious people, who were shouting, 'Now she bows down! now she bows down!' She exclaimed, 'No, I do not: it is you who have put me here; I can never bow down to gods of wood and stone, which cannot hear me. Only in Jesus Christ, the Son of God, the only Saviour of poor sinners, can I trust.' She was then dragged up; they took a rope to put round her throat, saying, 'Well, we will take you away and kill you!' She replied, 'Kill me if you will, the sooner I shall be with my Saviour in heaven; but I will not, I cannot, serve these foolish things.' They did not kill her; but for months she endured every kind of ill-treatment, and at last ran away to Abeokuta. The history of her journey is little short of a miracle, and reminded me of the angel opening the door for Peter.

"One of her companions in suffering had run away before; she told me she felt she could stand it no longer; she was weak in body and mind, and she feared they would lead her back to heathenism, so she would go away the first opportunity. She is the seventh child who has run away from her father's house; the former six went on account of the tyranny and cruelty of the father; but now they rally round him and help him with cowries to make charms, and to bribe the chiefs to be angry with us, and say, 'What a bad girl this is to go away, and what a bad thing this church matter is.'

"Another young woman has been set free; her intended husband refused to have her, and made her parents pay back what he had given for her, which they gladly did for fear lest she should run away. So she comes to church, and lives at home as usual.

"A young girl of sixteen years has been nearly killed by her father for coming to church; beaten with a cutlass till she could not feed herself, or turn on her mat. She has endured very much, but I fear she is giving way now; she does not come to church. On a week-day she visited me; I reminded her of the words of our Saviour, which she had learned with me, 'Whosoever shall confess Me before men, him shall the Son of man also confess before the angels of God; but he that denieth Me before men, shall be denied before the angels of God.' She wept, poor child, but alas! I saw her last Sunday go to fetch water from the brook, which, with every other kind of work, she had stoutly refused hitherto, even when they would not let her leave the house. She has told them for nearly twelve months, 'This is God's day!' Will you not pray for her, and for these young beginners in the ways of the Lord, that they may be kept, helped, and strengthened?

"Another has equally and patiently suffered the whip, the rope, and the chain, has been dragged about from one town to another, to make her forget about coming to church and serving God; but she was too much in earnest to forget by being carried to a far country. After some weeks of absence, she was brought back; her father promised her great things, clothes, beads, honour, and added, 'Now you will never go there?' pointing to the church. 'Father,' she replied, 'I am just the same as before, I will be a good daughter to you, I will earn cowries for you, only let me go to God's house, to hear His word and follow it, for this I cannot give up.' The father said, 'What strength do these white people give! what charm have they! Nothing will make these people give up!' and he nearly yielded. 'It is of no use,' he said, 'I am tired.' But his neighbours came about him, and gave him no rest till he promised to prevent his daughter coming to us. The mother came and said that if we would persuade her to worship idols as well, she might come to church. The girl has since often been sent to Ijaye to buy things; she was to go on Saturday, and come back on Monday; but then they found she could go to God's house there, so that was given up; and one Sunday she was called out of church, but did not go. On the following Sunday, hearing her mother getting the chain ready to tie her, she ran to us, and what a fearful noise we heard! The whole family came into our yard, and flourished about their swords and knives, which we knew they would not use: we left them till they were tired, and then they went away. The girl was then advised to go home and sit down quietly for that day, which she did; and, though the house is close to us, we heard no more noise. She visited me secretly a few evenings since, and told me her heart was in the same place, and that she would follow the way God had sent us to teach, unto death. They have told her they will carry her to those who sell slaves, and who send them far away; her answer was, 'Well, where you send me, I will go: God, the great God, my God, is in all the world.' You will readily believe how keenly we partake with them in their sufferings; though we weep, yet do we rejoice that they are so wonderfully supported; and we thank God that He has permitted His children to make such a good confession of their faith before so many.

"The father of one of these young women has this morning set her free to go to God's house, and to walk in the way she sees right; for he says, 'It is true what that white man says, it is no use to fight against God.' Another man is greatly troubled at what he has done, and is quite in an agony to see his child once more. The mother of a third now begs me to help her to find her child, her heart yearns after her whom she so fearfully persecuted, under evil direction. In other houses the cry is, about those who escaped, 'Oh, if it had not been for you, this would not have happened.' So our God has graciously made His arm to be felt among us, and many hear Him say, 'Why persecutest thou Me? it is hard for thee to kick against the pricks.' The Lord will not forsake His own work; when it pleaseth Him, He can put all His enemies to silence. Even these poor deluded heathen tell us, 'Have patience, white man; your words and ways are new, we are dark and have no sense, tell your word day after day, it will go into the ear, and bye and bye many will follow it' ". . . .

"*November 17th.* [1861]—My husband is much interested in translating the 'Pilgrim's Progress.' We indulge in the hope of taking it home to print before long, and we think it will be particularly interesting and useful to our Africans. This work has been a great pleasure to him, and helps to reconcile him to the quiet life he has been obliged to lead of late. Through God's mercy, I do not think I have had even a day's ailing since last November. Pray for us, and give thanks also, for God's mercy endureth for ever."

"*December 9th.*—We and our people have sold everything which we can turn into money, and the thought and burden of all that is upon us is getting almost more than we can bear. A few days ago I did get cast down, but our gracious God was merciful to us, as He ever is; our troubles are many, but His support is mighty. My dear husband's state is most serious; some nights ago he had hours of fearful coughing, and every moment seemed as if it might be his last; and we have not the least, the simplest, remedy to relieve him. He was much exhausted for two or three days, and one of our people, who could ill afford it, brought us a bag of cowries (about one pound's worth), and told us to take it and use it freely to buy meat and more strengthening things than beans, &c., which we are generally content with. That bag of cowries, which was to have been for our comfort, and especially for my poor husband, we had to give up, to rescue the daughter of the scripture-reader of Awaye from being sold. [She had been captured by the Ibadan people.] I nearly cried, yet we were thankful we had it, and could thus rescue the poor girl; and so gracious, and merciful, and faithful has our God been, that we have, after all, been living better than for some time past. We sold a counterpane, and a few yards of damask which had been overlooked by us; so that we indulge every now and then in one hundred cowries' worth of meat (about one pennyworth), and such a morsel seems like a little feast to us in these days. I have been buying to-day ten baskets of corn, and hope to buy five more to-morrow, for our children especially; and I was sadly afraid I could not even buy one basket in store this season; and so, time after time, is our want of faith put to shame, and also our faith revived and strengthened. Those baskets of corn are such a delightful sight to me this evening, that I can scarcely help running just to take a look at them, and be thankful. . . .

"*Jan. 1st.,* 1862.—Your kind hearts are, I well know, longing for tidings of us. We are weary for letters also, having had none since those written in June; we cannot help longing for home letters to perfect our New Year's Day, but we hope soon for the great treat of receiving the July, August, September and October mails, and some dollars to buy cowries with, for our daily needs. 1861 has passed away with its cares, sorrows, pains, and though last, not least, its many mercies; 1862 has commenced; we sometimes think it looks sad, dark and heavy, and we fear to tread it, but we know who is the same 'yesterday, to-day, and for ever,'—through war, sickness, all things, yes, through death itself. This has been the subject of my husband's address at our early morning service. There is a prayer meeting every morning at six or earlier, but on this morning we have it at seven, to give time for our people who are far off in this large town, and all came so bright and happy, truly enjoying it. They were here long before seven, for kind greetings, good words, and blessings. My thoughts and musings are many on this day, but I must come to our matter-of-fact history, especially as I have only three thin sheets of paper besides this. War, so-called war, is still going on, with very little of real war, but roads shut up, and parties out kidnapping. We, of the mission in Ibadan, are the chief and almost the only sufferers; depending on the coast as we do, and with no road: European necessaries and comforts we have long been

*Church and Mission House at Ibadan*

without, and cannot have again. My last pair of shoes are on my feet, and my clothes are so worn and so few, that if the war does not end soon, I shall have to come to a country cloth, and roll up like a native. These would be small troubles if we were in health, but my dear husband is a sad sufferer, and every bit of remedy or alleviation, in the way of medicine, has been for some months entirely finished. I have had two most severe attacks of fever, one in August, and one in November. I only began to get out on Christmas Day, to the great pleasure of our people, who said it would be no Christmas at all if I were not with them. And I have been getting better ever since, creeping up hill, and falling by degrees into all my various duties; but recovering is slow work, when even a cup of tea can now only be taken sparingly, by way of a luxury, as very little is left. Goat meat and yams, though good enough at other times, are not very nourishing or congenial now, and the season is fearfully hot. We do sometimes feel weary and cast down, and then cheer and comfort are given; we are mercifully helped on from day to day. Our Master's work is really going on; faults, infirmities, falls, are in our little church, but there are some truly travelling heavenward. November was a month of trial; evil doings among some of the Christians were revealed to us, and they were only sorry because they were found out. Candidates for baptism were unsatisfactory, and we were ready to cry, 'We labour in vain; and spend our strength for nought,' when our merciful Father, instead of punishing us for our murmuring and want of faith, gave us a wonderful sign that He Himself was in our midst, to own, to bless, to save, in the death-bed of one of our converts, whose conduct had been consistent in the few years since he joined himself to those who profess to be on the Lord's side. He left behind him a beautiful testimony to the truth and reality of the religion of the Gospel, calling the converts together, exhorting them, and taking leave thus: 'For me it is no more hard; through my Saviour the fight is fought; through my Saviour the battle is won; and I now, through His love, go to be with Him; but for you, my brethren, it is hard; you have to go on in an evil world, in a land where the devil is very strong; but hold on to Jesus, and all shall be well.' The last day he had strong convulsions, but, at intervals, happy looks and words, and when he could no more speak, on Olubi raising him, and asking if all was still well, with a happy smile he pointed his finger upwards, then folded his hands, as if in prayer, on his chest, and left his companions only to say, 'Blessed, indeed blessed, are those who die in the Lord.' It was a great comfort to us to have such a witness for the truth, and such a blessed entrance given to the mansions above; a soul safe from sin, Satan, and the evils and cruelties of a heathen land, of which none can have any idea but those who live in it. Thus a new song was put in our mouth, and in the refreshment of that we go on our way.

"There is a great talk that this war will come to an end before many months. We try to hope it, and if so, and we get a road and money and clothes for our children, (of which there are plenty waiting at Abeokuta) and everything to set all going comfortably, we may by the end of this year reach England, which refreshment we much need; but if the war lasts years, we cannot possibly leave, as far as we now see. But we look to Him, and lean upon Him, who is the Physician for body and soul, and who can keep us in sickness or health, in pain, and war, and troubles of various kinds, for His own good purposes. We pray that we may not be weary or faint, but seek only His will in all things, to go or to stay, patiently and willingly."

"*March 3rd.*—On the 13th February came our precious six months' mail; I had fifty letters for my share, and how happy was I. We are most fortunate, in all this war and confusion, that up to this time we have received all our letters from home.

"There has been much small-pox among our school-children, but all are going on nicely, it is made nothing of in this country; it has been raging in the town this year, and we know of only one death.

"On January 15th, one of my little girls fell from some steps outside our house, broke the inner bone of the arm, and dislocated the wrist. We did our best to put it to rights immediately; and because we could not make splints, and did not like to wait, my husband cut up the strong board cover of a German book, and I bandaged it up. My lotion was vinegar and water, and all went on admirably. The third night she was in dreadful pain, but after that she had no more. Those first nights I was very anxious about her, not trusting my surgical doings; so I never left her, and would not let any one touch her but myself for three days. After that, she was very happy in my room, with her picture-book and doll; and when I released the bandages she could again move her hand quite freely. I was greatly surprised at the perfect cure; all now to be seen is that the wrist is a little thicker than the other. So we have been helped over this trouble.

"I must tell you of a most useful gift. I have three pairs of new shoes! American shoes too, and from further in the interior. An American Baptist missionary sent me them from Oyo; they were his dear wife's, who died four years ago, after having been less than three months in Africa. Thus our daily wants are supplied, even in such a matter as shoes. Ah, how may we

> 'Praise God for all that is past,
> And trust Him for all that's to come.'

I am in good health, and my dear husband has longer intervals of rest from his trying cough than last year. If this war should end, and we could get a few comforts and necessaries about us, we shall almost forget weakness and want, and might yet be able to go on a year or two longer here. How happy this would make us, to carry on our work under the more favourable circumstances of peace; but we shall be rightly directed to go or stay, I truly believe; such goodness, such help, has mercifully been given us. The war has been a sad hindrance to us in many a way; preventing the completion of the second station in this town, where Mr. Jeffries is residing, and also the making of a third station, where a native teacher lives. We have managed to build a little house for him and his family lately; he was only in a borrowed room in a large compound, and that was not so pleasant; but as we and he have all helped, we made it for very few cowries, and it will be well worth what it has cost, even if we have to make the proper place next year. We sadly want the opening of the roads which the end of this war will bring; my children are so out of clothes, such a shabby little party they are, and there are so many nice boxes waiting for us, clothes, books, and slates, &c.; when I think of it all, I am sure we shall not have time to go home. I am nicely well, if only my dear husband should get as well! But all will be rightly, wisely, kindly ordered for us. Oh, how sweet it is to feel that every step is ordered for us, if we only seek grace to walk in it.

"There appeared to be good grounds for hope that peace would be concluded after the taking of Ijaye, which occurred in March, 1862, bringing such utter destruction upon the place, that, within a year, nothing but desolate and overgrown ruins remained to mark the spot where a flourishing town, containing upwards of sixty thousand inhabitants, had so lately stood. But, in the long contest, all the surrounding tribes had become involved in disputes with one another, some taking the part of Ibadan, and others that of Ijaye. The seat of war was eventually transferred to the Ijebu territory, which extended over the greater part of the country between Ibadan and the coast. The enemies of Ibadan well knew that to isolate would be to weaken it, and that to cut off its communication with Lagos, the market from which its supplies of ammunition were procured, might issue in its destruction. With this view, in fact, hostilities were still carried on with more or less of activity, and with varying success. . . .

"*May 30th.*—We are living just as we can, others helping us, out of their poverty. We get a yam here, and a yam there, and a little corn in the same manner. One of our converts yesterday lent us some cowries, which must, by pinching, last us three or four weeks, if possible; he had to borrow them from a heathen friend, before he could lend them to us. Dearest friends, you will think of us, and long to help us, but there is nothing left for your kind hearts to do for us, but to pray."

"*August 15th.*—I have a corner in the piazza, which I call my study. It is a funny little place, but very pleasant to me. Here I read and write, and receive any favoured visitors. Where there is wall, it is washed with a kind of red earth, but where it is of boards, they are very rough, and overlap one another. I took it into my head a little while ago to ornament it, for an amusement, and to enjoy it afterwards; so out of an old *London News* I have got some pretty English scenes, domestic groups, children, and animals, all of which are an immense delight to my little and big children, and form a never-ending subject of conversation when they are admitted there. . . .

# MARY KINGSLEY*
# (West Africa, 1893 and 1895)

Mary Kingsley, one of the best known women to have traveled in West Africa in the late nineteenth century, was born in 1862. Her early years were mostly confined to her home while her elder brother was engaged in travel to the exotic places that had occupied their father before his health declined. By the time she reached her early thirties, both parents had died, leaving her a small inheritance. This bit of money, in combination with the promise of a stipend for obtaining rare fish in West Africa, enabled Kingsley to fulfill her own travel dreams. Influenced by her father in the study of nonwestern people, Kingsley was also aided by her well-known scientist uncle, Charles, in obtaining rudimentary knowledge for preserving unfamiliar species of the fish she was to collect and return to England. Kingsley actually made two trips to Africa, one in 1893 and the second in 1895, which she combined in writing *Travels in West Africa,* from which the first excerpt included here is taken. (Some of the areas in which she traveled are actually considered to be Central Africa, rather than West.)

She arrived in Gabon after two months enroute from Liverpool, traveling between the Niger and the Congo, and experiencing one adventure after another. Her purposes were twofold. While collecting the fish kept her confined to mostly the river areas, Kingsley engaged in trade with the Africans she encountered as a way of learning their customs. As a budding ethnographer, Kingsley joined the increasing ranks of European travelers whose notebooks later became the sources of information on the people among whom they traveled. In this case, however, Kingsley was a young woman who moved in and out of African villages accompanied only by the Africans who guided her. Her memoir is replete with stories of her adventures on the often treacherous rivers she explored. And, for her times, Kingsley proved to be remarkably receptive to the African people she encountered. As to the missionaries with whom she often stayed, however, Kingsley was often critical and frequently prescient in questioning their relevance to African societies. In the first excerpt we meet

*Mary Kingsley, *Travels in West Africa,* London: Macmillan & Company, Ltd. 1897, 101–123; and Mary Kingsley, "Life in West Africa" lecture in the Sunday Afternoon Course at the South Place Institute, Finsbury, between 1895–1898 in *British Empire Series II,* 366–380.

43

# BIRKBECK

## Literary and Scientific Institution,

BREAMS BUILDINGS, CHANCERY LANE, E.C.

On Wednesday Evening, Oct. 13th, 1897,

AT EIGHT O'CLOCK,

# MISS MARY KINGSLEY

WILL DELIVER A LECTURE ON

# ➤ *West Africa.* ⬅

The Lecture will be fully Illustrated by the Oxy-
Hydrogen Light.

Admission, SIXPENCE.        Area or Balcony, ONE SHILLING.

Reserved Seats, TWO SHILLINGS.

*Members can obtain Tickets for the Reserved Seats, Area, or*
*Balcony, at Half-price.*

Prospectus, with List of Lectures, Classes, &c., gratis on application.

**THE BIRKBECK CALENDAR** (Price 6d., Post free 8d.), gives
detailed syllabuses of the Classes, the Text Books, particulars of
Examinations, Prizes, &c., with the list of successful Candidates
and the examination papers of the previous year.

1000  9-97      J. C. LARRANCE Steam Printer, 36, Beech Street, Barbican.

*Announcement of a lecture by Mary Kingsley*

Kingsley on her return to the French mission station in Lembarene, Gabon in today's Central Africa. The Protestant missionary, M. Forget, is dying. Kingsley uses the occasion of his death to comment on missionaries in general and African customs in the area. (Note a common misconception among these early travelers and pseudo-ethnographers when Kingsley refers to the cannibalistic Fan. The missionaries and unfriendly African informants were her sources. Kingsley never saw the Fan engage in cannibalism because they did not practice that habit.)

As Kingsley hems her skirt (reminding us how vulnerable she was as a female traveling mostly unaccompanied through uncharted areas), she comments on matters that are especially feminine in terms of interest: food and cooking, women's lives, and polygamy. Yet, Kingsley is also able to see universals: the breakdown of traditional African societies as the missionaries force European customs as part of conversion.

The second selection from Kingsley is a less well-known lecture she gave before a group of scholars and colonial servants back in England in the mid–1890s. Here we get a different picture of Kingsley: the ethnographer emerges to provide interpretations and speculations that may have given fuel to the colonial impetus then present in certain English circles. In this lecture, Kingsley is ambiguous as to the outcome on Africa as a result of the colonial impetus. On the one hand, the "civilized" Africans are those who have had contact with European culture. On the other, Kingsley recognizes the negative impact of Europe on Africa.

In a passing reference to British activities in settler colonies at the time, Kingsley forecasts another dimension of racial antagonism that would rear its head as the twentieth century dawned (albeit, in terms of problems for the white, not the black). "In . . . regions heavy populated by powerful Africans hanging about doing nothing beyond what they done for thousands of years, foreign labour from India is being imported—a thing which I am certain will only end in bringing in another problem for white men in Africa." She predicts, also, that the problem of imported labor is less likely to affect West Africa because of the forbidding climate. But, like all true imperialists, the African problems Kingsley lists are those whose long-run effects will bear upon the European colonialists.

In a humorous vein, Kingsley suffered indignities because of her sex. A French official refuses to take responsibility for allowing her to go unaccompanied, except for her African helpers, on a trip down some rapids. She had no husband. Her retort was that her crew were experts on the rapids "and as for the husband, neither the Royal Geographical Society's list in their 'Hints to Travellers' nor Messrs. Silver, in their elaborate lists of articles necessary for a traveller in tropical climates, make mention of husbands." And perhaps she enjoyed the gender reversal, when on the river, and with the current sweeping them into obstacles near the embankment, one of the Africa crewmen shouted to Mary "Jump for bank, Sar."

Kingsley returned to Africa at the age of 38, serving as a nurse during the South African (Boer) War. It was there that she died of enteric fever. But by the time of her premature death, she was widely renowned as an indomitable Victorian traveler. The Mary Kingsley Society of West Africa was founded soon after her death as a memorial to the well known woman writer and adventurer.

# Lembarene

On my return to Talagouga, I find both my good friends sick with fever—M. Forget very ill indeed. Providentially the *Éclaireur* came up the river, with the Doctor Administrator on board, and he came ashore and prescribed, and in a few days M. Forget was better. I say good-bye to Talagouga with much regret, and go on board the *Éclaireur,* when she returns from Njole, with all my bottles and belongings. On board I find no other passenger; the captain's English has widened out considerably; and he is as pleasant, cheery, and spoiling for a fight as ever; but he has a preoccupied manner, and a most peculiar set of new habits, which I find are shared by the engineer. Both of them make rapid dashes to the rail, and nervously scan the river for a minute and then return to some occupation, only to dash from it to the rail again. During breakfast their conduct is nerve-shaking. Hastily taking a few mouthfuls, the captain drops his knife and fork and simply hurls his seamanlike form through the nearest door out on to the deck. In another minute he is back again, and with just a shake of his head to the engineer, continues his meal. The engineer shortly afterwards flies from his seat, and being far thinner than the captain, goes through his nearest door with even greater rapidity; returns, and shakes his head at the captain, and continues his meal. Excitement of this kind is infectious, and I also wonder whether I ought not to show a sympathetic friendliness by flying from my seat and hurling myself on to the deck through my nearest door, too. But although there are plenty of doors, as four enter the saloon from the deck, I do not see my way to doing this performance aimlessly, and what in this world they are both after I cannot think. So I confine myself to woman's true sphere, and assist in a humble way by catching the wine and Vichy water bottles, glasses, and plates of food, which at every performance are jeopardized by the members of the nobler sex starting off with a considerable quantity of the ample table-cloth wrapped round their legs. At last I can stand it no longer, so ask the captain point-blank what is the matter. "Nothing," says he, bounding out of his chair and flying out of his doorway; but on his return he tells me he has got a bet on of two bottles of champagne with Woermann's agent for Njole, as to who shall reach Lembarene first, and the German agent has started off some time before the *Éclaireur* in his little steam launch.

During the afternoon we run smoothly along; the free pulsations of the engines telling what a very different thing coming down the Ogowé is to going up against its terrific current. Every now and again we stop to pick up cargo, or discharge over-carried cargo, and the captain's mind becomes lulled by getting no news of the Woermann's launch having passed down.

He communicates this to the engineer; it is impossible she could have passed the *Éclaireur* since they started, therefore she must be somewhere behind at a subfactory, *"N'est-ce pas?" "Oui, oui, certainement,"* says the engineer. The engineer is, by these considerations, also lulled, and feels he may do something else but scan the river *à la* sister Ann. What that something is puzzles me; it evidently requires secrecy, and he shrinks from detection. First he looks down one side of the deck, no one there; then he looks down the other, no one there; good so far. I then see he has put his head through one of the saloon portholes; no one there; he hesitates a few seconds until I begin to wonder whether his head will suddenly appear through my port; but he regards this as an unnecessary precaution, and I hear him enter his cabin which abuts on mine and there is silence for some minutes. Writing home to his mother, think I, as I go on putting a new braid round the bottom of a worn skirt. Almost immediately after follows the sound of a little click from the next cabin, and then apparently one of the denizens of the infernal regions has got its tail smashed in a door and the heavy hot afternoon air is reft by an inchoate howl of agony. I drop my needlework and take to the deck; but it is after all only that shy retiring young man practising secretly on his clarionet.

The captain is drowsily looking down the river. But repose is not long allowed to that active spirit; he sees something in the water—what? *"Hippopotame,"* he ejaculates. Now both he and the engineer frequently do this thing, and then fly off to their guns—bang, bang, finish; but this time he does not dash for his gun, nor does the engineer, who flies out of his cabin at the sound of the war shout *"Hippopotame."* In vain I look across the broad river with its stretches of yellow sandbanks, where the *hippopotame"* should be, but I can see nothing but four black stumps sticking up in the water away to the right. Meanwhile the captain and the engineer are flying about getting off a crew of blacks into the canoe we are towing alongside. This being done the captain explains to me that on the voyage up "the engineer had fired at, and hit a hippopotamus, and without doubt this was its body floating." We are now close enough even for me to recognise the four stumps as the deceased's legs, and soon the canoe is alongside them and makes fast to one, and then starts to paddle back, hippo and all, to the *Éclaireur.* But no such thing; let them paddle and shout as hard as they like, the hippo's weight simply anchors them. The *Éclaireur* by now has dropped down the river past them, and has to sweep round and run back. Recognising promptly what the trouble is, the energetic captain grabs up a broom, ties a light cord belonging to the leadline to it, and holding the broom by the end of its handle, swings it round his head and hurls it at the canoe. The arm of a merciful Providence being interposed, the broom-tomahawk does not hit the canoe, wherein, if it had, it must infallibly have killed some one, but falls short, and goes tearing off with the current, well out of reach of the canoe. The captain seeing this gross dereliction of duty by a Chargeur Réunis broom, hauls it in hand over hand and talks to it. Then he ties the other end of its line to the mooring rope, and by a better aimed shot sends the broom into the water, about ten yards above the canoe, and it drifts towards it. Breathless excitement! surely they will get it now. Alas, no! Just when it is within reach of the canoe, a fearful shudder runs through the broom. It throws up its head and sinks beneath the tide. A sensation of stun comes over all of us. The crew of the canoe, ready and eager to grasp the approaching aid, gaze blankly at the circling ripples round where it sank. In a second the captain knows what has happened. That heavy hawser which has been paid out after it has dragged it down, so he hauls it on board again.

The *Éclaireur* goes now close enough to the hippo-anchored canoe for a rope to be flung to the man in her bow; he catches it and freezes on gallantly. Saved! No! Oh horror! The lower deck hums with fear that after all it will not taste that toothsome hippo chop, for the man who has caught the rope is as nearly as possible jerked flying out of the canoe when the strain of the *Éclaireur* contending with the hippo's inertia flies along it, but his companion behind him grips him by the legs and is in his turn grabbed, and the crew holding on to each other with their hands, and on to their craft with their feet, save the man holding on to the rope and the whole situation; and slowly bobbing towards us comes the hippopotamus, who is shortly hauled on board by the winners in triumph.

My esteemed friends, the captain and the engineer, who of course have been below during this hauling, now rush onto the upper deck, each coatless, and carrying an enormous butcher's knife. They dash into the saloon, where a terrific sharpening of these instruments takes place on the steel belonging to the saloon carving-knife, and down stairs again. By looking down the ladder, I can see the pink, pig-like hippo, whose colour has been soaked out by the water, lying on the lower deck and the captain and engineer slitting down the skin intent on gralloching operations. Providentially, my prophetic soul induces me to leave the top of the ladder and go forward—"run to win'ard," as Captain Murray would say—for within two minutes the captain and engineer are up the ladder as if they had been blown up by the boilers bursting, and go as one man for the brandy bottle; and they wanted it if ever man did; for remember that hippo had been dead and in the warm river-water for more than a week.

The captain had had enough of it, he said, but the engineer stuck to the job with a courage I profoundly admire, and he saw it through and then retired to his cabin; sand-and-canvassed himself first, and then soaked and saturated himself in Florida water. The flesh gladdened the hearts of the crew and lower-deck passengers and also of the inhabitants of Lembarene, who got dashes of it on our arrival there. Hippo flesh is not to be despised by black man or white; I have enjoyed it far more than the stringy beef or vapid goat's flesh one gets down here.

I stayed on board the *Éclaireur* all night; for it was dark when we reached Lembarene, too dark to go round to Kangwe; and next morning, after taking a farewell of her—I hope not a final one, for she is a most luxurious little vessel for the Coast, as the feeding on board is excellent and the society varied and charming—I went round to Kangwe. M. and Mme. Jacot received me back most kindly, and they both looked all the better for my having been away. M. Haug and a young missionary from Baraka, who had come up to Lembarene for a change after fever, were busy starting to go up to Talagouga in a canoe, which I was very glad of, because M. Haug, at any rate, would be of immense help to Mme. and M. Forget, while they were in such bad health; only during his absence M. Jacot had enough work for any five men.

I remained some time in the Lembarene district and saw and learnt many things; I owe most of what I learnt to M. and Mme. Jacot who knew a great deal about both the natives and the district, and I owe much of what I saw to having acquired the art of managing by myself a native canoe. This "recklessness" of mine I am sure did not merit the severe criticism it has been subjected to, for my performances gave immense amusement to others (I can hear Lembarene's shrieks of laughter now) and to myself they gave great pleasure.

My first attempt was made at Talagouga one very hot afternoon. M. and Mme. Forget were, I thought, safe having their siestas, Oranie was with Mme. Gacon. I knew where Mme. Gacon was for certain; she was with M. Gacon; and I knew he was up in the sawmill shed out of sight of the river, because of the soft thump, thump, thump of the big water-wheel. There was therefore no one to keep me out of mischief, and I was too frightened to go into the forest that afternoon, because on the previous afternoon I had been stalked as a wild beast by a cannibal savage, and I am nervous. Besides, and above all, it is quite impossible to see other people, even if they are only black, naked savages, gliding about in canoes, without wishing to go and glide about yourself. So I went down to where the canoes were tied by their noses to the steep bank, and finding a paddle, a broken one, I unloosed the smallest canoe. Unfortunately this was fifteen feet or so long, but I did not know the disadvantage of having, as it were, a long-tailed canoe then—I did shortly afterwards.

The promontories running out into the river on each side of the mission beach gave a little stretch of slack water between the bank and the mill-race-like current of the Ogowé, and I wisely decided to keep in the slack water, until I had found out how to steer—most important thing steering. I got into the bow of the canoe, and shoved off from the bank all right; then I knelt down—learn how to paddle standing up by and by—good so far. I rapidly learnt how to steer from the bow, but I could not get up any pace. Intent on acquiring pace, I got to the edge of the slack water; and then displaying more wisdom, I turned round to avoid it, proud as a peacock, you understand, at having found out how to turn round. At this moment, the current of the greatest equatorial river in the world, grabbed my canoe by its tail. We spun round and round for a few seconds, like a teetotum, I steering the whole time for all I was worth, and then the current dragged the canoe ignominiously down river, tail foremost.

Fortunately a big tree was at that time temporarily hanging against the rock in the river, just below the sawmill beach. Into that tree the canoe shot with a crash, and I hung on, and shipping my paddle, pulled the canoe into the slack water again, by the aid of the branches of the tree, which I was in mortal terror would come off the rock, and insist on accompanying me and the canoe, *viâ* Kama country, to the Atlantic Ocean; but it held, and when I had got safe against the side of the pinnacle-rock I wiped a perspiring brow, and searched in my mind for a piece of information regarding navigation that would be applicable to the management of long-tailed Adooma canoes. I could not think of one for some minutes. Captain Murray has imparted to me at one time and another an enormous mass of hints as to the management of vessels, but those vessels were all presup-posed to have steam power. But he having been the first man to take an ocean-going steamer up to Matadi on the Congo, through the terrific currents that whirl and fly in Hell's Cauldron, knew about currents, and I remembered he had said regarding taking vessels through them, "Keep all the headway you can on her." Good! that hint inverted will fit this situation like a glove, and I'll keep all the tailway I can off her. Feeling now as safe as only a human being can feel who is backed up by a sound principle, I was cautiously crawling to the tail-end of the canoe, intent on kneeling in it to look after it, when I heard a dreadful outcry on the bank. Looking there I saw Mme. Forget, Mme. Gacon, M. Gacon, and their attributive crowd of mission children all in a state of frenzy. They said lots of things in chorus. "What?" said I. They said some more and added gesticulations. Seeing I was wasting their time as I could not hear, I drove the canoe from the rock and made my way, mostly by steering, to the bank close by; and then tying the canoe firmly up I walked over the mill stream and divers other things towards my anxious friends. "You'll be drowned," they said. "Gracious goodness!" said I, "I thought that half an hour ago, but it's all right now; I can steer." After much conversation I lulled their fears regarding me, and having received strict orders to keep in the stern of the canoe, because that is the proper place when you are managing a canoe single-handed, I returned to my studies. I had not however lulled my friends' interest regarding me, and they stayed on the bank watching.

I found first, that my education in steering from the bow was of no avail; second, that it was all right if you reversed it. For instance, when you are in the bow, and make an inward stroke with the paddle on the right-hand side, the bow goes to the right; whereas, if you make an inward stroke on the right-hand side, when you are sitting in the stern, the bow then goes to the left. Understand? Having grasped this law, I crept along up river; and, by Allah! before I had gone twenty yards, if that wretch, the current of the greatest, &c., did not grab hold of the nose of my canoe, and we teetotum-med round again as merrily as ever. My audience screamed. I knew what they were saying, "You'll be drowned! Come back! Come back!" but I heard them and I heeded not. If you attend to advice in a crisis you're lost; besides, I couldn't "Come back" just then. However, I got into the slack water again, by some very showy, high-class steering. Still steering, fine as it is, is not all you require and hanker after. You want pace as well, and pace, except when in the clutches of the current, I had not so far attained. Perchance, thought I, the pace region in a canoe may be in its centre; so I got along on my knees into the centre to experiment. Bitter failure; the canoe took to sidling down river broadside on, like Mr. Winkle's horse. Shouts of laughter from the bank. Both bow and stern education utterly inapplicable to centre; and so, seeing I was utterly thrown away there, I crept into the bow, and in a few more minutes I steered my canoe, perfectly, in among its fellows by the bank and secured it there. Mme. Forget ran down to meet me and assured me she had not laughed so much since she had been in Africa, although she was frightened at the time lest I should get capsized and drowned. I believe it, for she is a sweet and gracious lady; and I quite see, as she demonstrated, that the sight of me, teetotumming about, steering in an elaborate and showy way all the time, was irresistibly comic. And she gave a most amusing account of how, when she started looking for me to give me tea, a charming habit of hers, she could not see me in among my bottles, and so asked the little black boy where I was. "There," said he, pointing to the tree hanging against the rock out in the river; and she, seeing me hitched with a canoe against the rock, and knowing the danger and depth of the river, got alarmed.

Well, when I got down to Lembarene I naturally went on with my canoeing studies, in pursuit of the attainment of pace. Success crowned my efforts, and I can honestly and truly say that there are only two things I am proud of—one is that Doctor Günther has approved of my fishes, and the other is that I can paddle an Ogowé canoe. Pace, style, steering and all, "All same for one" as if I were an Ogowé African. A strange, incongruous pair of things: but I often wonder what are the things other people are really most proud of; it would be a quaint and repaying subject for investigation.

Mme. Jacot gave me every help in canoeing, for she is a remarkable clear-headed woman, and recognised that, as I was always getting soaked, anyhow, I ran no extra danger in getting soaked in a canoe; and then, it being the dry season, there was an immense stretch of water opposite Andande beach, which was quite shallow. So she saw no need of my getting drowned.

The sandbanks were showing their yellow heads in all directions when I came down from Talagouga, and just opposite Andande there was sticking up out of the water a great, graceful, palm frond. It had been stuck into the head of the pet sandbank, and every day was visited by the boys and girls in canoes to see how much longer they would have to wait for the sandbank's appearance. A few days after my return it showed, and in two days more there it was, acres and acres of it, looking like a great, golden carpet spread on the surface of the centre of the clear water—clear here, down this side of Lembarene Island, because the river runs fairly quietly, and has time to deposit its mud. Dark brown the Ogowé flies past the other side of the island, the main current being deflected that way by a bend, just below the entrance of the Nguni.

There was great rejoicing. Canoe-load after canoe-load of boys and girls went to the sandbank, some doing a little fishing round its rim, others bringing the washing there, all skylarking and singing. Few prettier sights have I ever seen than those on that sandbank—the merry brown forms dancing or lying stretched on it: the gaudy-coloured patchwork quilts and chintz mosquito-bars that have been washed, spread out drying, looking from Kangwe on the hill above, like beds of bright flowers. By night when it was moonlight there would be bands of dancers on it with bush-light torches, gyrating, intermingling and separating till you could think you were looking at a dance of stars.

They commenced affairs very early on that sandbank, and they kept them up very late; and all the time there came from it a soft murmur of laughter and song. Ah me! if the aim of life were happiness and pleasure, Africa should send us missionaries instead of our sending them to her— but, fortunately for the work of the world, happiness is not. One thing I remember which struck me very much regarding the sandbank, and this was that Mme. Jacot found such pleasure in taking her work on to the verandah, where she could see it. I knew she did not care for the songs and the dancing. One day she said to me, "It is such a relief." "A relief?" I said. "Yes, do you not see that until it shows there is nothing but forest, forest, forest, and that still stretch of river. That bank is the only piece of clear ground I see in the year, and that only lasts a few weeks until the wet season comes, and then it goes, and there is nothing but forest, forest, forest, for another year. It is two years now since I came to this place; it may be I know not how many more before we go home again." I grieve to say, for my poor friend's sake, that her life at Kangwe was nearly at its end. Soon after my return to England I heard of the death of her husband from malignant fever. M. Jacot was a fine, powerful, energetic man, in the prime of life. He was a teetotaler and a vegetarian; and although constantly travelling to and fro in his district on his evangelising work, he had no foolish recklessness in him. No one would have thought that he would have been the first to go of us who used to sit round his hospitable table. His delicate wife, his two young children or I would have seemed far more likely. His loss will be a lasting one to the people he risked his life to (what he regarded) save. The natives held him in the greatest affection and respect, and his influence over them was considerable, far more profound than that of any other missionary I have ever seen. . . .

The amount of work M. and Mme. Jacot used to get through was, to me, amazing, and I think the Ogowé Protestant mission sadly short-handed— its missionaries not being content to follow the usual Protestant plan out in West Africa, namely, quietly sitting down and keeping house, with just a few native children indoors to do the housework, and close by a school and a little church where a service is held on Sundays. The representatives of the Mission Évangélique, go to and fro throughout the district round each station on evangelising work, among some of the most dangerous and uncivilised tribes in Africa, frequently spending a fortnight at a time away from their homes, on the waterways of a wild and dangerous country. In addition to going themselves, they send trained natives as evangelists and Bible readers, and keep a keen eye on the trained native, which means a considerable amount of worry and strain too. The work on the stations is heavy in Ogowé districts, because when you have got a clearing made and all the buildings up, you have by no means finished with the affair, for you have to fight the Ogowé forest back, as a Dutchman fights the sea. But the main cause of work is the store, which in this exhausting climate is more than enough work for one man alone.

Payments on the Ogowé are made in goods; the natives do not use any coinage-equivalent, save in the strange case of the Fans, which does not touch general trade and which I will speak of later. They have not even the brass bars and cheetems that are in used in Calabar, or cowries as in Lagos. In order to expedite and simplify this goods traffic, a written or printed piece of paper is employed—practically a cheque, which is called a "bon" or "book," and these "bons" are cashed—*i.e.* gooded, at the store. They are for three amounts. Five fura = a dollar. One fura = a franc. Desu

= fifty centimes = half a fura. The value given for these "bons" is the same from government, trade, and mission. Although the Mission Évangélique does not trade—*i.e.* buy produce and sell it at a profit, its representatives have a great deal of business to attend to through the store, which is practically a bank. All the native evangelists, black teachers, Bible-readers and labourers on the stations are paid off in these bons; and when any representative of the mission is away on a journey, food bought for themselves and their canoe crews is paid for in bons, which are brought in by the natives at their convenience, and changed for goods at the store. Therefore for several hours every weekday the missionary has to devote himself to store work, and store work out here is by no means playing at shop. It is very hard, tiring, exasperating work when you have to deal with it in full, as a trader, when it is necessary for you to purchase produce at a price that will give you a reasonable margin of profit over storing, customs' duties, shipping expenses, &c., &c. But it is quite enough to try the patience of any saint when you are only keeping store to pay on bons, *à la* missionary; for each class of article used in trade—and there are some hundreds of them—has a definite and acknowledged value, but where the trouble comes in is that different articles have the same value; for example, six fish-hooks and one pocket-handkerchief have the same value, or you can make up that value in lucifer matches, pomatum, a mirror, a hair comb, tobacco, or scent in bottles.

Now, if you are a trader, certain of these articles cost you more than others, although they have an identical value to the native, and so it is to your advantage to pay what we should call, in Cameroons, "a Kru, cheap copper," and you have a lot of worry to effect this. To the missionary this does not so much matter. It makes absolutely no difference to the native, mind you; so he is by no means done by the trader. Take powder for an example. There is no profit on powder for the trader in Congo Français, but the native always wants it because he can get a tremendous profit on it from his black brethren in the bush; hence it pays the trader to give him his bon out in Boma check, &c., better than in gunpowder. This is a fruitful spring of argument and persuasion. However, whether the native is passing in a bundle of rubber or a tooth of ivory, or merely cashing a bon for a week's bush catering, he is in Congo Français incapable of deciding what he will have when it comes to the point. He comes into the shop with a bon in his hand, and we will say, for example, the idea in his head that he wants fish-hooks—"jupes," he calls them—but, confronted with the visible temptation of pomatum, he hesitates, and scratches his head violently. Surrounding him there are ten or twenty other natives with their minds in a similar wavering state, but yet anxious to be served forthwith. In consequence of the stimulating scratch, he remembers that one of his wives said he was to bring some lucifer matches, another wanted cloth for herself, and another knew of some rubber she could buy very cheap, in tobacco, of a Fan woman who had stolen it. This rubber he knows he can take to the trader's store and sell for pocket-handkerchiefs of a superior pattern, or gunpowder, or rum, which he cannot get at the mission store. He finally gets something and takes it home, and likely enough brings it back, in a day or so, somewhat damaged, desirous of changing it for some other article or articles. Remember also that these Bantu, like the Negroes, think externally, in a loud voice; like Mr. Kipling's 'oont, "he smells most awful vile," and, if he be a Fan, he accompanies his observations with violent dramatic gestures, and let the customer's tribe or sex be what it may, the customer is sadly, sadly liable to pick up any portable object within reach, under the shadow of his companions' uproar, and stow it away in his armpits, between his legs, or, if his cloth be large enough, in that. Picture to yourself the perplexities of a Christian minister, engaged in such an occupation as storekeeping under these circumstances, with, likely enough, a touch of fever on him and jiggers in his feet; and when the store is closed the goods in it requiring constant vigilance to keep them free from mildew and white ants.

Then in addition to the store work, a fruitful source of work and worry are the schools, for both boys and girls. It is regarded as futile to attempt to get any real hold over the children unless they are removed from the influence of the country fashions that surround them in their village homes; therefore the schools are boarding; hence the entire care of the children, including feeding and clothing, falls on the missionary.

The French government has made things harder by decreeing that the children should be taught French. It does not require that evangelistic work should be carried on in French, but that if foreign languages are taught, that language shall be French first. The general feeling of the missionaries is against this, because of the great difficulty in teaching the native this delicate and highly complex language. English, the Africans pick up sooner than any foreign language. I do not like to think that my esteemed friend Donna Maria de Sousa Coutinho is right in saying "because it is so much more like their own savage tongue," but regard this facility in acquiring it to the universal use of it in the form of trade English in the villages round them. Indeed, I believe that if the missionary was left alone he would not teach any European language, but confine himself to using the native languages in his phonetically written-down form; because the Africans learn to read this very quickly, and the missionary can confine their reading to those books he thinks suitable for perusal by his flock—namely, the Bible, hymn-book, and Bunyan's *Holy War*.

The native does not see things in this light, and half the time comes to the schools only to learn, what he calls "sense" *i.e.,* white man's ways and language, which will enable him to trade with greater advantage. Still, I think the French government is right, from what I have seen in our own possessions of the disadvantage, expense, and inconvenience of the bulk of the governed not knowing the language of their governors, both parties having therefore frequently to depend on native interpreters; and native interpreters are "deceitful above all things and desperately wicked" occasionally, and the just administration of the country under these conditions is almost impossible. . . .

But to return to the Mission Évangélique schools. This mission does not undertake technical instruction. All the training the boys get is religious and scholastic. The girls fare somewhat better, for they get in addition instruction from the mission ladies in sewing, washing, and ironing, and for the rest of it they have an uncommonly pleasant and easy time which they most bitterly regret as past when they go to their husbands, for husbands they each of them have.

The teaching even of sewing, washing, and ironing is a little previous. Good Mme. Jacot will weary herself for months to teach a Fan girl how to make herself a dress, and the girl will learn eagerly, and so keenly enjoy the dress when it is made that it breaks one's heart when one knows that this same girl, when her husband takes her to his village soon, in spite of the two dresses the mission gave her, will be reduced to a bit of filthy rag, which will serve her for dress, sheet, towel and dish cloth; for even were her husband willing to get her more cloth to exercise her dressmaking accomplishments on, he dare not. Men are men, and women are women all the world over; and what would his other wives, and his mother and sisters say? Then the washing and ironing are quite parlour accomplishments when your husband does not wear a shirt, and household linen is non-existent as is the case among the Fans and many other African tribes. There are other things that the women might be taught with greater advantage to them and those round them.

It is strange that all the cooks employed by the Europeans should be men, yet all the cooking among the natives themselves is done by women, and done abominably badly in all the Bantu tribes I have ever come across; and the Bantu are in this particular, and indeed in most particulars, far inferior to the true Negro; though I must say this is not the orthodox view. The Negroes cook uniformly very well, and at moments are inspired in the direction of palm-oil chop and fish cooking. Not so the Bantu, whose methods cry aloud for improvement, they having just the very easiest and laziest way possible of dealing with food. The food supply consists of plantain, yam, koko, sweet potatoes, maize, pumpkin, pineapple, and ochres, fish both wet and smoked, and flesh of many kinds—

including human in certain districts—snails, snakes, and crayfish, and big maggot-like pupæ of the rhinoceros beetle and the *Rhyncophorus pal-matorum*. For sweetmeats the sugar-cane abounds, but it is only used chewed *au naturel*. For seasoning there is that bark that tastes like an onion, an onion distinctly *passé,* but powerful and permanent, particularly if it has been used in one of the native-made, rough earthen pots. These pots have a very cave-man look about them; they are unglazed, unlidded bowls. They stand the fire wonderfully well, and you have got to stand, as well as you can, the taste of the aforesaid bark that clings to them, and that of the smoke which gets into them during cooking operations over an open wood fire, as well as the soot-like color they impart to even your own white rice. Out of all this varied material the natives of the Congo Français forests produce, dirtily, carelessly and wastefully, a dull, indigestible diet. Yam, sweet potatoes, ochres, and maize are not so much cultivated or used as among the Negroes, and the daily food is practically plantain—picked while green and the rind pulled off, and the tasteless woolly interior baked or boiled and the widely distributed manioc treated in the usual way. The sweet or non-poisonous manioc I have rarely seen cultivated, because it gives a much smaller yield, and is much longer coming to perfection. The poisonous kind is that in general use; its great dahlia-like roots are soaked in water to remove the poisonous principle, and then dried and grated up, or more commonly beaten up into a kind of dough in a wooden trough that looks like a model canoe, with wooden clubs, which I have seen the curiosity hunter happily taking home as war clubs to alarm his family with. The thump, thump, thump of this manioc beating is one of the most familiar sounds in a bush village. The meal, when beaten up, is used for thickening broths, and rolled up into bolsters about a foot long and two inches in diameter, and then wrapped in plantain leaves, and tied round with tie-tie and boiled, or more properly speaking steamed, for a lot of the rolls are arranged in a brass skillet. . . . A small quantity of water is poured over the rolls of plantain, a plantain leaf is tucked in over the top tightly, so as to prevent the steam from escaping, and the whole affair is poised on the three cooking-stones over a wood fire, and left there until the contents are done, or more properly speaking, until the lady in charge of it has delusions on the point, and the bottom rolls are a trifle burnt or the whole insufficiently cooked.

This manioc meal is the staple food, the bread equivalent, all along the coast. . . . It is a good food when it is properly prepared; but when a village has soaked its soil-laden manioc tubers in one and the same pool of water for years, the water in that pool becomes a trifle strong, and both it and the manioc get a smell which once smelt is never to be forgotten; it is something like that resulting from bad paste with a dash of vinegar, but fit to pass all these things, and has qualities of its own that have no civilised equivalent.

I believe that this way of preparing the staple article of diet is largely responsible for that dire and frequent disease "cut him belly," and several other quaint disorders, possibly even for the sleep disease. The natives themselves say that a diet too exclusively maniocan produces dimness of vision, ending in blindness if the food is not varied; the poisonous principle cannot be anything like soaked out in the surcharged water, and the meal when it is made up and cooked has just the same sour, acrid taste you would expect it to have from the smell.

The fish is boiled, or wrapped in leaves and baked. The dried fish, very properly known as stink-fish, is much preferred; this is either eaten as it is, or put into stews as seasoning, as also are the snails. The meat is eaten either fresh or smoked, boiled or baked. By baked I always mean just buried in the ground and a fire lighted on top, or wrapped in leaves and buried in hot embers.

The smoked meat is badly prepared, just hung up in the smoke of the fires, which hardens it, blackening the outside quickly; but when the lumps are taken out of the smoke, in a short time cracks occur in them and the interior part proceeds to go bad, and needless to say maggoty. If it is kept in the smoke, as it often is to keep it out of the way of dogs and driver ants, it acquires the toothsome taste and texture of a piece of old tarpaulin. I have gone into this bush cooking here in detail, so that you may understand why on the Coast, when a man comes in and says he has been down on native chop, we say "Good gracious!" and give out the best tins on the spot.

I may be judging the coast tribes too harshly if I include them with the bush tribes in my culinary indictment, so I confine my accusations to the Fans and up-river tribes, with whose culinary methods I have been more in contact, for when on the coast I have been either in European houses, or in those of educated natives who have partially, at any rate, adopted European ways of cooking. . . . I well remember M. Jacot coming home one day at Kangwe from an evangelising visit to some adjacent Fan towns, and saying he had had given to him that afternoon a new reason for polygamy, which was that it enabled a man to get enough to eat. This sounds sinister from a notoriously cannibal tribe; but the explanation is that the Fans are an exceedingly hungry tribe, and require a great deal of providing for. It is their custom to eat about ten times a day when in village, and the men spend most of their time in the palaver-houses at each end of the street, the women bringing them bowls of food of one kind or another all day long. When the men are away in the forest rubber or elephant-hunting, and have to cook their own food, they cannot get quite so much; but when I have come across them on these expeditions, they halted pretty regularly every two hours and had a substantial snack, and the gorge they all go in for after a successful elephant hunt is a thing to see—once.

There are other reasons which lead to the prevalence of this custom, beside the cooking. One is that it is totally impossible for one woman to do the whole work of a house—look after the children, prepare and cook the food, prepare the rubber, carry the same to the markets, fetch the daily supply of water from the stream, cultivate the plantation, &c., &c. Perhaps I should say it is impossible for the dilatory African woman, for I once had an Irish charwoman, who drank, who would have done the whole week's work of an African village in an afternoon, and then been quite fresh enough to knock some of the nonsense out of her husband's head with that of the broom, and throw a kettle of boiling water or a paraffin lamp at him, if she suspected him of flirting with other ladies. That woman, who deserves fame in the annals of her country, was named Harragan. She has attained immortality some years since, by falling down stairs one Saturday night from excitement arising from "the Image's" (Mr. Harragan) conduct; but we have no Mrs. Harragan in Africa. The African lady does not care a travelling whitesmith's execration if her husband does flirt, so long as he does not go and give to other women the cloth, &c., that she should have. The more wives the less work, says the African lady; and I have known men who would rather have had one wife and spent the rest of the money on themselves, in a civilised way, driven into polygamy by the women; and of course this state of affairs is most common in non-slave-holding tribes like the Fan. . . .

Now polygamy is, like most other subjects, a difficult thing to form an opinion on, if, before forming that opinion, you go and make a study of the facts and bearings of the case. It is therefore advisable to follow the usual method employed by the majority of people. Just take a prejudice of your own, and fix it up with the so-called opinions of people who go in for that sort of prejudice too. This method is absolutely essential to the forming of an opinion on the subject of polygamy among African tribes, that will be acceptable in enlightened circles. Polygamy is the institution which above all others governs the daily life of the native; and it is therefore the one which the missionaries who enter into this daily life, and not merely into the mercantile and legal, as do the trader and the government official, are constantly confronted with and hindered by. All the missionaries have set their faces against it and deny Church membership to those men who practise it; whereby it falls out that many men are excluded from the fold who would make quite as good Christians as those within it. They hesitate about turning off from their homes women who have lived and worked for them for years, and not only for them, but often for their fathers before them. One case in the Rivers I know of is almost tragic if you put yourself in his place. An old chief, who had three wives, profoundly and vividly believed that exclusion from the Holy Communion meant an eternal damnation. The missionary had instructed him in the details of this damnation thoroughly, and the chief did not like the prospect at all; but on the other hand he did not like to turn off the three wives he had lived with for years. He found the matter was not even to be compromised, by turning off two and going to church to be married with accompanying hymns and orange-blossoms with number three, for the ladies held together; not one of them would marry him and let the other two go, so the poor old chief worried himself to a shammock and anybody else he could get to listen to him. His white trader friends told him not to be such an infernal ass. Some of his black fellow chiefs said the missionary was quite right, and the best thing for him to do would be to hand over to them the three old wives, and go and marry a young girl from the mission school. Personally they were not yet afflicted with scruples on the subject of polygamy, and of course (being "missionary man" now) he would not think of taking anything for his wives, so they would do their best, as friends, to help him out of the difficulty. Others of his black fellow chiefs, less advanced in culture, just said: "What sort of fool palaver you make;" and spat profusely. The poor old man smelt hell fire, and cried, "Yo, yo, yo," and beat his hands upon the ground. It was a moral mess of the first water all around. Still do not imagine the mission-field is full of yo yo-ing old chiefs, for although the African is undecided, he is also very ingenious, particularly in dodging inconvenient moral principles.

Many a keen old chief turns on his pastor and asks driving questions regarding the patriarchs, until I have heard a sorely tried pastor question the wisdom of introducing the Old Testament to the heathen. Many a young man hesitates about joining the Church that will require his entering into the married state with only one woman, whom he knows he may not whack, and who, he knows, will also know this and carry on in all directions, and go and report all his little failings up at the mission, and get him into hot water with the missionary whose good opinion he values highly. And he is artful enough to know he enjoys this good opinion more as an interesting possible convert, than he would as a Church member requiring "discipline."

The worst classes of cases wherein polygamy troubles the missionary are those of boys trained in the mission school and married to school-trained girls. For a time they live according to Church ordinance; and then they keep it to the eye, and break it to the heart; and during this period of transition, during which the missionary fights a hard and losing fight for these souls against their inherited sensualism and sloth, they sink into a state that to my mind, seems worse than they would have been in had they never seen a missionary. But I will not go into the disintegrating effects of mission training here, because my opinions on them have no reference to the work done by the Mission Évangélique whose influence upon the natives has been, and is, all for good; and the amount of work they have done, considering the small financial resources behind them, is to a person who has seen other missions most remarkable, and is not open to the criticism lavished on missions in general. . . .

## Life in West Africa

Regarding the climate of West Africa, I have no hesitation in saying that it is a very deadly one for Europeans. This may seem a mere truism, but every now and again a dangerous nuisance of a person arises in England who says it is not so, leastways that it is no worse than India, and that men who die there have mainly got themselves to blame. People who say these things ought to go to West Africa and be buried there. I don't mind whether it is in a cemetery or in a swamp, but *somewhere,* because these foolish statements not only cost men who believe in them their lives, but detract from the hard-earned sympathy and honour due to the soldier, missionary, trader, and governmental official who work for faith and country in the West African regions. We have, moreover, no just ground for carrying on the hope that has been expressed so long—I found it the other day, in a book published in 1628, just as it is written to-day—that the climate will improve for white men. The average death-rate to-day, even if very little allowance is made for the influence of quinine and the better food-supply afforded by tinned foods, is very little less than it was in the seventeenth century, and if you consider the fact that the white population there in those days was undoubtedly greater than it is now, I fear the death-rate is rising, and it seems, though this has not been perhaps sufficiently tested yet, that the thing that was expected to be the salvation of white life there—drains—are not going to do much good.

Next we will take the native as a hindrance to improvement. In my opinion he is the greatest hindrance of all. I hardly dare express this opinion, for fear of being gone for by some of his more enthusiastic admirers; but as I am known to be an admirer of him myself, I will say it and take the consequences, for it seems to me that if the monogenity of the human race is granted, and had the African been that way disposed, there was nothing to have prevented his forming a great powerful culture state of his own before white aid or hindrance came. He flourishes in his climate; physically taken as a whole he is splendid; his country is fertile, rich in minerals from gold to coal, and well watered by a set of rivers which, also taken as a whole, you cannot surpass in the whole world. Mind, I do not say that it might have been expected he would turn out a European in form or civilisation, because we will allow his climate is too warm; but if it had been in him, there is no outside hindrance that would have prevented him rising to the level in culture of the Asiatic, as the little boys would say, all out of his own head. I daresay you wonder why I am always repeating those Germanic sounding words culture and culture level, but I am forced to do this to guard myself, for I do not say or believe that the African is inferior to the Asiatic, or to any of the other forms of coloured races; indeed, I regard him as quite their equal, and in main their superior. This, however, is a thorny subject which I will avoid, for, after all, it all depends on what you regard as the criterion of perfection in a race, and I have had it pointed out to me that my criterion in this matter would barely do credit to a cave man of the neolithic period; all I ask for in a race is courage, honour, a fine physical development, and an ability to make Nature its slave instead of being hers. In the three first of these the African can hold his own with the Asiatic; in the matter of Nature there is the excuse to be made for him that she is not a tyrant that he need battle with, but a nurse to him, and his arrangements with her give him as much comfort as those of other races—I think, on the whole, more; a swish mud native-built house is far more pleasant to live in than a corrugated iron one, though I am bound to confess I regard the African as an imbecile about roofs. He will make them in some districts of mud plastered on plaited sticks, flat, in the Moorish manner; they are nice enough in the dry season, though they are insidiously preparing afflictions for the wet, by cracking in the sun. When the first showers come they leak like lobster-pots, and on the arrival of the first big tornado, the chances are they come bodily in on you, accompanied by what seems like a belated section of Noah's flood. In other districts he still has his mud walls, but puts on a roof made of palm-thatch, picturesque in a way, and wonderfully dry as long as it stops on during a tornado; frequently it is not long, and away goes the roof with the tornado wind, and in comes the tornado rain, without, however, having in this case heavy chunks of roof mixed with it. Still it's a nuisance, and even during the dry season with no tornado about, a mat roof is too full of reptiles, insects, and rats to be a comfort. But if you want to know what an African roof can be, you must go where they make them of grass, like they do in Kacongo; they are, I assure you, not half so pleasant for the human being under them as they are for the scorpions, serpents, centipedes, spiders, and rats that live in them in a perpetual state of glorious war with each other; the line of retreat always being apparently into the house, usually in the form of the pursued letting

go all, as Brer Rabbit says, and coming kerblam on to you or the bed or
table if such things be present, failing these the floor; and when that
African equivalent to the spring cleaning charwoman comes, the driver
ant, all the inhabitants of the roof come down in a sort of rain, and you and
they leave the house with all possible rapidity by the one and only door;
which, as the drivers usually time their arrival for a wet dark night, is
inconvenient. The grass roofs are usually used with grass walls, and in
between the grass wall region, that is to say, the Kacongo and the swish,
that is to say, from Senegal to the Oil Rivers region, you get houses of
every range of neatness made with palm-mat walls, and the simple bark
hut of the Fan and their allied tribes; but I fear I have said harsh things
about the builders of all of them one time and another in spite of their good
points.

Then again take the African's canoe: a comparative ethnologist would
call it a dug-out, and class it as low in type. When you have to get into one
it strikes you as insecure, and insecure it is if you neither know how to use
it or sit in it. Moreover, you at first object to sitting in the lot of dirty water
that it contains, but you soon get over this, philosophically recognising
that the chances are you will soon be out of it into cleaner water, and after
that you may not require a canoe again, what with sharks or crocodiles,
&c., and the chances of simple drowning. Yet that canoe is also full of
good points, and when you get used to it, you see you can go through surf
in it that you could not in a white man's boat, and that on rivers and
swamps you can go in it where you could go in no other craft; while for
comfort, when outside circumstances are reasonable, there is no form of
boat half so pleasant; the rapid, gliding motion of a well-paddled canoe is
something more than comfort, it is a keen physical pleasure. This is the
case with many other things in what we may call the domestic culture of
the African; yet there is, I fancy, no one who would say the African,
judged by other nations, has reached a high point among the races of the
world. They have a sort of literature—a set of keen-witted proverbs,
showing an insight into human nature in its lower forms that is wonderfully
true; they have immense quantities of stories, riddles, and songs, things
that are a fascinating little world in themselves, yet again in a low form,
none of these rising to a grasp of great motives or noble enthusiasm. Their
language has no writing, yet that language, if it had been allowed to
develop unhindered, would have evolved one which would have put, in
point of difficulty, the grass writing of the Mongolians into the shade, for it
is a thing of three parts; underlying every word in it there is a strange
figurative thought form, and it is composed in itself of two parts, one part
only uttered by the tongue, the other part expressed by gesture. I have
seen members of that wild cannibal tribe, the Fan, catch words from my

lips with their hands regarding price to be paid for a thing, throw them to the ground and stamp on them, without uttering a syllable with their mouths; yet the whole of that action was a mass of words: and I have seen the silent oath of those who are under the Isyogo secret society, easily put in English words, as, Blast my arm if I don't tell the truth, and I have had spoken decisions that I have been asked to give in palavers when those decisions have been regarded as bad law, brought back to me in men's hands and laid at my feet, so that I might take those words up and look at them again, and I have swept away and swept away those parts that I knew was good law, and then waited, and having no answer have swept away again until the time came when the flaw in my law was reached; then came a burst of explanation and argument on the point—the whole of this is language in a broad sense of the word. Their religion, weird and curious as it seems to you at first, horrible as its results appear to you to the end, is a carefully, cleverly argued out conception of the status of Man in Nature. Their law is a law of Justice; I will not say without Mercy, because it has in it what *we* regard as Mercy, what they regard, and I am bound to say I regard too, as merely a part of Justice, that if any one does a thing against the law in ignorance that is not culpable ignorance, he or she cannot be punished therefor; but the administration of the law is such that much evil can thrive under it. Nevertheless, remember that in those great regions under fetich rule there are no unemployed, no paupers, no hospitals, workhouses, or prisons, and the African chief keeps order therein. Every man and woman's property is a thing that cannot be interfered with without due reason being given; the criminal, the idle, the sick, have all to be dealt with by the African chiefs, and they are treated in a way whereof African society is content, and herein lies much that would explain the failure of the African to rise above his present culture level. I have so often looked at them and thought, "Now I understand why Faust was to be handed over to Mephistopheles the moment he was content and satisfied with life; for what are you, Africans, strong, kindly at heart, keen-witted as you are, but the prey of the ruling races of the world?"

It would not be pleasant for me to say fully why I see why this has been, and why I see that this will be for long to come; I should have to say hard things of both white and black. But briefly I will say that I consider the African fails in enthusiasm, in power of combination, and in that restless desire for wealth and conquest, not conquest over the next-door tribe only, but conquest over the very powers of Nature themselves that characterise our race. He looks at things white men do, not with that awe usually credited to him; he thinks our things are queer, possibly dangerous, not necessarily desirable in every case, he soon gets used to them, and learns how to manage them, but he does not bother his head to make himself some like them; his imitation of white men's way is founded on a feeling that white men are big men, and he would like to be a big man too in a way, but it is a feeling more akin to vanity than akin to emulation; that it has not been a sound ground to build on has been amply shown by the effects of the treatment of Africans by the white man, a subject I will next briefly mention by saying I think we may safely assume both sides have been to blame. There are two things that the white is most virulently abused for by moralists, the slave trade and the liquor traffic, while the most common forms of criticism on the black is that he is an indolent brute, a fiendish savage or a child—irresponsible, ungrateful, lying, thievish, and so on, are thrown in on top as remarks by the way on his character.

I have not the space now, even had I the inclination, to sketch and criticise the actions of the white races in the matter of the slave trade and so on, but I beg you to remember the slave trade is not the sum total of white action on the African. Think of the thousands of noble-minded men and women who since 1490 have gone and lived and died in Africa, in the cause of the evangelisation of the African. Call these missionaries what you may—you have no right to deny that their constant aim has been the elevation of the African. Look back at the effects of similar efforts made by Christianity on the Teutonic tribes of Europe, and you see its success— then look at the history of the Roman Catholic mission to Congo, a mission that for 200 years held those Africans completely in its arms, and look at the Congo native to-day in the regions that mission ruled. The mission attempt to elevate the African mass seems like unto cutting a path through the African forest; you can cut a very nice tidy path there, and as long as you are there to keep it clear it's all a path need be, but leave it and it goes for bush. Nothing could have exceeded the willingness with which the Congoese welcomed the missionaries in the fifteenth century, nothing could have exceeded the attention they gave them and their teachings for many years. Yet when those Africans saw that the path they were making was not the easy path to earthly glory and prosperity they thought it was going to be, they let it go for bush. Take instances which you can find anywhere in Africa to-day of the children in mission schools being re-garded as satisfactory by the pastors, and listen to the constant complaint, that as soon as they are educated and have grown up, they do not utilise the instruction that has been given them in joining in the work of the mission, for the sake of their fellow-countrymen, but go away and take up with trade.

Now, after this dismal disquisition, you may say, then it is no use our troubling further about improving the African: but this simple way out is not available; for one reason, the African has demonstrated to be alterable in large masses, not by European means it is true, but by Mohammedan, and there is little doubt that from the point of view of culture elevation the alteration effected by the Mohammedans is an improvement. Then you may say, leave the African to the Mohammedan; but again you are not allowed to do *this,* for you have enormous African populations to deal with in the interests of empire and commerce, who have never been in touch with Mohammedanism, and humanly speaking will not be—such as the South African natives, and they must be what is called improved. Somehow or another their culture *must* be altered, so that they can assist in the development of the vast resources of their country; truly you will say they are used now, but who can regard the labour system of South Africa or the Congo Free State as a state of affairs either permanent or any credit to any one concerned. In other regions, heavily populated by powerful Africans hanging about doing nothing beyond what they have done for thousands of years, foreign labour from India is being imported—a thing which I am certain will only end in bringing in another problem for white men in Africa; and we have got enough, for while the white government is preventing the killing off the native population to a state which the native food production will support, *without* increasing the food production for the natives, and this can mean only a series of Mansion House funds for famines in Africa in the future; but as this is not a thing that will happen in West Africa from the importation of foreign labour, because the climate there kills the imported off, irrespective of colour, therefore if the West African does not alter and take to industry and so on, if ever his country falls truly under white control, and his population increases beyond his food supply, he will have to stagnate for a period and then tidy things up with some war, which will kill off the excess, and meanwhile white affairs will not prosper. It may be said, why should we wish to make white affairs prosper? Well, there are several reasons. You know what the West African is when left to himself: I like him, but still states of affairs like Coomassie and Benin and Dahomey necessarily attract humane attention and have to be put a stop to. Then for another reason the great riches of the country attract traders and so on; so leaving the African alone is not within the sphere of practical politics at all, therefore something must be done, and I wish to ask European civilisation if it is content to go on on the old lines, making a series of amateur empirical experiments at making him work, or rocking a cradle for him under the delusion that he is an interesting infant, as it has been doing these four hundred years?

If the African were a flighty-minded fiend, a lazy brute, or a child, the methods now in force, and that have been in force all these years, would have succeeded. In spite of all the noble and devoted lives laid down, in spite of all the blood and money, they have not. That he is not a fiend the African has shown by his treatment of Livingstone, Thompson, Barth, and a hundred others, least amongst whom am I; that he is not a child he has shown clearly to those who have traded with him, and by the individual Africans who have risen to a higher culture level under European and Asiatic education. I am aware that the educated African is said to invariably go fanttee, as it is called up here, and this picturesque and thrilling conduct of the educated African is supported by a few instances. But I need hardly assure you it is not the invariable custom; and there have been in the past and there are now living dozens of Europeanised Africans in West Africa, ministers, lawyers, and doctors, who would no more want to take off their store clothing and go cannibalising and howling about the bush than you would. Nevertheless, the African who turns into a Europeanised man is the exception that proves the rule, and whose isolated conduct misleads the white man, inducing him to go on on this old line, dazzled by the performance of one in a hundred thousand; we seem blind to the inertia of the great mass, that great mass that we have to deal with today in a state practically unaltered by the white work of four hundred years' duration.

Now I have said I would give a suggestion for the solution of this problem, and I humbly give it—it is, understand the nature of the African. If any of you want to make a great piece of machinery, or build a bridge, or a house, you succeed in your endeavour primarily from a knowledge of the nature of the materials you employ, and so you may succeed in dealing with the African if you will clear your mind of all prejudice and study what is the nature of man. Take him at his lowest. To my mind he is the most magnificent mass of labour material in the world, and he is, taken as a whole, one of the most generous, kindly, good-tempered races of men on earth; intellectually he is at any rate shrewd, and, strange to say, possessed of an immense wealth of practical common sense. Surely *that* is good stuff to go on, surely something ought to be done with it more economically and more humanely than is being done; but alas! you have got to understand him first, and the calm dot and carry one scientific observation of that African is not easy work. It is the work for the doing of which I go to West Africa, where I can get the native, between the Niger and the Congo, uninfluenced by European or Mohammedan culture, because the climate there is mainly composed of malaria, other disease microbes, and mosquitoes, so white men have in the main avoided it or died there; Mohammedans apparently don't mind these things, but the Mohammedan, at any rate in Africa, requires a sandy soil; give the hardy races of North Africa any amount of difficulty and danger you like, but as long as they have plenty of sand, and the chance of perishing now and again for want of water, they will flourish. In the region between the Niger and the Congo all of the sand seems dedicated by nature to the formation of banks in the rivers wherewith to impede navigation and form convenient lounges for crocodiles, and where there is more water about in rivers, swamps, and lakes than any sane man would wish for, without taking into consideration the terrific rainfall, and the constantly saturated state of the atmosphere, which makes you feel during the wet seasons—there are two a year in the equatorial regions—as if you were inside a warm poultice. Nevertheless, with all these disadvantages, that region between the Niger and the Congo is the ethnologist's paradise, and there the ethnologist who wants to study the nature of the African, unmixed with Semitic influences either Christian or Mohammedan, must go; for north of it there is Mohammedanised Lagos, beyond that the Slave, Gold, Ivory, and Grain Coasts that have had on them a stream of European influence since the fifteenth century. Behind these is the Sahara regions soaked in Mohammedanism. South of this forest belt region, between the Niger and the Congo, is the remains of the old kingdom of Congo, that for two hundred years was under the dominion—a dominion that did enormous good directly and indirectly—of the Roman Catholic Mission, and there you find strange fossilised fragments of their teachings in the native religion and legends to this day, though their great rule was terminated in the seventeenth century. The nature of the African thought-form in the region, therefore, between the Niger and the Congo, is the thing I have devoted my time to, recognising that with him his religion—his conception of the status of Man in Nature, is the ruling thing of his life and action; for whether he be altered by outside influence or no, the African can never say, "Oh, one must be practical, you know! That's all right from a religious point of view, but one must be practical." To be practical, to get on in this world, the African must be right from his religious point of view all the time, therefore to understand him you must understand that religious point of view to its very root, and go and study it in an unadulterated form.

The thing is worth taking up alike for humane as well as scientific reasons; though it is difficult, one has no right to dwell on its danger. No one need go out to West Africa without knowing the chances are they go out there to stay, and even if they should go out in ignorance, on landing they will be enlightened, and can take the next boat home. I remember on my first landing at a place where there are three small factories only, but which I had seen marked large on a map, asking a resident white if this was all the settlement. "Oh no," said he, "this is only the porter's lodge, I'll show you the settlement," and he took me to the cemetery; that cemetery justified the large lettering on the map. But settlements, even with the best of cemetery accommodation, are not the ethnologist's place; he must go right away into the fastnesses of the forest, sit and gossip at village fires, become the confidential friend of witch doctors and old ladies, and he must go alone without an armed expedition which will wall him off from the residential African. This sort of life he can comparatively easily lead, if he will learn the trade details of the locality sufficiently to enable him to pass as a trader; in the wildest districts he is reasonable to the African mind if he appears in this guise, and he is safer than he has any right to expect to be under the circumstances, and the amount of information he can pick up is immense, only, alas! that information is not arranged in a manner suitable for use in schools. Nevertheless, it is worth having. In past days, when Africa was left to the Europeans out there and the natives, the collection of ethnological information had merely a scientific and philosophic interest; now it has a greater one, for now European governments are undertaking to legislate domestically for the African from European offices. They cannot do this thing successfully unless they have in their possession a full knowledge of the nature of the people they are legislating for; without this, let their intentions be of the best, they will waste a grievous mass of blood and money, and fail in the end.

# MARY HALL*
# (Southern and Central Africa, 1904)

This formidable woman was actually the first female tourist to journey around Africa. And what a tourist she was! Since the scramble for Africa began towards the end of the nineteenth century, Hall's trip to Central Africa in 1905 was not only courageous but might also have been viewed as foolhardy. Indeed, it probably was so regarded by many of the colonial officials with whom she came into contact and on whom she depended for her supplies, her porters, and for guidance.

In 1904 Hall spent a year traveling around southern Africa, returning to England at the end of that tour. Setting out again in 1905 for Africa, she wrote in the book that emanated from her travels, that "I am the first woman of any nationality to have accomplished the entire journey from the Cape to Cairo, I think perhaps a simple account of how I managed to do it quite alone may be of some interest to many who, for various reasons, real or imaginary, are unable to go so far afield. I hope that a book, written from the woman's point of view, minus . . . the usual exaggerations incidental to all things African may be acceptable."

Hall's memoir thus begins with the exaggeration she hopes to avoid: Cape to Cairo was not the trip she made in 1905–06, beginning as she did on her return in Central Africa. "All alone" is an even greater distortion. Mary Hall was attended by colonial officials or missionaries in areas close to their stations. Otherwise, she was accompanied by two or three interpreters, and sometimes as many as forty porters and bearers. The fact that the interpreters and porters were African causes Hall to dismiss them as inconsequential.

Among Hall's goals was to travel from Lake Malawi to Victoria-Nyanza on the border between German Tanganyika, Belgian Congo, and British Uganda. In order to fulfill her ambition, Hall required vast amounts of equipment—all of which was obtained for her by one of the British colonial officers in British Nyasaland. She hired two youthful African

---

*Mary Hall, *A Woman's Trek from the Cape to Cairo,* London: Methuen & Co., 1907, 106–131, 221–228, 262–264.

interpreters, Mike and John, who were willing to go the length of the journey "that is if I ever lived to do it myself, on which point most people were very skeptical." She employed forty porters who were responsible for carrying Hall in her hammock (she disliked walking and especially climbing), and who had to bear all the supplies including her tent, folding bathtub, cooking utensils, and food enough for the entire party. Her personal traveling gear included numbers of dresses, hats, and other regalia necessary for dinner parties at European stations she visited along the way.

Hall was not an easy guest, nor a good traveler. Before embarking on her journey to Lake Victoria and Uganda, she first took a small boat across Lake Nyasa "alone" except for her two interpreters. As the only woman aboard, the captain was forced to turn the dining area over to Mary Hall. The cockroaches "were for ever on the warpath the hours of darkness. . . . At night my boys took out the table from the tiny saloon and replaced it with my bed. . . . the first streak of daylight [and] I called for my boys as soon as possible to remove the bed and bring in my bath. Until the table was brought back I knew it was entirely blocking up the narrow gangway outside, making the one officer of the boat furious." When not occupying the only closed space on the boat, Hall luxuriated in a deck chair most days—resting up for the nightly encounter with the cockroaches.

As she departed with her entourage for Lake Victoria, Hall may have harbored private doubts but outwardly she was undaunted. Her memory of the occasion: "There was I, one poor unprotected woman . . . going off with forty savage looking blacks" seems to have been written to stir sympathy among her readers. Instead one feels a measure of pity for the Africans who were under her command. The alacrity with which the European community permitted her travel suggests that the spinster tourist was viewed as her own best weapon, even in the wilds of untraversed terrain in the African heartland.

Wearing her "sateen dress" or other similar articles of clothing, reposing on her hammock, and seeming to have very little genuine curiosity about the African people she encountered, she wrote descriptive passages on the scenery. Hall and her party made the trip from Usumbora in German East Africa to the edge of Lake Victoria in about one month, traveling altogether 300 miles. They stopped occasionally to trade with local Africans ("mysterious savages"). But in the course of their journey, they climbed mountains, crossed swamps, and forded rivers—stopping along the way for Hall to enjoy her prepared lunch (the cook usually having preceded her); and afternoon tea. At those times Hall attempted to write if the sun was not too hot; and if she was not disturbed by the curious Africans who on occasion flocked to see "the white woman" (as she always referred to herself).

In the excerpt that follows we begin the trek at Usumbora and end when she dismisses the bearers and interpreters at the conclusion of their long and eventful journey. Hall's remark that it "was marvelous how well the whole caravan kept together" is nothing if not a tribute to her strength of will and her relentless determination. There is no question that the African members of her party found her difficult, but quite possibly only a demanding and narcissistic woman such as Hall could have undertaken such an arduous and difficult trip so early in the colonial period.

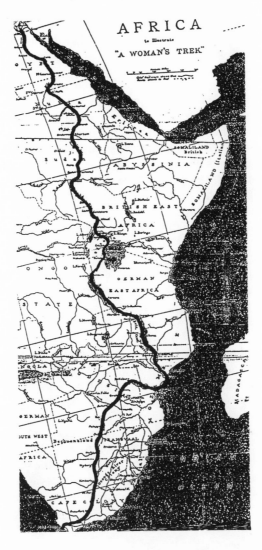

## *Usumbora to Kanyinya*

My caravan, numbering forty-two, got into line towards noon on October 9th. After some kindly words of encouragement and good wishes from the German officers, I was carried off in my machila [hammock], catching a last glimpse of my hospitable friends and hosts waving farewells from the little outlook at the angle of the Boma wall. The excitement of the start was enhanced by the thunder rumbling in the distance and the black clouds which looked ready to drench us at any moment.

The porters were followed for some distance by their relatives and friends, some of them, as a last little attention to their chums, carrying the machila and loads for a time, until I wondered whether, or not, the whole village was coming with me. But by degrees they dwindled away, and a certain amount of quiet ensued.

We made across country to the hills, which we began to ascend, and in about three hours pitched camp for the night. Round about my tent every four or five men built for themselves a charming little circular hut of interlaced grasses and reeds, thickly thatched with banana leaves. I expressed my regret to Mike [one of the interpreters] that it was too late to take a photograph, but he told me that it was of no consequence as they would build similar huts every day. My other men had never put up any kind of shelter, but always lay in the open, round the fires.

Towards evening I strolled to a small hill close by, whence I obtained a perfect view of the lake beneath, and the valley left by its receding waters. It was a glorious view, and I turned from it regretfully, thinking it was the last I should see of Tanganyika, but in this I was mistaken, as the following day I got several beautiful vistas as we ascended the heights.

When I returned to camp I found the men were busy doing up my bundles of salt, to prevent them getting wet. They are very ingenious and handy when they like. They had cut the dry stem of a banana plant and split it open, placing the bundle in the centre; then they drew up the strips of thin bark round it, and tied the whole together with strong fibre. It was a most satisfactory covering, and would resist any moisture.

I went to bed fully imbued with the idea that I should wake in the morning to find most of the men had deserted. Maffi also seemed suspicious of things in general, and neither of us slept very soundly. However, daylight revealed the full complement of porters, and I felt happier. The sun was overcast, but that kept the temperature cooler. These carriers had never seen a machila before, so were quite new to the work; consequently they went very slowly, and instead of my being in advance of the loads, as I had always been across the Tanganyika Plateau, we all kept together.

Later on, when we were doubtful as to the route, and might easily have gone astray if separated, it proved to be the best possible arrangement. One of the askari walked in front of the procession and one in the rear.

The road, as far as it reaches—about five or six hours' journey from the lake—is excellent, and broad enough for an army of soldiers to march along comfortably, eight or nine abreast. . . .

We travelled uphill all day, looking down upon banana groves and well-tended gardens in the valleys beneath us. The produce of these gardens is taken to the noisy market at Usumbora. About nine o'clock we came to the end of the engineered road. Hundreds of natives were at work on it with quaint little short-handled hoes, breaking up the earth and collecting it in small baskets to be distributed where needed for levelling purposes. The soil is of a bright red colour and forms a delightful contrast to the vivid green of the hills around.

While I was enjoying the prospect the porters had put down their loads, and most of them having found acquaintances among the road-makers, were telling them of the hopes and fears they entertained as to the hundred and one things which might happen before they met again, and of the wonders of the new calico and drapery they would bring back in triumph. I think the fact of their being members of a party to take a European woman so far, made them, in the eyes of their companions, men to be looked up to.

We continued our way along a very narrow track, which was very much more to my taste than the high-road we had just quitted. We had not gone far when the daily thunderstorm, which we had eluded the morning before, burst upon us, and in a moment we were in the midst of torrential rain. It was a funny, albeit mournful, sight to see the men, like drowned rats, literally drenched to the skin, which is about all they had on. I was fairly well protected in my machila, but rugs and pillows would not be kept within bounds and soon became very wet. As at night they formed part of my bedding, I was filled with unpleasant anticipations of an uncomfortable night with a severe cold to follow.

The tent was already pitched when I arrived in camp, but everything was wet and uncomfortable, so we set to work and dried what we could at the fires the men had made, and I luckily thought of my hot-water bottle, which was filled and used like a warming-pan to air my bed.

About midnight I awoke to find another heavy storm in progress, but I was then safely under cover, and hugging the clothes about me, soon fell asleep again.

After a storm everything is wet and more difficult to pack, and in consequence it was nearly seven next morning before we were on our way again. This was not so serious as it would have been a few days before: ever since we left Usumbora we had been steadily rising until we were now nearly on the top of the plateau, where the temperature was considerably lower, and there was not the same necessity to get to camp early, as even at mid-day it was not too hot. . . .

Every caravan is under the supervision of a "capitao," or "nympala," and one morning I caught sight of my capitao driving along two young calves which I knew did not belong to me. This I felt required explanation, and I immediately called Mike to help me to investigate the matter. The men evaded my questions as much as possible, but at last had to confess that they had taken the cattle in order to force the proprietor to give us a goat. This being quite contrary to my ideas of justice, I called a halt, and made the owner come to my side. He was in a frantic state of excitement, and it was pitiable to see him, rushing from one side of the machila to the other, clapping his hands to salute me, while all the time he kept an anxious eye on the rifle of the askari. My inability to speak the language increased the difficulty of the situation, and I tried my hardest by signs, to pacify and assure the poor fellow that he would be fairly treated. By his wild expression of despair and dumb show of running a knife across his neck, I understood that, even if I cut his head off, he had no goat to give me. Decapitation was far from my thoughts, especially as goat-flesh held no alluring charm for me. I explained that I had no wish for a goat, but suggested that if he had any milk or eggs, either would be acceptable, and an equivalent in salt should be given to him. At this he went away greatly relieved, taking his calves with him, and a few miles further on, I was told that he had overtaken us, bringing about three quarts of milk. I think that my judgment in the case proved far more satisfactory to the man and myself than to the askari.

We were fortunately in camp that day before the rain commenced, but while I was writing in the afternoon, the wind blew a fearful gale and nearly overturned my tent, which caused a great scamper among the men to peg it down more securely. I was most thankful it had not happened in the night, as they are then not easily aroused, and the consequences might have been serious.

The storms pass as suddenly as they come, and when this one had spent itself I walked to the village close by. It was enclosed by a stockade made of dried reeds and grasses, which met overhead at the entrance, forming an archway.

The women in general were a little afraid of me, for, never having seen a white woman before, they evidently felt that they were in the presence of a strange being, whose customs and habits might prove dangerous.

In this particular village they were less timid; one of them was very intelligent and amusing, and so quick at gesture that we carried on quite an animated conversation by its means.

I was not favourably impressed with the beauty of some of the hairdressing styles here. I noticed one little girl walking about with her hair done in a number of thin, hanging plaits, caked with oil, and looking just like so much mud. I learned afterwards that this unattractive fashion is a mark of distinction, and only the daughters of chiefs are allowed to adopt it.

After I had looked over the little huts, and before leaving, I gave each woman standing round a *hela*—about a halfpenny. Mike told me with a very superior air that they had no idea what it was, never having seen money before, and they were going to wear them as ornaments. However, the askari soon enlightened them as to their value for barter, as later I saw them running about very happy, with some oily-looking fluid in the palms of their hands, which Mike said was "nose-oil," meaning a kind of snuff. The soldiers had given it to them in exchange for the *helas*.

By the fourth day we were well up on the plateau, 6,000 feet above the sea, and the view of the hills in all directions was glorious. Our course for some time lay along a high ridge, from which I overlooked a vast scene of undulating country, stretching away to the horizon. It was just as if the wild, rolling billows of the sea had been suddenly solidified and changed into mountains and valleys, over which we had to trace our tortuous way.

After a while we had to descend slightly, and the men wriggled my machila through a banana grove, where I got picturesque glimpses of the porters through the thinner parts of the foliage, wending their way onwards along the winding path. The banana plants grow to a great height, and it seemed like passing through a dense wood, with occasional rays of sunlight penetrating the branches, and making more vivid the bright emerald green of the leaves on which they glinted.

In this part of the country the chief of a district is designated a "Sultan," and, although perhaps not in strict accordance with *Burke,* the title is usually applied to the headman of the village.

At my next halting-place the Sultan was away, so I made my state call on the Sultana. I generally found it more agreeable to my nasal organs to pay my respects in the open air, but sometimes the people considered they were honouring me more by receiving me inside their dwelling. It was so on this occasion, and I had to go down on all fours to make my way into the hut, through an opening 3 feet square, bumping my head and face against innumerable bits of carved wood and curious objects done up in grasses, hanging at the door as charms to keep away sickness and evil spirits. It could hardly be called a dignified entrance on my part, but all seemed pleased to see me.

The conversation might have been both intellectual and improving had the Tower of Babel never existed for our confusion; as it was, our ideas were exchanged somewhat in this manner. My hostess said what she had to say to the askari, the askari translated it into Swahili to Mike who put it into English for me, so that our talk was neither fluent, rapid, nor reliable. I must confess that my attention flagged during the process, but it gave me time to notice a few of the characteristics of the people.

They are of a refined type; very tall and slim, with dark brown oval faces, not at all like the typical broad-nosed, thick-lipped negro. If you divide Africa roughly into three parts, the middle section from east to west is peopled by the Bantu race, of which there are endless divisions and subdivisions, but they are all classified as Negroid.

The previous day I had noticed a man with his face besmeared with yellow daubs of paint, but as a rule they are not disfigured in any way.

Later on that afternoon, when I was wandering round, I saw a particularly athletic-looking black talking to the porters, and when I asked who he was, Mike informed me in a solemn manner that he was the milkmaid (herdsman). Large herds of cattle were to be seen, and judging from the land under cultivation there must be a considerable population; but as soon as they got wind of a caravan, they fled in all directions, or concealed themselves. I must say I missed the friendly crowds rushing out to salute us as they did on the Tanganyika Plateau. Though they made a hideous din at the time with their shouting and screaming, they afforded me much amusement, and left behind memories of a wild but well-disposed people.

At the camping-grounds, however, the villagers always seemed to be on very good terms with the askari and porters, and offered me handsome presents. At first I did not accept all they brought, but I soon learned that I was expected to take everything, and divide what I did not want for myself among the carriers.

My men proved themselves a good set of fellows, and having settled down to the routine of safari, I now felt confident that none of them would desert.

The next day I had my first experience of their cleverness in overcoming the difficulties presented by nature. We had to cross several rivers, which are very formidable obstacles, not as regards the actual streams, which are generally neither wide nor deep, but because they are bordered by half a mile or more of papyrus grass, 20 feet high, growing in a fearful quagmire, through which we had to make a passage.

On these occasions the baggage had to be put down and all hands requisitioned for the task of getting me across. They would set to work with a will to cut down the giant grass until they made sufficient space to force the machila through. I never thought it would stand the strain put upon it, and at times there were ominous creakings which were most alarming. The over-anxiety of the men very nearly caused my downfall several times; they had a habit of clutching the canvas body of the machila to help in lifting the weight, and if they did not happen to take hold of both sides simultaneously I was nearly tipped out. When we were safely across, and the first foothold firmly established, there would be a tremendous hullaballoo and general rejoicing. The course of the rivers being through deep valleys, we nearly always had a steep hill to climb immediately after crossing, so before proceeding I generally gave the men time to recover after their extra exertions.

I was taken up the hills backwards, and in this way I got a good view of the river and grass we had just struggled through; looking at the expanse of swamp from above, it seemed an insuperable barrier, and I felt very proud of my bearers for having done so well.

In past ages these must indeed have been mighty rivers, but are now so overgrown that there is only a comparatively narrow waterway coursing through the masses of papyrus.

As the crow flies, we did not progress much that day. The men had had a very trying time, so we camped early, and I think we were all glad of a rest. Our arrangements were made much more quickly now than when we started, as each man knew exactly what was expected of him, and where his load had to be placed. One or two would go at once for water, some would fetch wood, others built the kitchen, while the rest combined in creating the little mushroom village of green huts which always sprang up, as if by magic, in the vicinity of the tent.

The first day that we killed fresh meat, Mike gave me to understand that I was expected to take what I wanted for my own use and apportion the remainder of the animal among the men. I found it cut up and placed neatly on banana leaves: all was there, even to the intestines, every atom of which the natives boil to flavour their cereal food. The skin is considered the perquisite of the man who kills the animal. It is always very carefully pegged out to dry, and then becomes part of the owner's wardrobe, or is perhaps converted into a bag to carry his flour.

Goat is not bad eating when well cooked, but atrocious otherwise; and as my *chef* did not excel in this branch of the culinary art, I contented myself with the liver and enough flesh to make a little soup. My personal boys and the askari were given a fair proportion, and the remainder was divided between the six Uganda porters, they being the only ones who would eat either goat's flesh or mutton, the others only condescending to beef, which they never got until we reached Bukoba.

At most halting-places a large quantity of bananas was brought to me, and I always took care that the men who did not eat meat had the greater part of them.

At one place when the chief called upon me I asked if he could let me have any eggs or chickens, whereupon he stopped and hastily picked some grass, which he rolled excitedly in his hands, then threw it on the ground before me and rushed away. I thought I had given mortal offence, and wondered what I should do to propitiate him, when it was explained to me that his action simply signified that all he had was placed at my feet; that he would show me all honour, and fulfil, if possible, my slightest behest.

That evening the men became very jovial; there was a great deal of dancing, shouting, and clapping of hands, and evidently they were having a very good time. When the moon was full they always had some festivity, and liked to sit up late. The paymaster of Usumbora had given me a whistle, and I used to blow it when I thought it time for all to be asleep, and I seldom had to use it twice. If I did have to repeat the signal, it was always after they had indulged in a generous supply of "pombé," which has the same tongue-loosening properties as Bass or any other brew when taken in large quantities.

The next morning, after tramping for about two hours, we had a long delay, trying to enlist some men from the village to give us their help in crossing the Livuvu River, which lay a few miles ahead. I gathered that it was a very risky undertaking, as it was a *bonâ-fide* river, and might be deep. If it proved very appalling, I determined—rather than be carried across in the men's arms and probably be dropped in the middle—to retire to a secluded spot, there divest myself of my garments, and walk through the water in my mackintosh. I also planned that I would first have the tent pitched on the opposite side, and a hot bath prepared, to follow the cold one as soon as possible.

After working it all out in my mind, I was rather looking forward to the excitement, and was a little disappointed to find that the difficulties had been overrated. We happened upon the river at a favourable season, and found it was not too deep for the men to ford; but I was afraid the machilla might hang too low, so I made them first take it across empty, so that I might see for myself how it went. I decided it was feasible, and we made a start. They carried it on their heads, and at the deepest part I took hold of the poles and drew myself up as high as possible, while some of the men assisted me to retain the position as long as necessary. I landed dry and triumphant, one more obstacle successfully overcome.

Although we had escaped one wetting, it looked as if our dry season was not to be a long one. I hurried the men on with the tent in the hope of being in time to avoid the coming storm, and we just managed to do it.

That afternoon I dealt out "poso" to the porters. At roll-call they all stood in a semicircle facing the tent, and those who remembered the particular appellation they started with answered when it was read out. A native always has a "Mukowa," which is his patronymic, but he has another by which he is commonly known, and this he changes according to fancy. For example, my boy registered himself as "Michael Mike," because his former master's name was Michael, and now, for aught I know, he may be figuring with another employer as "Mary Molly."

I now made these men decide upon their names, and promise to keep them until I broke up the caravan. Accordingly they were re-registered in a book by Mike, who wrote down their names, in a hand which would do credit to an English Bank clerk. He then ticked off each man in a most business-like way as he came to receive his pay. The small, red glass beads were all done up in bundles of three fundos, costing one rupee. Each man received one fundo, which is ten strings of about a foot long. This was his allowance for four days' food, and put into English money works out at a fraction over one penny farthing per day.

The askari are very important personages in their own estimation. They each had an attendant boy, also a light, low tent between them, and I used to see far better straw being taken to their quarters than to mine. They also had the pick of what food was to be got in the villages. In their khaki uniform they looked fairly smart, but *en déshabille* quite the reverse. They then wore a waistcoat over a shirt which hung outside their long, loose Turkish trousers of white calico; and on their feet they wore easy shoes about three sizes too large. In this get-up they lounged about in dilapidated old deck-chairs, with a "this-is-what-we-do-in-the-army" kind of air, which amused me intensely.

I had only just finished giving the men their "poso" when a terrific storm broke over us, and, as the trench round the tent had not yet been dug, I was flooded out.

As I went on I grew wiser, and was very strict about this. Tired or not, the men had to make the trench the moment the camp was pitched, which in the end saved both them and me much trouble and discomfort.

As soon as the rain ceased all my things were removed from the tent and the wet earth scraped away. Several small fires were then lighted inside, the warm ashes from which were afterwards spread about to dry the ground; when that had been done, the driest leaves that could be found were brought in and placed under the ground sheet, and the tent once more became habitable.

Altogether our pitch that day was not a success; we were too near the river, from which a reeking dampness was arising, and I sincerely hoped we should suffer no evil consequences. Naturally I was very anxious to avoid a chill, which would render me so much more liable to develop malaria, or any of the other ills that flesh is heir to, especially in Central Africa.

So far I had been fortunate enough to escape everything of the kind and had no desire to fall sick in the midst of that wild plateau, miles away from assistance and medical aid. It would have been impossible to obtain any invalid nourishment, and I only possessed quinine and a few preventives rather than restoratives in the way of medicine. Whenever I allowed my mind to dwell on such possibilities, my utter aloofness was brought vividly home to me, and I had to banish any such pessimistic ideas as promptly as they occurred.

The air was often saturated with moisture at night. Sometimes my tent would be quite wet in the morning, and the damp atmosphere penetrated even into the interior. When I took off my clothes on going to bed I had to put them away in a tin box, otherwise they would have been too damp to put on next day. Even my hair-brush was affected, and the bristles became quite soft—in fact, everything in the tent was moist, and it was a perfect marvel how I escaped ague and rheumatism.

The following morning Mike met me with the news that we should have many "waters and muds" that day, and he was quite correct. I was torn, dragged, and pushed over five rivers, or at any rate over as many bends of two rivers. I found it quite impossible to get at the facts of the case from the men, as the rivers were so winding, and natives can never enlighten one on such points.

My machila came through the ordeal with flying colours, and after that I felt it would stand anything. It was tested at most appalling angles. The man at the end of one pole might be on a firm conglomeration of earth and grass, raised a foot or two from the mud, while the man at the same end of the other pole was sunk to his knees in the slush, so that the machila was tilted to a most alarming degree, and I was obliged to cling on like grim death to a pole, or anything I thought would support me, shouting (at the same time) directions to every one.

The carriers were most willing, but had very little forethought, and by this time it was evident to me that in any emergency I had only myself to rely upon.

I knew we must be making endless pictures for the camera as we forced our way through the undergrowth, and felt so sorry that it was impossible to take them, for it would have been interesting to have had some tangible reminders of these exciting scrambles. But even, had there been any one with me capable of taking photographs, they would have been very diffi-cult to get, as the grass was yards over our heads and the light consequently not good enough for a snap-shot. Time exposures would have been out of the question under such critical conditions.

I have learnt by experience that many things seem very terrible until something worse happens. We had got over the difficulties and dangers of crossing the rivers, which at one time we had regarded as almost insurmountable, but there were far more dangerous "rocks" ahead. These took the form of hundreds of infuriated savages, who made me feel as if my wild career were to be brought to a sudden termination, and with my quietus the worst predictions of the majority of those with whom I had discussed my journey, fulfilled.

There was no road of any kind to help us find our way across the plateau. We were only following native tracks, which are most mystifying to any but the initiated, and it was therefore the business of the askari to see that we had efficient local guides to conduct us from one landmark to the next, in the direction in which we wished to go. These one of the soldiers would get from the villages we passed, or sometimes he would catch some unwary being along the way, and regardless of any excuse that might be made, would force him to accompany us. It was absolutely necessary that, by fair means and foul, we should get a guide, but I am afraid the askari did not always try the fair means first.

On the morning in question I overtook the loads, all deserted on the ground, and at a little distance there was a great hubbub among the carriers, who were breathless with excitement. At the very moment that I arrived upon the scene, a soldier rejoined the party with a poor trembling wretch in his clutches. It appeared that the askari had been into the village which lay a little off our route, and the inhabitants, seeing them coming, had fled. After giving chase, this was the only one of the fugitives they could capture. I tried to soothe the man with kind words, which of course, had no meaning to him; but Mike made him understand that I should be much obliged if he would consent to show us the way, that no harm should be done to him, and that he should have a present of salt when he had conducted us to the next point of our journey.

This little disturbance occupied some time, and the sun was getting high in the heavens; so without further delay we proceeded, taking the man with us.

We at once descended into a deep, narrow valley, which he had to cross, and when my machila was reversed to carry me backwards up the opposite side, I saw on the ridge, where a few moments ago not a soul was visible, hordes of natives gathering. Then they came racing helter-skelter down the hill with what seemed to me quite unnecessary speed, their numbers increasing from all sides.

They presented a most warlike and terrifying appearance, brandishing their spears above their heads as they ran, while their long, fringy draperies floated out behind them in the breeze.

I anxiously consulted Mike what he thought they were doing, but he did not seem much concerned, and replied in an indifferent tone, that they were only following their chief. However, I knew it was not safe to assume from his manner that there was no danger. From my experience of the natives, I knew that they were absolutely unimaginative, and that a catastrophe, which any one of ordinary intelligence could foresee, might actually overwhelm them before they would think of making any preparation to meet it. So I said, "Yes, but I am sure that they are following us too, and I am afraid that we shall have trouble because of the man we have brought away with us."

By this time we had reached the top of the hill, and my machila had been turned round again with my face looking forward, so that I was not at all easy in my mind as to what might be taking place in the rear, and I urged Mike and the askari to keep me well posted in every movement of the pursuing natives, and to be sure and tell me when they were near.

After a few minutes, which seemed like weeks to me, Mike informed me, "They are now getting close."

I had by this time braced myself to face the position. I meant at the worst to die game and have the wounds in front; so in less time than it takes me to write, I was out of the machila and had taken up a place under a solitary tree. As I chose this position there sprang into my mind a picture of St. Sebastian riddled with arrows, and I mentally substituted myself and spears.

I awaited the approach of the enemy sitting on a box of food, which I hoped I might live to want, even although it was in tins.

Nearer and nearer came the infuriated mob, until they drew up just in front of me. A small group, whom I took to be the Sultan and his headmen, separated themselves from the general rabble, and came a little forward. The uproar was so great that I could scarcely hear myself speak, so I requested the Sultan and his retinue to remain, and let the others retire to a distance.

Rooted in my memory, I have a picture of them as they obeyed and squatted on the ridge of the hill, with their gleaming spears held upright, and silhouetted against the sky. I could not help admiring the warlike, savage spectacle, although I shuddered to think that at the first sign of the chief those same picturesque spears would perhaps be hurled at me in wild fury.

In the midst of such unusual excitement and surroundings, with the blazing vertical sun and the unclouded sky above, hopelessly distant from any succour should it be needed, I, a solitary white woman faced the dusky chief, and the parley began.

During the dual translation of the conference, I had time to see that the Sultan was a young fellow of about twenty-four, with a lightish brown skin, well oiled and polished, his head shaven except for a circle of about 3 inches of hair on the top, and another at the back. He was tall and slim, and held himself extremely well. He wore what had once been a piece of bark cloth, which, after much wear, frays out and becomes like a long fringe. It was bound at the top with a coarse native cord of plaited straw, looking in the sun like gold braid. This garment was fastened over one shoulder, and hung to about the knees, giving him a decidedly picturesque if bizarre appearance.

His anger was at white heat, but outwardly he was very calm and dignified, and stated his case concisely.

"Your soldiers," he said, "have been to the village in my absence, and seized one of my men, besides carrying off spears which were dropped by others in their flight."

I expressed my regret, and told him that it was not with my sanction that this had been done; neither did I know that any spears had been brought away, and I assured him that they should be returned at once. This appeared to mollify him somewhat, then I explained to him that it was quite necessary for me to have a guide. I said that I should be very glad if he would allow some one to come with me as far as the next river, and he answered to the effect that nothing would give him greater pleasure; two or three men should be sent, but he could not spare the one we had taken, as he was a herdsman and was needed to milk the cows.

I felt that I had taken a new lease of life when we came to this amicable understanding. There was a visible stir among the men in the background, who began to feel that "the white Queen" and their own Sultan were evidently coming to terms, and that bloodshed would be unnecessary. I think my own porters had remained so calm because they never doubted the omnipotence of the white skin to overcome any difficulty.

The Sultan posed for his portrait, which I greatly prize as a memento of one of the most thrilling incidents of my life. He then presented me with a brass wire bracelet from his arm, and I returned the compliment with much salt, after which we parted the best of friends.

Had the chief and his followers been more hasty, or less willing for an explanation, the consequences might easily have proved fatal to me, but as it turned out, the incident was a striking example of what can be effected by a little common courtesy even among so-called savages.

These justly angered, but now happily pacified people wended their way back to their village in a much quieter manner than they had left it.

We continued on our way for about 8 miles, and camped on an eminence in a dry atmosphere. I had not been there long when word was brought to me that the Sultan had sent me a fine goat as a present, so I felt I must have impressed him as favourably as he had me.

We were then just a week out from Usumbora. I had quite settled down to the life, and found it most fascinating, especially in dry weather. When thinking over the events of the past few days, I felt that so far, I had been very lucky, and I trusted that any other difficulties which might present themselves in the future, would be surmounted as successfully as those which had overtaken us already. . . .

Once or twice during the journey I had to talk very seriously with the men. For instance I found them one afternoon sitting about the camp looking very glum, and on inquiring the meaning of the general depression, I found that they had had no food, as they considered it too dear in that neighbourhood, and declared they could not afford to buy it.

I felt they must not go on short commons after working so hard, so I reminded them of the "poso" allowance they had received regularly all the time, and pointed out to them how little they had been obliged to spend hitherto, having had such plentiful supplies from the presents brought to me. I told them I was surprised that now, simply because things were a trifle dearer and presents not so plentiful, they were so foolish as to go without food. I assured them that if I did not eat I should certainly be ill, and so would they; and I finished by saying, "Till now if any of you have been ill, I have been pleased to let you off your work until you were better, but if you do not eat to-night and are ill to-morrow, it will be entirely your own fault, and I shall knock off a day's pay from every man who cannot carry his load."

I am glad to say that the justice of my argument came home to them. I saw a smile flit across the faces of one or two of the leading spirits, and knew I had won the day. They roused themselves from their gloom and said they would go at once and get some provender. It only requires a little tact and firmness to manage these overgrown children. . . .

The next day we entered an avenue of metawa trees, which continued almost without interruption as far as Bukoba. Planting these trees is an excellent idea of the Government, as they make the high-road between their two important stations on the Victoria Nyanza—Mwanza and Bukoba—very pleasant. The surface of the road was soft to the men's feet, which they thoroughly appreciated after the rough experience of the last few days. We were now almost at our journey's end, and on reaching camp I gave them their "poso" for the last time.

In calculating at Usumbora what quantity of beads and salt I should require, no allowance was made for any delay, and had any detention occurred I should have become insolvent. As it was, I had to eke out what salt and beads remained by a few bundles of pice (an Indian coin equal to about a halfpenny). Fortunately I had brought a few hundred of these, done up in rolls of twenty-five, but even they would have been of little use had we not been so near a large settlement.

I tried to get a little writing done here, but it was perfectly hopeless. The people were numerous, and each individual made some excuse to interrupt me. Men sauntered up to the tent, touched their hats, or rather their heads, and said "Jumbo" (good-day), and then stood and stared their hardest. The women came and sat at my feet, and conversation ensued with one of them somewhat in this style.

She began with what sounded like, "Chere cura cara mene bo."

I was not going to let her think that the white woman could not talk, so I answered, "Yes! Certainly; I have never doubted it."

Then she made another remark, and I replied. "Very likely; but then, you see, it has never been put to me in quite that way before." And so we went on, until we both realised the absurdity of the situation, and burst out laughing.

The Sultan's headman was almost inside the tent, lost in admiration of my writing capabilities, and children were scampering about, looking very jolly in their bead and shell attire; but they were shy of me, and beat a hasty retreat when I turned in their direction.

The previous day we had skirted the north end of Lake Ikimba, which, as far as I could see, was fast becoming, like all the other rivers and lakes, a vast papyrus swamp. It was surrounded by park-like country, with a range of hills to the east, round which we had to work our way to reach Kanazi. About two hours before we got there, at a turn of the road, our first view of Victoria Nyanza burst upon us. The men grew very excited, and ran on shouting and dancing, and my own joy was so great that I felt very much inclined to get out of the machila and join them.

After forging our way across the plateau for a whole month, surrounded by dangers known and unknown, to be at last within sight of our goal was almost too much for us all. The sense of immense relief at the consummation of my wishes, made me realize how tense my feelings must have been all the time.

When we arrived at Kanazi I found there was a very good house for white people, and I was told the Commandant of the district always occupied it when he passed that way, so I felt I was safe in doing the same. The previous night had therefore been my last for some time in a tent, and I could not have believed how attached I should become to my portable home. Nevertheless, I found it very delightful to have two rooms, in any part of which I could stand erect.

In the afternoon I sat outside on the verandah, which was raised a few feet from the ground, and I was soon beset by a small crowd below, making loud personal remarks in an unknown tongue. At one time they concentrated their attention on some part of me under the table, so I just lifted my dress and let them see my high laced mosquito boots. And then, much to their amusement, I mimicked the way they had looked me up and down. The intricacies of European dress were a source of never-failing interest to the native. Once, on the plateau, I felt rather cold, and put on some gloves—about the only time I wore them—and the men could not understand them at all. I had to take them off and on several times for them to see how I did it.

The camp yard at Kanazi was a scene of great activity that day. My own poor men were very tired and quiet, but there was another set of porters with Government loads, in charge of some askari, making a good deal of noise, and I felt as if I were back in the every-day noisy world again.

The *capitao* of the village sent in not only a goat, some milk, eggs, and good bananas, but also a lettuce, some spring onions, and a cabbage. I had almost forgotten the taste of such luxuries!

Kanazi is beautifully situated on a small bay, and has a glorious view across the deep blue lake. Islands, both small and large, occur here and there, and cast their reflections in the water. They are probably the home of many a feathered family, being densely wooded and intensely green.

It was delightful to sit on the verandah resting, and I lounged there luxuriously, watching some lovely little birds with bright yellow breasts, which were taking a good splashing bath in a pool in the hollow of a stone, and then hopping about preening their gaudy plumage. I longed to tarry awhile amid such charming surroundings, but it was impossible, as I did not know when the steamer would be at Bukoba, and I also had to consider the men, who were anxious to finish their work, get their money, and return home.

When the afternoon grew cool I went to see Sultan Kahigi's house. He was away himself, but his *capitao* took me round. It was a big, rambling place, and like the mansions of most of these chiefs, very sparsely furnished. He was having some additional rooms built for his wives, and meanwhile they were lodged in huts outside. I called upon his sister and two of the young wives, one of whom was dressed in a long green drapery, and the other in yellow. They were sitting under the shelter of their door, and covered their faces when I came near, so I chaffed them in dumb show about it, putting a handkerchief up before my own. They saw the joke at once and soon let the drapery drop. One was decidedly fascinating, with an olive skin, oval face, and beautiful soft eyes; the other was rather more of the negro type.

Mike, as usual, was interpreter, and I asked them, with his aid, if they would come to London with me and then I pretended to carry one off. She held back, saying, "What will my husband do?" I replied, "Oh, never mind him; I will get you another in London," at which she laughed gaily.

I induced all three to accompany me a little way, and I made the pretty one link her arm in mine, and so we walked along, to the evident amusement of those around. They all enjoyed the fun, and late that evening, to show their good-will, a plate of butter was brought to me as a present from the ladies.

It always struck me as sad that the women of that class had so little to do. Intellectually I believe they are capable of better things, but their narrow life affords no scope for any mental effort. . . .

During the month [the men] had been in my service we had traversed the districts of Arundi, Kyasa, Ruanda, Karagwe, and Kianga, and had covered over 300 miles of country described . . . as most difficult and trying, consisting of a tangled mass of mountains, many of the intervening valleys being only a few hundred feet wide. . . .

My men that day, like B'rer Fox, "lay low," but they were very much "on the spot" the next morning when I had promised they should have a bullock as a tip, for behaving so well on sofari.

I had been advised to let Mike and John [another interpreter] return across the plateau with the porters, as it would be safer for them than travelling alone, so all that day we were very busy in various ways. Boxes and bundles had to be rearranged, and household washing done, then as I felt responsible for the tent on its way back to the kind lender, that had to be packed securely, not only to preserve it, but to prevent it being used on the journey. I also had letters to write, which I wished Mike to leave at the different places we had touched at, so when the paymaster came and asked me to come out and inspect the bullock, as it was too wild to be brought into the yard, I felt I had not the time to spare.

I heard afterwards that the men could not possibly kill it, and that finally it was shot by an askari, who divided it among them, and, according to the report of an eye-witness, each man grabbed his share with avidity, and there and then devoured it with such gulosity that, in less than half an hour after its death, only the hoofs remained. I must confess my surprise at hearing this, as during the march the few men who had eaten meat were most particular in cooking it. It was fortunate for my peace of mind that I did not discover these carnivorous tendencies sooner, although I rather regretted not having seen the savage orgy.

The following morning I made the men file past me, and handed to each the promised rupees. It was good to see their faces light up with pleasure at the sight of the money, and I equally enjoyed giving it to them, as I felt it had been honestly earned. I was very pleased indeed that I could send them back to Usumbora with such a satisfactory report.

They rushed to the market and stores with their newly acquired wealth, and when they returned before starting, they were all gaily attired in either coloured calico or bark cloth, which will serve them for years. Then I had to make final arrangements with Mike and John; the latter had been a very good boy, but Mike had been decidedly trying at times, although he was really most capable and spoke English fairly well.

When they had all departed, I felt a great weight had been lifted from my mind, and that once more I was free for a while from the turmoil and worry of a caravan. . . .

# MARY ELIZA BAKEWELL GAUNT*
## (West Africa, 1911)

Australian born, Mary Gaunt was another early traveler to Africa, one who insisted on traveling "alone" as the title of her memoir indicates. Gaunt was one of the first women to enroll at the University of Melbourne (1881), although marriage kept her from earning a degree. Early widowhood then provided her with the opportunity to write and to travel. With the small amount of capital her husband left her, Mary Gaunt went to England where she successfully wrote and published a first novel. The income from that book, commissions on a travel volume, plus free passage to West Africa, enabled her to carry on the Bakewell family tradition of visiting far-flung parts of the British empire.

Enroute to The Gambia, her first stop, Gaunt met the Governor of the colony on board ship. Since Gaunt was armed with letters of introduction from the Colonial Office, her host immediately offered her the opportunity to travel around The Gambia, including a trip up river on the *Mungo Park*. Like Hall before her, Gaunt is conscious of being the lone "white woman" on this expedition, writing about meeting an African chief who has come to register a complaint with the District Commissioner, her traveling companion on the voyage. Unlike Hall, however, Gaunt is more humble: "I should have liked to have been worth looking at . . . coal dust was in my hair . . . and my skirts had picked up most of the multifarious messes . . . on the unclean deck." Travel in European attire was not easy for a woman in those days, but Gaunt, like her sister travelers elsewhere at this time, would not have considered trousers.

While any number of European women were in Africa by the time Gaunt arrived (1911), she is critical of the British for what she regarded as their reticence in bringing their wives to the outposts where they were stationed. The French and the Germans, Gaunt observed, almost always had families in attendance. One English official remarked that his wife's complexion would suffer were she to be exposed to the tropical sun. Gaunt's response: "Possibly it is because I am an Australian . . . that I

---

*Mary Gaunt, *Alone in West Africa*, London: T. W. Lowrie, 1912, 59–78.

*Mary Eliza Blackwell Gaunt*

resent very much the supposition that a woman cannot go where a man can." What seems to have upset her, however, was more the possibility of the "intermingling of the European and the daughter of Ham." Urging, even editorializing that British "women must be encouraged to come out. Every woman who follows in her footsteps makes it easier for those to follow."

Another strongly held opinion in which Gaunt differed from her mostly English hosts was in matters pertaining to health. She believed in the open air theory. Wherever Gaunt went, she refused to sleep under mosquito nets. She argued often with various health officials, always holding the view that fresh flowing air was a better catharsis against malaria than screening, netting, or closed windows—all of which she encountered during the several months she traveled around West Africa, but which she summarily rejected ("a sane and sober life in the open air day and night" was what she preached). Ironically, though Gaunt's views were medically incorrect and eccentric, she never succumbed to malaria (or any illness) during the course of her stay in what was often referred to as "the white man's grave."

From The Gambia, Gaunt moved down the coast to Sierra Leone, confining her visit to mostly the capital of Freetown. Moving on to Liberia, frequently referred to as "the American colony," Gaunt's observations are unflattering but also revealing. The following excerpt covers her visit to Liberia, where she offers firm, if unique, opinions on all manner of people she encounters and events she witnesses.

On to Guinea, Gaunt comes back under the control of the Colonial service, whose protective practices are the source of strong resentment: "I found stirring within me a very masculine desire . . . to be allowed to take care of myself. . . . They were looking after me because they were emphatically sure the coast is no place for a lone woman." With relief, Gaunt escaped to German Togo and briefly journeyed into French West Africa (still arguing her fresh air philosophy), before ending her trip on the Gold Coast.

While Gaunt is often refreshing and at times entertaining, her oft repeated views pertaining to the differences between the races evidences her to be another standard bearer of pseudo-scientific racism. It is important to keep in mind, also, that she came from a wealthy Australian family where society was highly stratified by race. What Gaunt reveals in the selection included here is the attitude of most middle-class people of her generation regarding empire, and towards those who were caught up in the yoke of colonialism. "The native who has had contact with the white man is but on the first rung of civilization. Between black and white there is that great and unbridgeable gulf fixed, and no man may cross it."

*Mary Eliza Bakewell Gaunt*

## *Liberia*

No one on board the *Zaria* really believed I would land in Liberia. When I heard them talk I hardly believed it myself, and yet being there it seemed a pity not to see all I could see. The captain and officers were strongly of opinion there was absolutely nothing to see whatever. If it was madness for a woman to come alone to the Coast, it was stark-staring madness that almost needed restraining in a strait-waistcoat to think of landing in Liberia, for Liberia of all the countries along the Guinea Coast is the one most disliked by the sailors, most despised, and since I have been there I am inclined to say not without reason. For of course I did land; I should have been ashamed of myself if I had not, and I spent the best part of a fortnight there, and thanks to the kindness of His Britannic Majesty's Consul spent it very comfortably indeed.

Liberia is America's experiment in the way of nation-making even as Sierra Leone is Great Britain's, and if I cannot praise the Creole of Sierra Leone I have still less admiration for his American cousin.

In the second decade of the last century philanthropists began to consider the future of the freed slave in the United States, and it was decided that it would be wisdom to transport him back to the continent from which his forefathers came, and let him try there to put into practice the lessons he had learned in the art of civilisation. Bitter is the slur of black blood in the States; bitter, bitter was it ninety years ago when the forlorn little company who were to found a civilised negro state first set foot on their mothers' land. America was but young among the nations in 1822, so she took no responsibility, made no effort to launch these forlorn people in their new venture, or to help them once they were launched. . . .

It must have been a very forlorn little company of people who landed on a small island at the mouth of that unknown river in 1822. They called the island Providence Island, and there they were cooped up for some weeks, for the people on the shore, warlike savages who brooked no master, objected to the newcomers, and it was some little time before they could set foot on the mainland and found their principal town of Monrovia. That was nearly ninety years ago, but very far inland they have never been able to go, for though Liberia takes up quite a large space on the map it is only Liberia in name. The hinterland is held by fighting tribes who resent any interference with their vested rights, and make the fact particularly clear.

The outlines of the history of Liberia I had known vaguely for many a long day even to the name of Monrovia their capital, so called after President Munro, [sic] and it seemed to give point to the story to sit on the deck of the ship that swung at her anchors just beyond the surf of the river mouth. At least they had chosen a very beautiful place. Blue sky, blue sea, snow-white surf breaking on the bar, and a hillside clothed in dense greenery with palms cutting the sky line and the roofs of houses peeping out from among the verdure, that is what I saw, and the captain was emphatic I had seen the best of it. I did not doubt his word then, and having been ashore I am bound to confess he was right.

But the difficulty was to get ashore. I had a letter to the British Consul, but I had not sampled the kindliness of British Consuls as I had that of the Governors, and I did not know exactly what he would say. "I wonder if there is an hotel," I said doubtfully to the captain, and he sniffed.

"You couldn't stay in a negro hotel."

I sent off my letter to the Consul and waited, and a little cloud came up out of the sea and spread over all the sky, and it rained, and it rained, and it rained, and it rained. The sky was dark and forbidding, the sea was leaden-coloured, the waves just tipped with angry, white foam, and the green hills were blotted out, the decks were awash, the awnings were sopping and wept coaly tears, and the captain said as if that settled it, "There, you can't possibly go ashore." But I was by no means sure. Still there was no letter from His Majesty's Consul. Morning passed on to afternoon, and afternoon waned towards evening and still there was no letter. A ship on a pouring wet day is just about as uncomfortable a place as one can be in, but still I was inclined to accept the captain's opinion that Monrovia without someone to act as guide, philosopher, and friend would be a worse place.

No letter, and the captain came along.

"I must get away before dark." He spoke as if that settled it, and he was right, but not the way he expected.

I felt I simply could not go without seeing this place, and I decided. "Then I'll go ashore."

"You can't possibly."

"Oh yes, I can. They won't eat me."

I don't know though that I was quite comfortable as I was dropped over the side in a mammy chair into a surf boat that was half-full of water. The rain had stopped at last but everything in that boat was wet, and my gear made a splash as it was dropped down.

My soldier brother had lent me his camp-kit for the expedition.

"Can't possibly hurt it," said he good-naturedly. "It's been through two campaigns. If you spoil it, it shall be my contribution; but you won't."

I accepted, but I thought as I sat on the bedding-roll at the bottom of that very wet boat, with my head not coming above the gunwale, that he did not know Africa. I hoped I should not have to sleep on that bed that night, because it was borne in on me it would be more than damp.

Luckily I didn't. We crossed the bar, and the ragged, half-naked Kroo boys, than whom there are surely no better boatmen in the world, begged a dash [tip] "because we no splash you," as if a bucket or two of salt water would have made much difference, and I gave it and was so absorbed in the wonder as to what was to become of me that I gave hardly any heed to the shore that was approaching. When I did it was to notice that all the beauty I had seen from the deck was vanishing. Man's handiwork was tumble-down, dirty, dilapidated, unfinished. I stepped from the boat to a narrow causeway of stone; it is difficult to get out of a boat five feet deep with grace, more especially when your skirts are sopping, and I stepped from the causeway, it was not above a foot wide, into yellow mud, and saw I was surrounded by dilapidated buildings such as one might see in any poor, penniless little port. There were negroes in all stages of rags round me, and then out from amongst them stepped a white man, a neat and spick-and-span white man with soldier written all over him, the soldier of the new type, learned, thoughtful, well-read.

"Mrs Gaunt?"

I said "Yes" with a little gasp, because his immaculate spruceness made me feel I was too much in keeping with the buildings and the people around us.

"Did you get my note? I am sorry I only got yours a couple of hours ago."

Oh, I understood by now that in Africa it is impossible for a note to reach its destination quickly, and I said so, and he went on to arrange for my accommodation.

"If you will stay at the Consulate I will be delighted, but it is a mile and a half from the town, and I have no wife; or there is a boarding-house in the town, not too uncomfortable I am told."

There could be but one answer to that. Of course I accepted his invitation. . . . It was broken to me regretfully that I would have to walk; there is no other means of progression in the negro republic.

Such a walk as it was. Never have I met such a road. It was steep, and it was rough, and it was stony as a mountain torrent; now after the rain it was wet and slippery and the branches of the over-hanging trees showered us with water as we passed. . . .

The Consulate is a fine two-storied building with wide verandahs and a large hall where we generally sat, and that hall was very inadequately lighted by some excellent lamps. The Consul didn't understand them and the negro servants didn't understand them, and darkness was just visible and I determined as soon as I knew my host well enough to ask him to let me have a turn at his lamps. Such is the power of a little knowledge; when I left the Consulate it was lighted as it should be, but that first night we spent in a dim, religious light, and I felt I was going to enjoy myself hugely, for here at last was something new. The Gambia and Sierra Leone had been too much regulation Tropics; all that I had seen and done I had at least read of before, but this was something quite different. This had all the glamour of the unknown and the unexpected. I am bound to say that His Majesty's Consul did not look at things with the same eyes. He didn't like Liberia, and he said frankly that things might be unexpected in a measure but he always knew they would be unpleasant. But I went to bed that night with the feeling I was really entering into the land of romance.

Next morning I told my host I would go and see the town.

"But I shan't go by the short cut," I added emphatically.

"What short cut?"

"The way we came last night."

"That's not a short cut," said he, and he smiled pitifully at my ignorance of what was before me. "That's the main road." . . . [to] the Liberian College where the youth of Liberia, male and female, are educated. It is a big building built of brick and corrugated iron, in a style that seems wholly unsuited to the Liberian climate, though viewed from a distance it looks imposing in its setting of greenery. They teach the children algebra and euclid, or profess to do so—evil-tongued rumour has it that the majority of the Liberian women can neither read nor write—but to attain that, to them useless knowledge, they have to scramble over without exception the very worst road I have ever met.

But the road only matches the rest of the place. Monrovia is not only an ill-kept town, it is an outrageously ill-kept town.

Many towns have I seen in the world, many, many towns along this west coast of Africa, so I am in a position to compare, and never have I seen such hopelessly miserable places as Monrovia and the other smaller Liberian towns along the Coast. The streets look pretty enough in a photograph; they are pretty enough in reality because of the kindly hand of Nature and the tropical climate which makes vegetation grow up every-where. There is no wheeled traffic, no possibility of getting about except on your own feet, and in consequence the roadways are generally knee-deep in weeds, with just a track meandering through them here and there, and between the roadway and the side walk is a rough gutter, or at least waterway, about two feet deep, and of uncertain width, usually hidden by the veiling weeds. Occasionally they have little gimcrack bridges appar-ently built of gin cases across these chasms, but, as a rule, if I could not jump as the wandering goats did, I had to make my way round, even though it involved a detour of at least a quarter of a mile.

And the houses in the streets were unlike the houses to be seen any-where else on the West Coast, and, to my mind at least, are quite unsuited to a tropical climate. They are built of wood, brick, or, and this is the most common, of corrugated iron, are three or four stories high, steep and narrow, with high-pitched roofs, and narrow balconies, and many windows which are made with sashes after the fashion of more temperate climes. The Executive Mansion, as they call the official residence of the President, is perhaps as good a specimen as any and is in as good repair, though even it is woefully shabby, and the day I called there, for of course I paid my respects, clothes were drying on the weeds and grass of the roadway just in front of the main entrance. Two doors farther down was a tall, rather pretentious red-brick house which must have cost money to build, but the windows were broken and boarded up, and one end of the balcony was just a ragged fringe of torn and rotting wood. So desolate was the place I thought it must be deserted, but no. On looking up I saw that on the other end of the balcony were contentedly lolling a couple of half-dressed women and a man, naked to the waist, who were watching with curiosity the white woman strolling down the street.

A great deal of the Liberian's life must be spent on his balcony, for the houses must be very stuffy in such a climate, and they are by no means furnished suitably; of course it is entirely a matter of taste, but for West Africa I infinitely preferred the sanded, earthen floor of my friend the Jolloff pilot's wife to the blue Brussels-carpet on the drawing-room floor of the wife of the President of the Liberian republic. But, as I have said, this is a matter of taste, and I may be wrong. I know many houses in London, the furniture of which appears to me anything but suitable.

It was quaint to me, me an Australian with strong feelings on the question of colour, to be entertained by the President's wife, a kindly black lady in a purple dress and with a strong American accent. She had never been out of Africa, she told me, and she had great faith in the future of Liberia. The President had been to England twice. And the President's sad eyes seemed to say, though he hinted no such thing, that he did not share his wife's optimism.

"We have lovely little homes up the river," she said as she shifted the array of bibles and hymn-books that covered the centre-table in the drawing-room to make room for the tray on which was ginger-beer for my refreshment, "and if you will go up, we will make you very welcome."

She would not let me take her photograph as I desired to do; possibly she had met the amateur photographer before and distrusted the species. I could not convince her I could produce a nice picture.

I never saw those "lovely little homes" either. They certainly were not to be found in my meaning of the words in Monrovia or any of the Coast towns, and up country I did not go; there was no way of doing so, save on my own feet, and I felt then I could not walk in such a hot climate. There may be such homes, I do not know, for between this good, kindly woman and me was the great unbridgeable gulf fixed, and our modes of thought were not the same. In judging things Liberian I try to remember that. Every day it was brought home to me.

The civilised black man, for instance, is often a great stickler for propriety, and I have known one who felt himself obliged to board up his front verandah because the white man who lived was wont to stroll on *his* balcony in the early morning clad only in his pyjamas, and yet often passing along the street and looking up I saw men and women in the scantiest of attire lounging on their balconies doing nothing, unless they were thinking, which is doubtful.

Dress or want of dress, I find, strikes one curiously. I have times without number seen a black man working in a loin cloth or bathing as Nature made him, and not been conscious of anything wrong. He seemed fitly and suitably clad; he lacked nothing. But looking on those men in the balconies in only a pair of trousers, or women in a skirt pure and simple, among surroundings that to a certain extent spoke of civilisation, there was a wrong note struck. They were not so much barbaric as indecent. It was as if a corner of the veil of respectability had been lifted, the thin veneer of civilisation torn off, and you saw if you dared to look the possibilities that lie behind. I believed all the horrible stories of Vaudooism of America and the West Indies when I saw the naked chest and shoulders of a black man leaning over a balcony in Monrovia, and yet I have been only moved to friendliness when the fetish man of an Ashanti village, with greasy curls flying, with all his weird ornaments jingling, tom-toms beating, and excited people shouting, came dancing towards me and pranced round me with pointing fingers that I hope and believe meant a blessing. Can anyone tell me why this was? Was it because the fetish man was giving of his very best, while the half-civilised man was sinking back into barbarism and looking at the white woman gave her thoughts she would deeply have resented? Was it just an example of the thought-reading we are subconsciously doing every day and all day long without exactly realising it ourselves?

The people of Monrovia, there are over 4000 of them, seem always lounging and idling, and the place looks as if it were no one's business to knock in a nail or replace a board. It is falling into decay. It is not deserted, for the people are there, and presumably they live. They exist waiting for their houses to tumble about their ears. There is a market-place down in Waterside, the poorest, most miserable market-place on all the African coast. The road here, just close to the landing-place, is not made, but just trodden hard by the passing of many feet. Here and there the native rocks crop up, and no effort has been made to smooth them down. Above all, the stench is sickening, for the Coast negro, without the kindly, sometimes the stern guidance of the white man, is often intolerably dirty, and if my eyes did not recognise it, my nose would. In all the town, city they call it, there is not one garden or attempt at a garden. The houses are set wide enough apart; any fences that have been put up are as a rule broken-down, invariably in need of repair, and in between those houses is much wild growth. The scarlet hibiscus covers a broken fence; an oleander grows bushy and covered with pink roselike flowers; stately cocoa-nut palms, shapely mangoes are to be seen, and all over the streets and roadway in the month of January, I was there, as if it would veil man's neglect as far as possible, grew a creeping convolvulus with masses of pink cup-shaped flowers—in the morning hopeful and fresh and full of dew, in the evening wilted and shut up tightly as if they had given up the effort in hopeless despair. Never have I seen such a dreary, neglected town. It would be pitiful anywhere in the world. It is ten times more so here, where one feels that it marks the failure of a race, that it almost justifies the infamous traffic of our forefathers. It was all shoddy from the very beginning. It is now shoddy come to its inevitable end.

For all the great mark on the map, as I have said, the settlements at Monrovia do not extend more than thirty miles up the river; elsewhere the civilised negroes barely hold the sea-board. They are eternally at war with the tribesmen behind, and here in Monrovia I met half a dozen of the prisoners, dressed in rags, chained two and two with iron collars round their necks, and their guard, a blatant, self-satisfied person, was just about as ragged a scarecrow as they were. Not that the victory is by any means always to the Liberians, for a trader, an Englishman, who had been seeking fresh openings in the hinterland where no Liberian would dare to go, told me that though the tribes are not as a rule cannibals, they do make a practice of eating their best-hated enemies, and he had come across the hands and feet of not a few of the Liberian Mendi soldiery in pickle for future use.

To keep these tribesmen in check, the Liberian, who is essentially a man of peace—a slave—has been obliged to raise an army from the Mendis who inhabit the British protectorate to the west, and so he has laid upon himself a great burden. For, unfortunately, there is not always money in the treasury to satisfy this army of mercenaries when they get tired of taking out their pay in trade gin or tobacco. Poor Liberians, threatened with a double danger. If they had no soldiers the tribesmen within their borders eat them up, and if they have soldiers, war they must have, to provide an outlet for energies that otherwise might be misdirected.

I left my kind host with many regrets and Monrovia without any, and I went on board the *Chama* which was to call at Grand Bassa and Cape

Palmas, and if I did not intend to view them entirely from the ship's deck, at least I felt after my visit to Monrovia it would hardly be necessary for me to stay in either of these towns.

They bear a strong family resemblance to the capital, only they are "more so." The tribes see to it, I believe, that there is no communication with the capital except by sea, and the little communities with their pretensions to civilisation are far less interesting than the people of an Ashanti village who have seldom or never seen a white man.

I landed at Lower Buchanan, Grand Bassa, early one morning. The beach simply reeked of human occupancy. They do not trouble about sanitation in Liberia, and the town itself looked as if the houses had been set down promiscuously in the primeval bush. Perhaps there were more signs of wealth than in Monrovia, for I did see three cows and at least half a dozen hairy, razor-backed pigs on the track that was by courtesy the principal street, and it must require something to support all the churches.

I suppose it is the emotional character of the negro that makes him take so largely to religion, or rather, I think I may say, the observances of religion. The question of the missionaries is a vexed one, and on board the *Chama* was a missionary who made me think. She was a pretty young girl who had left home and father and mother and sisters and brothers and lover—ah, the lover was evidently hard where all had been hard—to minister to the spiritual needs of the people who dwelt behind Cape Palmas. . . .

But if ever I saw the wrong side of Christianity I saw it here in Liberia. Monrovia had many churches, all more or less unfinished, all more or less in decay, and here in Lower Buchanan three corrugated-iron churches within a stone's throw of one another constituted one of the chief features of the town. It was early on a Tuesday morning, the best time for work in a tropical climate, if work is going to be done at all. On the beach the Kroo boys were bringing from surf boats the piassava, the fibre that grows in the swamps and constitutes a large part of the Liberian export, but in Lower Buchanan itself the greater part of the inhabitants that I saw were in church. I entered that church.

Such a tatterdemalion crew! God forbid that I should scoff at any man's faith, but here cleanliness is practically divorced from godliness, and I can honestly say that never in my life have I seen dirtier bundles of rags than that congregation. A woman in a costume a scarecrow would have despised, her head adorned with a baby's hat, the dirty white ribbons fluttering down behind, was praying aloud with much unction, shouting that she was a miserable sinner, and calling upon the Lord to forgive her. The negro loves the sound of his own voice, and again I must claim that I do not scorn any man's sincere faith, but that negro lady was thoroughly enjoying herself, absolutely sure of her own importance. The ragged scare-crows who listened punctuated the prayer with groans of delight, and the only decent one amongst them was a small girl, whose nakedness was hidden by a simple blue-and-white cloth, and she was probably a house-hold slave. For these descendants of a slave people make slaves in their turn, perhaps not men slaves, but women are saleable commodities among a savage nation, and for a trifling consideration, a bottle of trade gin or a few sticks of trade tobacco, they will hand over a girl-child who, taken into the household without pay, holds the position of a servant and is therefore to all intents and purposes a slave. This is really not as bad as it sounds; her position is probably quite as good as it would be in her own tribe, and as she grows older she either marries or forms some sort of alliance with a Liberian. Loose connections and divorce are both so common that she is no worse off than the ordinary Liberian woman, and the admixture of good, strong virile blood may possibly help the future race. At least that is what I thought as I watched the congregation at prayer. They sang hymn choruses so beautifully as to bring tears to my eyes, and then they came outside and abused me because I wanted to photograph them. Had I been they, I should have objected to going out to the world as specimens of their people, but they need not have reviled me in the blatant, coarse manner of the negro who has just seen enough of civilisation to think he rules the universe. I did not press the matter, because I felt it would be ungracious to make a picture of them against their will. But clearly the lovely little homes were not in Lower Buchanan. Nor were they in Cape Palmas.

Far be it from me to say that plantations of some useful description do not exist. They may; I can only say I have seen no evidences of them in three of their towns or near those towns. I will put it on record that I did see some cabbage stalks behind some broken railings opposite the Presi-dent's house in Monrovia, but that was absolutely the only thing in the shape of a garden, vegetable, fruit, or flower, that I did see in the environs of the towns. You can buy no fruit in Monrovia, no chickens, no eggs. Bananas and limes have to be imported. Meat is only to be had at rare intervals, and living is so frightfully dear that when the British Consul had, during my stay, to provide for a distressed British subject who had been unfortunate enough to get adrift in the land, he had to pay six shillings and six-pence a day for his board and lodging—a bare room, not over-clean, with a rough bed in it, and board that did not include meat, but consisted chiefly of manioc or cassava which is what the majority of the Liberians live on themselves.

The country as a matter of fact lives on the Custom's dues which reach about £70,000 a year and are levied not only on the goods that they themselves use but on those the unfortunate natives on the hinterland require. No Liberian is a craftsman even of the humblest sort. The Kroo men are fishermen and boatmen; men from Sierra Leone, the Gold Coast, and Lagos, with an occasional Vai tribesman thrown in, are painters, smiths, and carpenters. The Liberian, the descendant of the freed slave, despises these things; he aspires to be a gentleman of leisure, to serve in the Government Service, or in the Church, to walk about in a black suit with a high collar and a silver-mounted cane. Then apparently he is happy even if he come out of the most dilapidated house in Monrovia. There are, I believe, exceptions. I wonder, considering their antecedents and the conditions under which they have had to exist, whether one could expect more. Possibly it should be counted to them for great righteousness if any good men be found among them at all. But taken as a whole the Liberians after close on ninety years of self-government must strike the stranger as an effete race, blatant and arrogant of speech, an arrogance that is only equalled by their appalling ignorance, a race that compares shockingly with the Mandingo or Jolloff of the Gambia, the stately Ashanti, a warrior with reserve power, or the busy agricultural Yoruba. These men are gentlemen in their own simple, untutored way, courteous and dignified. The Liberian is only a travesty of the European, arrogant without proper dignity, boastful with absolutely nothing in the world to boast about unless it be the amazing wealth of the country he mismanages so shamefully. For Liberia is a rich country; it has a soil of surpassing fertility, and it seems to me that almost anything in the way of tropical products might be produced there. That nothing is produced is due to the ignorance and idleness of these descendants of slaves who rule or misrule the land. Since the days of the iniquitous trade, that first brought her into touch with civilisation, West Africa has been exploited for the sake of the nations of the western world. No one till this present generation seems to have recognised that she had any rights. Now we realise that the black man must be considered at least as much as the white man, who has made himself his master. Now most settlements along the Coast are busy, prosperous, and, above all, sanitary. Only in Liberia, the civilised black man's own country, does a different state of things prevail; only here has the movement been retrograde.

An end must come, but who can say what this end will be. . . .

# ANNE LOUISE (HAY) DUNDAS*
## (Tanganyika, 1921)

Despite Gaunt's admonitions to British wives early in the twentieth century, a few women (including Lady Lugard) had followed or accompanied their Colonial officer husbands to Africa. Others came in increasing numbers, especially after World War I. Anne Dundas, whose new husband was a District Commissioner in East Africa, began her honeymoon en route to Tanganyika in 1921. Dundas kept a diary of her experiences from arrival on the coast until she and her husband, Kenneth, departed in 1923.

Germany lost all her African possessions as part of the post-Armistice reparations in 1918–19. England took over German East Africa (Tanganyika) and the Colonial Office hastily divided the colony into administrative districts. The Dundas' were assigned to a remote area in Chagga country "three degrees south of the Equator and two hundred fifty miles inland from the East African coast." In her diary, Anne Dundas recorded the transition from gradual immersion into the tropics, into the closed world of the colonials abroad, and into her own household domain.

As she makes her way into this new and strange African land, Dundas is awed by the natural scenery she encounters: the bright sunny days with the "velvety folds and ridges" of the mountains in the distance. Night falls quickly in Africa with the stars "appearing suddenly." The hours of darkness are quiet except for the wild animals that stalk—and which posed a threat when Dundas and her husband went on camping trips. The mosquitoes, likely to be anopheles and carriers of malaria, plagued Europeans and Africans alike. But for most colonials, the "protective" net is an imperative, while most Africans did not have access to mosquito nets in the postwar era. Maintaining good health was a problem for those posted in Africa. Dundas was often ill and sometimes took refuge in a Roman Catholic mission station to recuperate. She mentions the unfamiliar heat, the lack of physical activity, and, of course, the mosquitoes.

Hers is a touchingly frank story. Like most colonials abroad, Dundas

---

*Anne Dundas, *Beneath African Glaciers,* London: H. F. & G. Witherby, 1924, 46–65, 172–176.

*Anne Louise (Hay) Dundas*

carries the flag before her, but unlike some she was not committed to uplifting the natives. Her initial contact with African male servants proved unsettling but soon she came to appreciate that they tried to accommo- date. Like most mistresses in the colonies, Dundas adjusted to linguistic demands. In her case, she learned what is referred to as "kitchen Swahili" (enough to communicate on matters domestic).

Where the traveler might complain about hotels, types of food, and problems with her porters, the traveler also came and went. Dundas' memoir is unique in that she stayed in one administrative district for two years, although she did undertake occasional travel—official and unof- ficial—with her husband. "An official safari for the government repre- sentative means travelling on foot some sixty to a hundred miles. . . . [meetings with local chiefs included] all matters pertaining to taxes, ownership and use of water furrows, agriculture, marriage and divorce are brought before the white *Bwana Mkuba* [big man] for discussion and treatment." Taxes were imposed by the colonial government; and land ownership, including that pertaining to farming, was not regarded as an individual right until after the colonial period.

Leisure activities were readily available in areas where there were small concentrations of Europeans. In the following extract, Dundas talks about the golf course and tennis club that were built by African labor but open only to the whites among whom she notes there were none of the class distinctions one would have found at home. The colonial world of yes- teryear included evenings at the club where the men would come fully attired in coat and tie; and their wives in good dresses, and on weekends often in formal apparel. In the following text, Dundas refers to the veranda she turned into a ballroom when guests came to visit. Men outnumbered women, and Dundas tells about the men who "were kind enough to don feminine garb" to round out the sexes. It is possible some of these men were homosexuals, as the colonial service had its complement of them but few discussed sexuality openly (or in print) in those days.

Where no club was available, as was the case in Dundas' district, she mentions the ritualistic and medicinal "sundowner," which was consumed at the homes of the few whites in the community on a rotational basis. Community was important to the colonials. Some were posted together at one place, then shifted separately elsewhere only to come back together in an entirely different part of the world a few years later. Anne Dundas talks about the widening circle in the "human chain" that bound them in an otherwise alien environment.

East Africa contained a significant Indian population; and because of the long familiarity the British had with these subjects in India, many administrators favored them over the British. Dundas describes an Indian

*Anne Louise (Hay) Dundas*

tea party she attended. The babies look like "luscious chocolate drops decorated by a French confectioner." The maypole dance was "performed by weary-looking, bandy-legged men." While it *is* possible the "Hindu sisters" Dundas refers to were actually Hindu, the fact that they were "hidden" from the men and because the party celebrated the Aga Khan, it is more likely that these women were actually Ismaili Muslims.

Rituals and beliefs differed between the African colonized and the colonizers. Female circumcision, which Dundas notes is the "ceremonial of womanhood," was not a familiar custom to Europeans, although Dundas is incorrect in saying that it "is peculiar to Africa." It is also practiced in the Middle East and among some Muslim populations elsewhere in the world. Her description of events surrounding the ritual is one of the earliest accounts provided by a female participant-observer. Boys, if circumcised at all in the Europe of her day, were usually operated on in hospital when but babes. In many African societies, and as Dundas notes among the WaChaggo [pl.], it is the male rite of passage to adulthood.

Isolation to Dundas meant challenge. She believed in keeping in touch with European civilization as much as possible, yet she displayed an interest in and curiosity about "this strange world of black 'savagery'" that surrounded her.

## Life in an Out-Station

The making of a new home in a new country is not without its thrills for even the most blasé of women.

The rail trip from the coast to the interior of Tanganyika is a minor excitement in itself, albeit one awaits in vain the longed-for "hold-up" by stampeding wild elephants, or the unannounced advent of man-eating lions through the open window. Such stirring scenes have been enacted on East African railways within the memory of present settlers, but alas! these experiences were not for us in 1921.

The extremely primitive weekly "Express," the discard from some abandoned railway in Central India, makes a deceptively smooth exit from Tanga station, but with the first hint of increased grade its good behaviour ceases; the two dilapidated engines snort and jerk violently, as if wishing to shake off some section of the long and loosely linked tail which drags helplessly behind. One is fortunate if one's *vis-à-vis* is a cheerful relative, undisturbed by a sudden lapful of femininity hurled upon him. The iron dragons belch fire with true Fafnirian vigour, and showers of red-hot embers pour in at the open windows, settling on the luckless traveller whose interest in the passing scenery outweighs his discretion.

These pampered and self-important little engines are fed with wood, and one has to endure not only the constant spark-dropping, but endless waits for fuel, which is piled up at the roadside and loaded into the tender by slow-moving natives. Often a quarter of an hour is consumed in whistling them out of their near-by huts. Meantime only quick action prevents the peppering of one's travelling gown into holes, if it is not actually in flames. Frantic search for safe cover proves fruitless, and one finally settles down nervously in the centre of the compartment and resigns oneself to the inevitable discomfort caused by the "Big Berthas" ahead.

Within two hours of Tanga the foothills of the Usambara highlands appear, and here one sees the first velvety folds and ridges which make the lower mountains of Africa seem less barren than the forestless heights of other countries.

With the approach of twilight the serrated peaks rise higher against the fast purpling sky; one thinks of Valhalla and almost expects to see the Valkyrie hosts float from some dark recess into the flaring afterglow of the sunset, which succeeds the darkening shadows for a brief moment and then quickly fades into night.

There are no half-tones in Africa to bridge her changes, the notes are sharply defined. The hot tropical day follows fast on the sunrise; the evening shadows are hovering about before the sun has fairly set, and the black mantle of night is quickly silvered with countless stars, not arriving singly as in European countries, but appearing suddenly, as if a curtain had hastily been drawn from the face of the heavens, revealing the stage set for night.

Anyone who has lived in Africa knows how awesome are her hours of darkness; a stillness of death pervades the sleeping world of humans, yet one is ever aware of the wild life which silently creeps from cover with the approach of night, and imagination peoples the thick bush with crouching lions and velvet-footed leopards, and every dancing firefly becomes a glowing eye set in the head of some savage beast.

Within the carriage *de luxe* reserved for our use on this first journey we were beset by countless mosquitoes if we ventured outside the protecting sleeping-nets, and from the leaky roof, during sudden showers, a miniature waterfall descended upon the berths, so that sleep was well-nigh impossible. Sheer excitement of one's first night journey in Africa would, in any case, keep one awake, and a sudden stop between stations brings the same chill of apprehension as the slowing-up of a transatlantic liner off the Newfoundland icefields. Raised on a shaky elbow, the "tenderfoot" keeps vigil through the long hours, and awaits painfully the first streak of dawn. Then comes relaxation as the tropical mugginess of atmosphere yields to the fresher air of higher altitudes, and with a cool morning breeze stirring the bush, which closes in on both sides, one's potential enemies return to their lairs and sheer weariness claims a willing victim.

The terminus of the direct line to the foot of snow-capped Mount Kilimanjaro was our destination, and was to be our first home in Africa—a thought which for one, at least, held infinite possibilities and excitements. This one had been told in England that the arrival of the weekly train at an African Government post was treated as a great event, and that even the sophisticated journeyed to the station to greet arrivals, be they strangers or one's nearest and dearest, and one had scoffed at the idea as an unbelievable provincialism. Yet how this same one's heart thumped with anticipation as the train slowed up and emitted its last snort at the little white-washed station! The prophecy was fulfilled! There were half-a-dozen European faces under khaki helmets and—could it be—the genial smiling face of a *woman*!

Not even the sudden deluge of rain which descended upon the gala outfit could despoil that first welcome of its pleasure, and while a kindly official removed once spotless white shoes, and assisted the struggle into rubber boots, one contemplated with equanimity the sea of mud and water outside, and longed to do battle with it; for half-a-mile away, at the top of the hill, was there not a wee house which was to be a "home" for two years, and which one had never seen, not even in a picture!

A cup of tea served by the hospitable station-master heartened us for the plunge-bath outside, and excitement drove one on, unmindful of the deluge and the feet of clay which grew heavier with each step in the clinging mud. The old inhabitants plodded along conversing cheerily, but the new-comer gasped and struggled, apparently unobserved, and all but sat down ignominiously. No one of the party seemed to realise that for her this was the beginning of life's greatest adventure. So determined was she to see nothing unpleasant in the surroundings, that the few dilapidated shops and Greek hotels scattered along the road were mere architectural shadows, not to be examined until one's whole-hearted attention had been given to that small temple on the acropolis—a temple disparagingly referred to by sceptical relatives at home as "that three-roomed hut."

With the memory of the tin-roofed Government "homes" clustered about Slough and various other abandoned military depots in England, imagine one's surprise and joy, at the end of the long muddy street, in suddenly facing a hill-side avenue of straight little cypress-trees, suggesting the Riviera, and ascending through them, beneath a pergola dripping purple bougainvillæa blooms, to a rose-embowered, enchanting little white-stone bungalow, from whose spacious verandah one had an uninterrupted view to the far horizon, with its yellow and mauve mountains! What booted it that the furnishings consisted of two dilapidated iron beds, four straight-backed chairs and five or six well-worn pieces of Government furniture? There was space; there was a view; there was a woman's vision to create beauty from apparent ugliness, and it was "home," however humble. . . .

To the woman who is without imagination and resources Africa must soon become a slough of despond, in which she flounders helplessly. She must be able to create her diversions, forget her aversions and devote herself whole-heartedly to the discovery of good in everything, for the new civilisation reveals her delights only to those who have the eager eyes and ears and heart of the explorer; to all others the book is closed. Amusement, companionship and ordinary healthful exercise the woman must create from very little material, for in few of the Government stations of the interior are they to be found ready-made. She is fortunate if she finds half-a-dozen white women within fifty or a hundred miles, and if congeniality with those women would be an improbability in Europe, it behoves her to cultivate its possibility to the utmost in Africa. To hold oneself aloof from anything which spells European civilisation is quite as destructive as to withhold one's interest in the strange world of black "savagery" which surrounds one.

Equatorial Africa is not a white man's country in its broadest sense, for no country can be such where the menacing sun compels the wearing of a heavy helmet throughout the hours of daylight.

"To be pleased with everything and please everyone in the place" should be an eleventh commandment in the outposts of the Empire, and the twelfth, "To withhold nothing that is yours from your neighbour," and that means not only one's heart and brain and kindly impulse, but all one's worldly possessions. Woe be to the woman who believes herself independent of her fellow-exiles in Africa! The day will come when visiting hordes descend unannounced upon her household, when chairs, beds, china and silver must be requisitioned from her neighbours, and when diversions must be created with as little material at hand as is apparently possessed by the conjurer who produces a clucking chicken from the bystander's pocket.

It is this necessary camaraderie in a new country which breaks down the walls of self-centredness and lets in a flood of warm, humanising influences which one is prone to believe unnecessary in an older civilisation. The lesson is not learnt in a day. Old prejudices and predilections must be faced and put to the death when they evince antagonism to the interests of the community. Here is no question of the highest in authority receiving a homage and consideration which is not honestly striven for by integrity of purpose and genuine kindness. What one gives one receives. As this is true of things spiritual, so it is of the material, and bread cast upon the waters often returns in most unexpected ways.

Even Mother Nature is ever ready to play her part in the distribution of the greatest good to the greatest number. So simple a gift as a packet of marigold seeds donated to a friend some eight miles distant on the mountain, after flowering generously on the heights, returned its numerous offspring via a water-furrow to the garden of the original donor, there to burst into thousands of golden blooms along the banks of the stream.

Flowers, fruit and a share of all delicacies pass from the more fortunate to the less. Everyone has something to share at one time or another with his neighbour. The gardenless house may be inhabited by a good shot, and a brace of birds returns in the emptied flower-basket of his artistic neighbour, who knows no distinction between a spruce partridge and his edible relative. When a sheep is slaughtered, or one's cherished suckling pigs reach the proper gastronomic stage, the owner divides all with his brother officials, keeping for his personal use only what suffices for one or two meals. If the Swahili cook, after many painful efforts, succeeds in producing an eatable cake, it is forthwith carried to the community tennis court to be eaten by everyone with the community tea, served between games.

Thus the social isolation of life in Africa acts as a stimulant to one's better nature and a corrective to the selfishness which is often engendered by the luxury and ease of modern civilisation. All possible effort is put forth by the more important members of these tiny communities to draw everyone into such sports and amusements as can be crowded into the cool evening hours, for only by making others feel their importance in the general social scheme, can sufficient members be mustered for real competition, and competition, we know, is the life of many things besides trade.

For purposes of general amusement and recreation there are practically no "class" distinctions, save those of colour and race. Everyone, be he clerk or peer, is entitled to the privileges of Club and Sports, unless he prove objectionable to the majority. The mere fact of his residence, whether permanent or temporary, grants eligibility to his share of the social life of the little colony.

Where else could you find a community of some twelve or fifteen European men supporting a two-court tennis club and a fair nine-hole golf course reclaimed in a year from impassable bush plains? The cheapness of black labour in Africa naturally aids in the metamorphosis, but it also requires good-fellowship, the downing of all social barriers and cheerful sharing of comparatively heavy expense among the none too generously paid Government officials.

After the games of golf or tennis, small parties gather at the various houses for the evening drink, which is rated as indispensable to health in the tropics, where the evening air calls forth the lurking germs of fever. "Small chop" (sandwiches) accompany the sundown medicine of Scotch or rye, and the time from six-thirty to eight o'clock passes in the telling of tales (some "out of school"), the recounting of varied experiences in other parts of the world, and discussion of happenings, political and otherwise, "at home." A name is casually mentioned by a new-comer: "Oh yes, he was stationed with me on the Gold Coast," breaks in the "old timer," and so the circle ever widens, and new links of interest are forged in that human chain of younger sons who have gone forth to represent the empirical Mother.

Occasionally there is an Indian tea-party to enliven the station, not that the party itself is anything but lugubrious—from the impassive faces of the hosts to the rather lukewarm beverages served—but the funereal toasts proposed in halting English by the unsmiling master of ceremonies to the representatives of the Great English Government afford intense, though unintentional, amusement to the Europeans present. Not a word of the long speech learned and recited by the well-meaning official toast-master is understood by his brother Indians, so the response of the European *Bwana Mkubwa* (great master) is usually made in Swahili, quite as unintelligible to the majority of the European guests because it is far too correct to be understood by the ordinary dabbler in that difficult tongue.

When "honours are even" we resume our seats at the long table and nibble our cake and chocolate, whilst our hosts (wearing their shirt-tails outside their trousers) hover about, solicitous for our comfort.

On momentous occasions, such as the birthday celebration in honour of the Aga Khan, the High Priest of all Ismailia Mohammedans, the entertainment embraces a maypole dance performed by weary-looking, bandy-legged Indians, with the ever-present waving shirt-tail, each man holding a coloured cotton streamer in one hand and two sticks in the other. With these he strikes first at those held by the man in front, and then behind, more or less in unison with the discords emanating from a wheezy harmonium, which occupies the place of honour in the centre of the circle. Added diversion is sometimes afforded by an obtrusive *m toto* (child), his mouth filled with kerosene oil, spitting vigorously into the flame of a lighted match, thereby producing intermittent fireworks, which are loudly applauded by the exhausted maypolites. This subject for the S.P.C.C. being reluctantly banished from the foreground, a group of high-voiced little schoolboys, dressed in diminutive frock-coats plus the junior shirt-tail, indulge in a dialogue on the value of money versus education (in which, of course, virtue is bound to be its own reward), or some such laudable subject.

As the entertainment at this stage is growing rather thin, and our hosts appear somewhat anxious and weary, the European ladies adjourn by invitation to view their Hindu sisters, hidden from vulgar male curiosity. These also are celebrating in mild fashion the birthday of their great religious patron; but here is real beauty—soft, dusky flesh, drowsy black eyes, tiny brown hands, and lovely clinging silks of various hues, silver-bordered, framing the delicate features and falling in soft drapings to the feet, covering the coarse day garments, which are just visible as the little bodies sway and bend in homage to the absent hero of their mystical religion.

Everywhere about the floor of the inner sanctum lie wee brown babies, sleeping peacefully in their stiff, gold-lace caps, looking not unlike luscious chocolate drops decorated by a French confectioner.

This charming private view ends the evening's entertainment, and the official guests, after expressing their gratitude for the hospitality, depart in close formation, so that the blessed anthem of *God Save the King* may be rendered but *once* by the "band"—it being the custom to greet all European officials and speed them homeward by this suitable selection, sometimes unrecognisable as rendered by a native orchestra, and decidedly painful when repeated some twelve times of an evening.

The Indian "party" is a rare Sunday afternoon event, for which all Europeans turn out in their best day clothes—almost the only opportunity afforded for any dress, save tennis and dinner.

One of the saving graces of life in a British station is the unvarying observance of the small conventions which mark the society of civilisation. A man may be the only European official, with no neighbour nearer than one hundred miles, but he and his wife (if he has one) will dress as carefully for their lonely dinner as if in the midst of a London season, and the gleaming candles, the flowers and quiet unobtrusive service are considered as essential in Africa as in Mayfair or Upper Fifth Avenue.

It is something of a shock to a European woman new to the country, and accustomed to good English servants and possibly the luxury of a personal maid, to be confronted by a household staff of four or five black "boys" understanding no word of English. It requires patience and cultivation of the art of pantomime to reach a common ground of understanding between mistress and "maid," but the boys are very quick to observe, very willing to learn, usually honest and rarely impertinent, and one soon acquires sufficient words of the strange language of the native to make oneself understood.

It is a musical language when correctly spoken; there is something infinitely more gracious in the Swahili house-boy's *"Ahsante, mem-Sahib"* ("Thank you, Mistress"), than in the stolid silence of the American servant or the hypocritical "thank you, madam," of the English after-war parlour-maid. The spotless white *kanzu*, not unlike the old-fashioned night-shirt, which reaches to the bare feet, and a finely embroidered white linen *fez* covering their shaven heads, gives the African servant a dignity unknown to the southern "nigger" of civilisation, with his loudly checked shirt, ill-tailored suit and bulldog-toed yellow shoes. The *kanzu* is the costume worn by all male Swahili coast-dwellers, and in the interior has been adopted not only by the house-boys serving European masters, but by many natives of the better type. Otherwise the accepted costume of the native of the Kilimanjaro country is a draped cotton cloth or blanket. The *totos,* or small children, are blessedly unhampered by anything more than a string of beads, and their pretty brown bodies seem amply clothed at that.

When one is a new-comer to the district and the bride of a *Bwana Mkubwa,* one is given a series of surprise parties by the principal wives of the native chiefs. An imposing appearance they make, followed by less important members of their household bearing gifts of fresh eggs, chickens, the skin of wild animals, or a rudely carved flower-holder. These women have an unmistakable look of caste, with finely chiselled features and enviable dignity of bearing. Hand-shaking is usually indulged in between the wives of chiefs and the wives of their white officials, and although these black aristocrats look clean enough, after a few such greetings the European woman retires hastily to her bathroom for a vigorous hand-scrubbing, as the native woman eats all her food with her fingers, and, it may be surmised from their stickiness, licks them "clean" afterwards.

Until we took up our residence there had been little or no dancing in the district, and as this seemed an essential and healthy recreation, we utilised our spacious cement-floored verandah for a ballroom, and started a "series" of fancy-dress parties. The floor, hand-polished with native beeswax and turpentine and rubbed to Mansion House perfection by many bare black feet, was quite dazzling on the first occasion, when with visiting officials and their wives we numbered some six women and twenty-four men, several of whom were kind enough to don feminine garb for the evening to equalise the sexes. Gibson girls, veiled ladies of the harem, bonneted and hoop-skirted Victorian flirts, with stiff Sisal curls, summer triflers with shady hats and flowered voile gowns, made a bevy of maidens equalled only by a 'Varsity musical comedy, and although somewhat highly coloured as to complexion and decidedly free as to leg action, they added greatly to the zest of the occasion in their borrowed sex and plumage.

Most of these costumes were made under male supervision by the local Indian tailors, and were a complete surprise to the ladies present, which spoke well of the ingenuity and resourcefulness of the transplanted Englishman.

The weekly train often brings notables, from home or abroad, who expect amusement or instruction for a week or more, and there are always lesser officials travelling to and from the coast, with an occasional "bigwig," such as a judge, a mighty hunter or that *rara avis*—a Governor. These travellers usually bring their tents, cooks and personal servants, but one is expected, if possessed of a vacant room, to receive them as houseguests, be they strangers or friends. When honoured by the official visit of the Governor one "takes up one's bed and walks" to the nearest neighbour, who usually discovers an unoccupied crevice in his two- or three-roomed house for the extra guests. Otherwise the "hosts" take to tents and make a picnic of the affair, finding much enjoyment in dining as guests at their own table without the attendant anxieties and struggles with the kitchen staff. These unexpected visits are often a pleasant break in one's quiet life, though not unattended by difficulties when one considers that the most imposing residence consists of three rooms and a verandah; but as Africa is the country *par excellence* for the creation of something from nothing, behold a charming house of banana leaves quickly erected for the accommodation of one's guest, another for his kit, still another for his servants, and when the green leaves become dry and dusty the miniature village is pulled down and another erected in the course of a few hours by skilful natives. If one wishes to present a really smart appearance, one has a guest-house, with thatched roof, mud walls, white-washed and green-shuttered, and furnished with whatever is movable from the mansion to the hut.

It is surprising what a concealing dress of pretty chintz will do for an unlovely black iron bed, and our European sisters might well take cognisance of the ingenuity of the African hostess. One grows inordinately proud of one's resourcefulness after a time, but possibly this is pardonable in a country where the accomplishment of anything savouring of European civilisation is attended by so many difficulties.

Life is not all a bed of roses in Africa; there is always the lurking fear of fever and ill-health from many sinister causes. At nightfall one's legs must be encased in mosquito boots practically all the year on the coast and six months in the interior, as the countless variety of gnats, mosquitoes and biting flies hover about under dinner-tables and chairs to feast upon the unfortunate females who prefer a pretty slipper and silken ankle to sensible, though unlovely, protection. To be compelled to wear ugly knee-length leather boots as the complement of a diaphanous evening frock is a sore trial for any fastidious woman, but the wise ones do it, and thus avoid one of the fever dangers of Africa, although not all mosquitoes are malaria-carriers. One is told by the oldest inhabitant to take heed only of the mosquito that stands on his head while biting, but before one has decided whether the intruder has entered head first or tail first the deadly work may be accomplished, and after a lapse of three weeks one knows the answer.

In Africa, avoiding the various intrigues against longevity becomes a daily sport, and for men, unless stationed in a particularly poisonous district, it seems a fairly healthy country. Women suffer from many causes—unaccustomed heat, glaring light, the difficulty (which many never attempt to overcome) of making themselves understood by the native servant, lack of accustomed activity, social and physical, all play havoc with her more delicate mechanism. Here again the personality, resourcefulness and character of the woman enter into the making or marring of her own life, and that of others associated with her in voluntary exile from all that is familiar, and from the so-called amenities of civilisation. If she occupies the long hours of enforced inactivity and pulsing heat with good books, restful memories and happy plans for the future, if she conscientiously studies the language, history and customs of the native races surrounding her, if she lends herself and all she has to the life of the little station, if she determines to miss nothing that has ministered to her comfort and well-being in the Old World, and to be content with what is afforded in the New, if she loves the blue skies that smile on her flowers, the silver stars that glisten through the night, if she fears nothing, and, above all, allows her sense of humour full play over the rough surfaces of daily living, then will the heart of Africa open itself to her and she will have learned that the "perception of the inexhaustibleness of Nature is an Immortal Youth. . . .

## Quaint Customs and Beliefs

What the native does not know he presumes his ancestors were informed of. The exact meaning of many such beliefs are now not to be ascertained, because those who introduced them lived under conditions which no longer obtain, and there is no clue to their ideas. But what they *did* and observed it is not only wise to follow suit in, but essential, because the ancestors may too easily resent a departure from their rules and habits. Thus a smith must teach his son to become a smith, just as all his ancestors did, for the ancestral shades will not permit their art to become extinct among their descendants. The spirits are thus also guardians and preservers of custom, and those who offer slight to those customs are afflicted or become ceremonially unclean. Ceremonial purification may then be performed by certain medicines or magical performances, but most often by specific rites which are known only to elders of a special grade.

Most ancient, perhaps, of all ceremonies is that of circumcision—so ancient indeed that its origin and object are lost in antiquity; certainly natives themselves have no idea why it exists. But the antiquity and mystery of the rite make it most sacred among all customs. It is practised by the great majority of Bantus, and marks the transition from childhood to manhood.

Equally venerable and sacred with the circumcision of males is the corresponding rite of the females, a practice peculiar to Africa. Both these ceremonies are always attended by much celebration, and as the young Wachagga boy or girl approaches the period of dawning manhood or womanhood, both sexes look forward eagerly to the ceremonials attending this transition from childish pursuits to the more serious duties of life.

Preparation for these ceremonials goes hand-in-hand with instructions to both sexes on the duties and responsibilities devolving upon each after their bodies have been duly purified and consecrated to the great end—parenthood.

The ceremonial of womanhood for the young girl is of a personal and private nature, and is not without its compensations. The operation by a skilled old woman of the clan is performed on the girls singly in their own huts, surrounded by their female relatives, and is preceded by the decking out of the girl's person with all the "family jewels." The young throat and breast are fairly weighed down with great ropes of vari-coloured beads; a belt of the same encircles her waist and thighs, and on the legs and arms are worn great iron bracelets and strings of bells.

Seemingly everything possible is done to divert the child's thoughts from the ordeal in prospect. Gifts of goats, grain and household utensils are brought by the relatives and friends if they be of a well-to-do circle, and on this day the girl is presented by her mother with her own hoe and a cooking-pot, the symbols of the woman's domestic rule in the realm allotted her.

After the operation the girl is joined by her family in the hut, and is there anointed with fat by her father and all the female members of the family. She then joins her young companions (who may or may not have been through the same ordeal) and they become the centre of an admiring circle of dancers—youths and maidens—who link arms and surround the young girl who has just achieved womanhood.

Sometimes one, more often three or four, of the newly initiated maidens dance slowly backwards and forwards in the hollow of the ever-widening circle, their bells and clanging iron ornaments giving forth a rhythmic musical note as they bend their knees and swing to and fro on the tall staffs presented by the father of each for this momentous occasion.

Often an elder sister (with little beauty to boast of, but making the most of this opportunity to shine in public) directs the steps of the younger girl, walking and dancing backward and forward before the much-bedecked little sister, stamping, clapping and chanting a weird tune at intervals in unison with the clanging iron bells and anklets of the *première danseuse*.

It is also the privilege of the mother, or sister, of the young principal to receive gifts of money, trinkets or grain from the guests. For this purpose the woman who dances before them carries on her staff a large cloth bag, open-mouthed, and modestly invites the donations of stray shillings from the onlookers. One notices that though the dancers never stop, there is much surreptitious observation of the bag and its slowly increasing bulk.

On the day when I was permitted to make personal observations of these ceremonials I happened unawares on the celebration, following the tinkling bells across native fields till they led me to the feast in a near-by banana grove, and unfortunately I had no coins with me, as this was the first celebration I had ever actually witnessed, and I was unaware of the custom of donations to the newly initiated. I was soon made conscious of my delinquency by the disappointed look on the young girl's face as the bag was uplifted in vain before me.

This time of initiation is, to the budding belle of black Africa, fraught with infinite romance. Often her betrothal dates from this eventful day, and if it has preceded it the day of celebration will be marked by special favours from her betrothed and his family.

On this day, or later, after her complete recovery, the father of the young man she is to marry will probably give her a goat or sheep. His mother may give her a set of milk gourds and platters of fat. The young man of her heart will at this time, or later, hang a necklet of bright-coloured beads about her neck in the presence of assembled guests, and this betokens that she is his chosen bride, and may not be wooed by other suitors.

Following on these rites comes, among most tribes, an initiation cere-mony, signifying the final entry into manhood and womanhood, and most generally accompanied by instruction in the "whole duty of man," and the sphere of woman's activity. . . .

# JOAN ROSITA TORR FORBES*
# (East Africa, 1917)

Joan Rosita Torr was born in 1890 in rural Lincolnshire. Her father was a Member of Parliament and a member of the landed gentry. Rosita, the eldest of six children, had a conventional upbringing before marrying Colonel Robert Forbes and going to India as a colonial wife. The marriage was an unhappy affair of short duration. Soon after they were posted to Australia in 1917, Rosita requested a divorce and took off on a whirlwind trip around the world. Stopping in North Africa, Forbes developed a fascination with both the Arab culture and language. She stayed on and published her first book from Libya two years later. This was a study of the hair-raising adventure that took her to the Kufra Desert in 1920.

Disguised as a Muslim, and taking the name Khadija, Forbes traveled with an Egyptian diplomat and explorer. Combining the flair and sense of adventure of Richard Francis Burton and T. E. Lawrence, Forbes, however, was seriously limited in where she was allowed to go. Both the Italian government and local Arab authorities attempted to prevent Forbes and her companion from attempting their journey to Kufra. Her disguise and the fact that they slipped away from their party in the dead of night accounts for the fact that Forbes and her companion managed to escape their opposition. In successfully traveling to, and meeting with the desert dwellers, Forbes became the second European to accomplish this feat. The first—a German man—died soon after his explorations of the area.

After her successful adventures in the Kufra, Forbes and her companion returned to Egypt by way of the Siwa oasis. While she was in Egypt, Forbes continued studying Arabic—having covered her earlier linguistic deficiencies with claims that her mother had been a Circassian slave from the Black Sea area. She also wrote a dramatic account of the difficult trip (*The Secret of the Sahara: Kufara,* New York, 1921).

Following her marriage to another British military officer, Forbes again donned her disguise. She went to Morocco, where she visited the Moroccan chief, al-Raisini, famous for kidnapping and holding his hostages for ransom. For reasons we may never know, Forbes captivated al-

*Rosita Forbes, *From Red Sea to Blue Nile: Abyssinian Adventure,* New York: Macaulay & Co., 1925, 86–91, 102, 108–109, 111–112, 119–167.

*Joan Rosita Forbes*

Raisini. Not only was she successful in interviewing him, he provided her with enough background material to enable Forbes to write a brief account of his life.

Forbes then set off for the "Empty Quarter" in South Arabia. The British government was more successful in thwarting her efforts than the Italians had been in Libya. Because of troubles in the area, Forbes was forbidden to venture into that vast unexplored desert. When her plans failed, Forbes turned to Ethiopia, accompanied by photographer Harold Jones, with whom she made a film. The dark haired beauty, who "dressed in high heels" and wore "huge Ascot hats," donned jodhpurs and spurs to travel on horseback through the empire in 1922. Forbes and Jones (her second in command), were assisted by numbers of Ethiopians. They arrived at Assab, the Red Sea port, and journeyed to Harar, the ancient Muslim city where Richard Burton was held captive back in the mid-nineteenth century.

By the mid-1920s, the area was under the control of the central Ethiopian government. Ras Emru, a cousin of the Regent and governor of the province, provided them with hospitality and then set the two on their way with a retinue to servants and pack animals to ease their passage into the interior of the country. En route to Addis Ababa, the capital, Forbes observed carefully and amassed considerable data on Ethiopian customs.

When they reached Addis Ababa, Forbes met with Queen Zaiditu (Judith). Later, they met the Regent, Ras Tafari and his wife. Many of the dreams for his country related by Ras Tafari to Forbes were carried out by the Regent when, in 1930, he became Haile Selassie I.

Forbes and Jones were only in Ethiopia a few months. Her study "Concerning Women" was therefore impressionistic. Nevertheless, Forbes' account was the first of its kind to be made available in the west. While the documentation is presented as pertaining to Ethiopian women, keep in mind that Forbes and Jones were accompanied by Amhara interpreters and guides. (The Amhara are an ethnic-linguistic group who dwell mostly in the central highlands.) Thus, the customs described generally deal with women living mostly in the Shoa province, in the central part of the country.

After her comparatively peaceful sojourn in Ethiopia, Forbes and her husband traveled to South America. She also made frequent trips to India, where she "preferred staying with rulers of the princely states." She lectured widely in both Europe and the United States before her death in 1967.

*Joan Rosita Forbes*

# A Forest City

Addis Ababa, the "New Flower," became a capital in 1896 when Menelik extended the village he had created four years previously, forbade wood-cutting and ordered the wholesale plantation of gums, so many by each family. It lies in a bowl between Entoto, 10,000 feet high, and other mountains which form the rims of the scented, shallow curve, lined by thousands of mushroom huts and tens of thousands of trees. The air is honey-sweet, and so strong that one forgets how little one can sleep at such an altitude—nearly 8,000 feet. The sunshine is palely dazzling without the usual black and white contrast of African light. The forest is like a myriad spears, their steel quivering in the wind and, amidst its metal blueness, are scars which are white stone-built houses roofed with corrugated iron, and mud specks which are huts. The little hills, down which the roads fling themselves in a tumult of rock and boulder, are dwarfed by the gibbe (palace) of the Empress. This is a conglomeration of different architectures, flat roofs, peaked, shed, house and pavilion, while the highest of all the buildings is like a Greek temple.

If all the cities of the world have some different and essential spirit, surely Addis Ababa's is the most elusive, for it is neither barbaric nor conventional, lawless nor tame, but something sturdily independent, proud of a tradition which it takes for granted, unassuming beneath a varnish of self-consciousness. I did not stay long enough in the forest town to realize more than that, in her violent contrasts and in her gentle violence, Addis Ababa is typical of her people. There are a few modern buildings—a hotel, the bank of Abyssinia, the Legations, and, of course, the palaces of the royal family, but the huts outnumber them, smother them, as a self-sufficient simplicity outweighs the influence both of Africa and Europe. Among the 60,000 inhabitants are a large quantity of Levantines, Armenians, Greeks and Syrians, as well as Indians and yellow-skinned Yemenese, but they are superimposed on the native life and remain detached from it, an excrescence though they control the business and industry of the capital. Were they swept away to-morrow, the essential Addis would be unchanged.

There are half a dozen motors, which progress tank-fashion over roads that are often either trenches or earth-works, but the camel is the four-wheeler, and the mule the taxi.

Topees and felt hats of all shapes and sizes go side by side with the priests' white turbans, with shaven head or curls close wound in the end of a *chamma*, [traditional white gauze shawl], but over every throng float the grass parasols, like sails bellying in the breeze.

The life of the city radiates from the markets, where are packed thousands of peasants, merchants, speared hillmen, men-at-arms; women on foot and on donkeys; my lord on a stallion, with squires at his stirrups, my lady, closely muffled on a mule, are wedged into a human tapestry, but dominated by the palace and the churches. So the priesthood dominates a religious and little educated race, but always under the throne which theoretically owns all the land, has right of life and death over every subject and can claim his labor in peace, or his sword in war. It is a feudal system, framed by the astuteness of Menelik [II], who saw the danger of the hereditary races, each the war lord of his province, and gradually substituted his own governors, dependent on the central authority at Addis, but it is a feudal system administered by a liberal-minded Regent.

Africa is primitive and, below the surface, smoulder the embers of an ancient violence, but, here again, Abyssinia is not Africa, for, like the smiles and the gestures of her people, her violence is gentle.

The murderer may be hanged in public by a particularly slow and careless process, or handed over to an execution at the hands of his victim's family, which must be a replica of the crime he has committed, but the Abyssinians hate taking life. Rather than kill a horse with a broken leg, they will let it linger in uselessness, while no one would think of destroying any of the hordes of dogs which act as city scavengers, and make the night unbearable with their insistent barking. We heard of old tortures, now almost obsolete; we saw relics of these things, but, however stern and simple the justice of Ethiopia, its severity cannot be compared to that of Islam in fanatical Lybia and Asir, or in Raisuli's Moroccan mountains.

In Addis no one rides alone. Always a groom or a couple of serfs, a few riflemen or a boy with a fly-whisk run alongside, their number varying according to the importance of their master, and no one walks who can afford any kind of beast. In fact I think it is bad form to have any walking muscles and, when the great are forced to take a few paces, they are supported under the armpits. Consequently traffic is congested, yet there are far more bows than jostling, and an unfortunate kick by the heels of his mule may land a rider in prison, or on the gallows, for accidental manslaughter is punishable as murder.

So, in this land of outward conflict and inward assurance, the contrasts between white robes and earthen huts, between the tentatives of modern science and the network of custom and tradition, even between Christianity and sunburned superstitious Africa, are all expressed in Addis Ababa. This woodland town is as complex and intriguing as the problems which beset her unconquered race.

Our first morning in Addis was spent in paying off the caravan, all of whom affixed greasy thumbmarks, by way of signature, to a receipt which ran into several pages of Amharic language. After that we were free to go out fishing with the camera. Addis is a difficult place to photograph, because trees block every view, and distances are prodigious, when considered from muleback. It is nearly an hour's ride up and down hill and across rivers, from the hotel, markets and business quarter to the Legations, with their attractive gardens set in miles of woodland. On the way we found all sorts of excitements. A motor might be encountered, in which, case there was a pell-mell rush of riders for the nearest turning. Worse still, some misguided modern had introduced the first steam wagon, and the sight of this half a mile away was sufficient to send every animal into convulsions. At the end of our first encounter with it, [Harold] Jones "cinemaoperator" was draped gracefully round the ears of his mule, with the saddle tangled in its mane, while I, having dismounted with much haste and no dignity, was attached to one end of a rein, while my beast seasawed between earth and sky, his velvet trappings slipping further tailwards with each plunge. The last of these landed us, inextricably confused, in the ditch.

"It is a country mule. It is not used to the town," said the charming stranger who rescued me.

"Perhaps it is a little bucolic," I retorted, dusting myself gingerly.

The river beds, narrow clefts between the rocks, were always amusing in the morning, when most of the population seemed to be engaged in washing, themselves, their clothes, or their household effects. The boulders were shiny with soap, the water foamed with it, and snow-white *chammas* drying in the sun contrasted with the dark figures of their owners glistening after a vigorous scrubbing.

From eight o'clock the dust rose like golden pollen over flocks and herds coming into the city, with here and there a long-horned bull charging across the street till the ropes from horns and heels were taut in opposite directions, and this was always the moment chosen by a camel caravan to wind itself into the figure eight, so popular with these supercilious beasts. The grain market was a hive of industry up till noon and massed with donkeys bulging with leather sacks; Gourages, the porters and manual laborers of the capital, sturdy in their sheepskin coats; Galla women, the oil thick in their fuzzy plaits; horses with their backs scarred as if by grids; attractive girls of the city with the neat ribbed heads, a baby or a gourd rolled up on their backs; the toga-like *chammas* of the citizen, and the tallow-stained shifts of the peasant.

Wandering, apparently quite happily, among this crowd were generally several couples of debtor and creditor or accuser and accused, linked together with a four-foot chain. In Abyssinia no one may be imprisoned until he is proved guilty, so this is a convenient method of ensuring that the defendant does not escape. If a man accuses a woman of some crime, he has to produce a female relation to be chained to her until judgment is given, while the reverse holds good, of course, in the case of masculine debtor and feminine creditor. The couple remain chained, night and day, and they are generally sent to live in the house of some mutual friend or other person of confidence.

Sometimes we passed impromptu courts of justice, conducted with much explanation and gesture in the midst of an interested crowd. On these occasions any passer-by may be called in as judge, to settle the disputed ownership of beasts, petty thefts or damage. He takes his duties seriously, and listens patiently to the various witnesses, who often illustrate their story, mimicking the dragging away of a sheep, and the purloining of grain, with much histrionic talent. Plaintiff and defendant may be called upon to back the truth of their statements in kind, so that if the first exclaims, "I will lay a sheep that my words are true," the judge may ask the second with how much honey, grain, or hides he will wager his accuracy. The loser forfeits not only his case, but the livestock or produce with which he has backed it, but the verdict of the unofficial judge is always accepted.

Of course important cases go before a court, where the old religious, civil and penal code, based on Mosaic law, is administered by justices, the chief of whom is the Afa Negus, "Mouth of Kings", with priests as assessors, since only these can understand the obsolete Geze into which the 4th century Fetha Negast [codification of laws] was translated at a later date. The sovereign alone can impose penalty of death, so murderers are sent to Addis to be tried, and the law decrees that these must be killed by the nearest relative of the murderer in the exact manner in which the victims were slain. In olden days this must have given rise to considerable cruelty, when the murderer was handed over to the vengeance of a distraught wife or father, but now, if the blood payment is not accepted, and if the crime is not one to necessitate a public hanging, the condemned is taken to the hollow beyond the railway station. His own people go with him to claim his body, the family he has wronged follow and, up to the last moment, there is wild argument between them, the one offering, the other refusing, bribes which increase in size as the parties approach the graves of the criminals' valley. Among these, the guardians of the law hand over the prisoner, or in some cases prisoners to the avenging families, and withdraw a few paces to watch that no torture is committed. The whole thing is done quickly and decently. The assasin is held down by stalwart relatives of the deceased, while the widow or head of the family deals the first blow with a knife, or shoots, according to how the original crime was committed. If necessary, as may be the case if a woman is avenging the stabbing of her husband, the murderer is despatched by other relations. The police then approach and demand if the punishment has been carried out. The avenger of son or brother announces, "Menelik, *yemut,*" "By the death of Menelik, it is," after which oath, the most formidable in the Abyssinian vocabulary, the body is claimed ty waiting parents, who have stood by to see fair play and if, by chance, breath still remains in it, as sometimes occurs if the unofficial executioner is old or excited, it is carried to the nearest hospital. Should the man recover he is considered to have paid the penalty, for with the dread "By the death of Menelik," the family of the murdered have acknowledged quittance of the blood debt.

While we were in Addis, one such execution took place beyond the gum-trees in the sunlit hollow. In this case, as the man was a notorious malefactor, a crowd of two or three hundred gathered at a distance. The condemned, with his arms pinioned behind him, had to be dragged down the slope by two guardians, during which process he shouted of the number of men, elephants and lions he had killed. A man with a sword stood by, while two relatives of his latest victim shot him through the head at a few inches range. The first rifle misfired, but death must have been instantaneous.

Immediately the executioners retired in favor of the dead man's friends, who carried him, under a sheet held like an awning, to where the grave-diggers were already working. The affair, primitive, humble and impressive, took three minutes from the first appearance of the condemned to the removal of his body. No excitement or curiosity was displayed by the audience, for these men are accustomed to do all the business of their lives in public and in the open air. Not only this, but they like to settle such business themselves.

There are no lawyers in Addis Ababa, except in the Consular courts, which deal with disputes between their own nationals. In cases where a European and an Abyssinian are concerned, the former's consul is admitted as an assessor and, when his conclusion does not correspond with that of the Abyssinian President, the case is referred to Ras Tafari [Regent, later Emperor Haile Selassie], soldier, statesman, social reformer, to whom the phrase might be permitted, *"l'état c'est moi."*

I was anxious to meet the heir-apparent to such great difficulties, perhaps to greater opportunities, for I felt that he, representing the best and broadest of Abyssinia, might prove the key to her puzzle. I went to tea one afternoon in a big house on a hill, with a long European dining-room—white walls, chintzes and thick carpets—a charming room which looked on to a garden, beyond which were a lion-crowned gate and a section of khaki bodyguard. The Ras and his wife, the Princess Menen; were sitting side by side on a sofa, he in a big royal-blue cloak, she in a black one bordered with red, over a *chamma* fine as spiders' webs. They rose to welcome me and I found myself before a man of middle height, slight and strong, with slender, finely modelled hands that grasped mine firmly. Hands are very indicative of character and the Regent's are both practical and artistic. He did not misuse them in excessive gestures, but gave an impression of stillness and assurance. It was delightful to talk both to Prince and Princess, for there was evidently much sympathy between them. They shared their interests and, best of all, their laughter. Ras Tafari talks French and Arabic and made use of both in his shrewd questions concerning my travels, but the Princess speaks through an interpreter. I remember we discussed Siam, which I had seen, and which interested them as a native, independent kingdom, cobwebbed in old customs, but attracted towards modern progress.

"I hope it won't develop too fast," I said, "the old traditions are so interesting."

The Ras smiled and his face lit up, till he no longer resembled the kings of Judah, three thousand years dead, who were his ancestors. The smile was keen and kind, and there was very nearly a twinkle in it, as he contested the charm of the new against the old, of the useful and productive against the wasteful and picturesque.

Servants brought in the most delicious tea I have drunk outside Hongkong, where tea-making is a rite, concerned with a score of canisters and half a dozen pots. While we ate particularly engaging cakes, rather shamefacedly, for our hosts fasted, I thought how curious it was to discuss motor routes and irrigation with a man whose features might have been stamped on Solomon's coins. Most of all, it was amusing to find that the Princess and I agreed on such divergent subjects as marriage and Palestinian personalities!

I rode back after sunset when the trees were a scented mystery and, between them, a thousand fires twinkled out of the huts. The smoke was like mist, eddying blue among the eucalyptus. Against the last stains of orange the spears were transferred into feathers, their tips entangled in the jeweled net of the sky. The mule picked its way sedately. Its hoofs clopped to the accompaniment of a thread of sound, throbbing and insistent. It was a lyre played far up the hill, where flames shifted between smoke and shadow. I was impatient lest the footsteps shuffling after me should break the illusion. Scent and the silence of the forest were like an iridescent glass, blown so fine that a note of music might shatter it. . . .

A voice spoke from the darkness of the hotel entrance, "Gabra Gorgis is in prison," it said.

"In prison," I gasped, wondering what frightful crime our cook had committed.

"Yes, the Abyssinians are not allowed to walk down the hill after dark without a permit, so surely now, since he is a stranger here, he is in prison!"

I laughed with relief. . . . After all the charm of an illusion is that it cannot endure.

The morning, fortunately, brought the release of our henchman, for which he was devoutly thankful, as prisoners are not fed by the State, but depend on their friends for supplies.

"Derselaam!" exclaimed the cook, "and I know no soul in the town except the son of my aunt, and he is dead!"

For a few hours he shadowed our footsteps, and even accompanied us when we went fishing with the six-inch lens, which enabled us to catch the sellers of honey and wax unaware, or the merchants haggling in a Bond Street of piled *chammas,* or the slave girls gossiping while their earthenware pots overflowed at the well. Traffic moves slowly in Addis, because friends stay to talk in the middle of the street, but these stalwart water-carriers, thick-ankled, shorn or curly-headed, always seemed to have more to say than anyone else. Gossip I suppose is the privilege of the confidential slave!

While we were watching the struggle at a well, where the water is free to all who are either sufficiently patient or sufficiently ruthless to get near it, Ras Tafari rode by. Half a hundred officers and chiefs rode with him. White-clad riflemen ran beside and behind. There must have been nearly a thousand of them, but they were lost among the crowd which surged around and among them. The Regent was stopped a dozen times by citizens, determined to lay some plea before him, and he responded with grave good humor, aware perhaps of the possessive feeling with which he is regarded. One man had walked all the way from Harrar to make his appeal, for, in the Ras' own province, the sentiment is not so much that they are his people, but that he is their own, belongs to them, is the last and surest court of appeal, prince and brother, and man!

Gabra Gorgis, the black soldier . . . considered the Ras as a sort of feudal divinity, more easily approachable and much more logical than any celestial being. "If only I could speak to him, he would give me back my work," he said, and once again we heard the story of a post lost for most complicated and divergent reasons.

That night we dined with the Ras and Princess Menen. The electric light, gold plate, gold lettered, menus wreathed in roses, printed by the Regent's private press, most of all the delicious food which made me suspect that a chef had been lured from Paris, showed our host's appreciation of Europe, but the crowd of servants in immaculate white and the gorgeous cloaks of the Abyssinian guests, Dejezmatch Haile Salessi, [sic] uncle of the Regent, and Feterari Desta Damtu, the good-looking husband of his thirteen-year-old daugher, introduced a touch of Africa.

While we drank champagne or *tedj* [Ethiopian wine] and ate the most marvellous creamy concoctions out of Venetian glass, we talked of Abyssinia.

"She seems to me so self-sufficient," I said. "You need Europe less than any other country I know."

"We need European progress only because we are surrounded by it," said the Ras. "That is at once a benefit and a misfortune. It will expedite our development, but we are afraid of being swamped by it."

"There is no fear of that, for it is only the townsman who is adaptable. Show him that a thing is good and he will at once adapt it, but no flood of modernity could sweep the peasant off his feet!"

"Yes," agreed the Regent, "there is a great difference between the two. The citizen is not afraid of the new. He is the least fanatical of people, always ready to welcome Europeans and to profit by their knowledge."

"In one way peasant and townsmen are alike. They both have the qualities of a ruling race," I add.

The Ras asked for explanation.

"The Arabs are the people I know best," I replied, "so I judge Eastern peoples by comparison with them. Arab and Abyssinian are equally hospitable, but the former is afraid of foreigners and very suspicious of them, because he is not sure of himself. Whereas your people, at least in the south, are broad-minded in their attitude towards strangers."

"In fact their assurance approaches arrogance," suggested the Ras. "It is a pity that they have had to learn that there are adventurers among the 'red men' as they call you. Originally we took our knowledge of Europe from the chivalrous Portuguese, who helped us in our long wars against Islam, and from the Jesuits who accompanied them—the most intellectual of the priesthood—but, since those days, all sorts of foreigners have come here, and the Abyssinian has had to learn to distinguish between them."

I quoted the Arab saying, "a man must learn from his pocket."

The Ras smiled. "All knowledge is good," he said, and told me of the means he was taking to encourage it. He has built a hospital near his house to supplement the excellent American organization under Dr. Lamb, for which the Crown gave a grant of land. His printing-press is designed for the publication of educational works, but, in order to propitiate the clergy, who are opposed to any innovation, at present, it is dealing only with religious books.

"The church stands for freedom, the clergy for slavery!" interpolated an Abyssinian.

A college for one hundred students is in course of construction, electric light is being planned for the town. A flour-mill and wood-working machinery have been imported, as well as pumps and pipes to supply the town with water, and a large cotton plant, consisting of forty-two machines, destined to deal with all stages of cotton manufacture. I believe the idea for the last originated with the Empress, who was much concerned for the people, when, three years ago, the price of *abu gedid,* the coarse white sheeting chiefly of Japanese or American manufacture from which all trousers and shirts are made, rose to 13 reals a length. She ordered wholesale planting of cotton and began to plan the construction of a factory for ginning, spinning and weaving the home-grown material.

"Will it pay?" I asked the Ras.

"Nothing new ever pays," he answered. "This is an educational experiment. I want to teach the people the value of industry. At present the majority bury, or otherwise hide their money. They've no other idea of investment than to loan it to anyone who will promise them high interest."

"It will be splendid if you can interest them in trade."

"A beginning has been made. The market used to be open only one day a week and the town was deserted for the other six. Now you see the streets full of merchants, always ready to do business. I am encouraging every new form of commerce, after the example of the Emperor Menelik, who used to remit customs on any original goods imported into the country. He gave loans to merchants who wanted to start on progressive lines and told them, 'bring all new goods to me. I will see they are sold. Don't be frightened of innovations.'"

"He must have been a remarkable man," I said.

"He was, and he had complete power over his people. He could do what he liked with them."

Menelik, of course, had the prestige of a conqueror and this counts for much in Abyssinia, where every man is a soldier, but, though his victories and the glamour of his personality united the country, he could not make a nation out of it. He left to his successor a heritage of problems, first among them the responsibility of ruling such races as Galla, Dankali, Somali and Shanakil, unlike in religion, language, and mentality. He left a country loosely knitted together and so recently that the stitches are still visible. Whether they will prove durable is as yet uncertain. Tigre, Shoa, Amhara have so long been different kingdoms, temporarily united from time to time by emperor or king, that it is doubtful if anything but a common enemy, or the dread of European absorption, could weld them into one nation. Racially the Shoan stands apart, for he had intermarried with the wild races on his borders and there is a strong negroid tincture in his blood. Though Amharic is the *langage diplomatique* of Abyssinia, each old kingdom has its own dialect, besides which there are Geze, the language of priests, also spoken in Tigre; Arabic and Galla, both known outside the bounds of their peoples; Tigri, which is more than a dialect, and such tongues as Gouragi, Harrari, Dankali, and others. Apart from the subject races, each Abyssinian state has its hereditary influences and interests, and the welter of past jealousies, racial or family, contribute to the political disorders of to-day. The feudal lords of the north resent the curtailment of their powers and the centralization of authority in Addis.

The Regent is therefore faced with the problems, not only of the present, but of the unyielding past. He has to deal with character, and human nature is immutable, except in a crucible of war or other emotion. The peasants, who are the backbone of Ethiopia, are biblical in their pastoral simplicity, contented with the sunshine and their marvelous climate, dull-witted, sometimes courteous and hospitable, sometimes uncouth and surly. Money is a passion with most of them, but, in the wilder districts, it is represented by cartridges or other local necessities. The townfolk are curious, interested in anything new for a time, but they are cautious and rarely frank. It is very difficult to induce an Abyssinian to express his real thoughts and intentions. Partly out of innate politeness, he invariably says "yes," and of course it is not always possible for him to carry out his promises. No Abyssinian understands the value of time—to-day, to-morrow or next year are the same to him.

Before I left Addis Ababa, I came to the conclusion that the reigning Empress, Zaiditu, daughter of Menelik, had inherited many of her father's qualities. Tactful and shrewd, she is at once the motive force behind many schemes for social improvement, and the mediator between the priests who represent the old world and the Regent urging the claims of the new. Her statecraft is so clever that, while she approves and aids Ras Tafari's policy of development, she is still the champion of tradition. Very wisely she deals with the older clergy, hedged in by custom, telling them: "Let us wait and see if this new thing does not turn out to be good." No one criticizes her. Lonely, aloof, a little pathetic in a state and dignity which she uses as a background, conscious of its value, but never, I think, overwhelmed by it, she is a force which counts in Ethiopia and which will be largely responsible for its independent progress. "Small I am like Queen Victoria," she is supposed to have said on her coronation, "great like her I hope to be."

While we were in Addis Ababa, the Empress and her court were in mourning for the seventh anniversary of the death of Tahitu, Menelik's consort, in memory of whom a great feast was to be held at which five or ten thousand people would be fed. Custom insists that the reigning sovereign shall take part in every form of national life, so the Empress was busy supervising the hospitable preparations, and would see no one, not even her ministers. "I am busy in the kitchen," she reproved those who sought audience, but the courtesy which is an Abyssinian characteristic caused her to send us a message that, if we cared to come to the palace at seven next morning, she would receive us before beginning the work of a long and varied day.

We got up with the sun and rode below a canopy of gums. The mists woven with the shuttles of dawn hung cold between lilac and cactus hedges. It was a blue world, where the huts were damp toadstools in a forest. Men rode muffled to the eyes in their cloaks. As we climbed up towards the Gibbe, to which all roads seem eventually to lead, we passed some one hundred slaves bearing red-swathed baskets on their heads—bread for the palace breakfast, or perhaps for the morrow's feast. The sentries at the gate were shrouded in hoods and cloaks. Through a succession of irregular, stone-walled yards, full of riflemen, splendidly trapped mules, servants and officials, we were led by an usher, whose long wand was often used to make way for us. The Gibbe covered a square mile or more of ground, and in the center of its maze of courts, among acres of thatch, mud, iron and stone, are the two pavilions, with outside staircases and tiered balconies in which the Empress lives.

Zaiditu, daughter of Menelik, the lion of Judah, Queen of the Kings of Ethiopia, received us on the second floor, in an octagonal pagoda-like room, spread with fine carpets and hung with portraits of Menelik and his consort. There was no furniture except the three seats placed for us and the lower chair on which the Empress was enthroned, her feet on a velvet cushion, behind her one lady in waiting, on either side, her chamberlains and priests.

Zaiditu, like so many of the queens of history, is very small, but her stature is magnified by an impressive dignity of manner. When we were presented to her, her mourning necessitated a plain, dark cloak, and only her eyes and cheeks appeared between the muffling folds of gauze. Even the hand we touched was covered in the same white, silky stuff, but the great black eyes, set powerfully under a broad forehead, were characteristic. They were intelligent and quiet, with the wisdom of a 3000-year-old descent and the peace of much thought. The audience was short, for the Empress insisted that she must set an example of industry to the domestic hive which stirred and ground, baked, roasted and brewed. After a few minutes talk about my travels and gracious wishes for the northern journey, which she and the Regent had done everything in their power to facilitate, she left us to photograph the town from her balcony.

At last we had found the one uninterrupted view in Addis Ababa, for, beyond the palace roofs, the trees dropped to a ravine and climbed again, rank after steel blue rank, to the houses and the markets and, crowning all, the octagonal cathedral, backed by the mountain mists. We saw the tiny figure of the Empress pass across the yard, a velvet umbrella, fringed green and black, held over her head, a group of courtiers around her. On one side the lions of her country roared from their cages. On the other a hornbill marched along the grass, ruffling its feathers in the sun. The painted woodwork was gilded. The soldiers bared their heads as they sat in rows along every wall. Priests began to chant near the massive throne-room, which opens onto a sheet of mountain and valley. A smell of incense drifted into the air, and other more savory odors came from the town of canvas which constituted the banquet hall. Small boys pushed past us, very important with their burdens swathed in velvet. A few rose petals fluttered at our feet and I remembered the rose used to be sacred in old Tigre where incense was made of the petals. It was all very simple and its simplicity saved it from being tawdry or barbaric.

The palace courts were fuller on the afternoon we went to visit the Itchegue, the Administrator of the Abyssinian Church, who controls all clerical property and staff.

The funeral feast was finished. Hundreds of priests, thousands of chiefs, officials and their followers had been fed on the raw meat which makes warriors, washed down with golden, insidious *tedj*. The men-at-arms were smiling, fatuous and loud-voiced, the slaves could not control their laughter. In each dark face the mouth gaped full and red, while the bloodshot eyes were bold. The lions, too, had been glutted with fresh meat and they took no interest in the throngs which passed their cages. Satisfied and full-lipped, the courtiers, in their white robes, were talking lazily, with vague smiles. The Empress had presided on a curtained dais, high above the carpeted canvas hall, where, across trestle tables lined with guests, slaves presented raw carcasses of oxen, slung from poles and covered with strips of silk and velvet, to the ready knives and teeth. Now she had retired to her own rooms, and court and street were crowded with her departing guests.

"His Holiness awaits you," smiled a bowing usher, as we watched peaked capes of riders go bobbing down the hill above the gleam of rifle barrel or silver prayer sticks.

In the thirteenth century, the sainted Tekla Haimanot ordained that the Ethiopian archbishop, the Abouna, should always be an Egyptian appointed by Alexandria, as a link between the Coptic Church of Egypt and the Abyssinian Monophysites who acknowledge the immaculate conception of the Virgin, concede but the one nature to Christ, ordain that priests must marry as deacons once for eternity, and were condemned as heretics by the sixth century Council of Chalcedon. Tekla Haimanot, fearing that the isolated position of his country might cut her off from civilization, proffered as a remedy the continual introduction of Alexandrine culture, so the Abouna is, as ever, an Egyptian from the desert monastery of St. Anthony, knowing little of local custom. Consequently the functions of the Itchegue, sometimes called the Black Pope, are comprehensive and important. His writ runs through every church in a land said to contain a million religious subjects, and it went with us, inscribed under a golden seal, to help us in our work.

The Itchegue received us in a panelled room faintly scented, as if with the breath of old ritual. A velvet cloak, gold-edged and embroidered, fell to his feet. His high white turban was covered with a flowered veil and he held an exquisite golden cross. Beside him was a table laden with leather-bound manuscripts, the characters painted or inscribed on vellum. Against the wall crouched several priests in saffron cloaks, relieved by the great square crosses of Abyssinia. The Itchegue approved of our project to cinema for the first time the rock-hewn, thirteenth century churches of Lalibela.

"If you go as far as that," he said, "you will see the best that is in our country," and we noticed how keenly he observed us under lids drooped in apparent indifference.

"I understand the power of the Church if she has many men like that," I said to Jones as we rode through the thronged enclosures, where rifles and peaked cloaks of warriors' turbans and satin capes of priests, cream, embroidered *chammas,* velvet saddle-cloths fringed with gold, or white ones splashed with great crimson crosses, were blended into a sun-gilt tapestry.

The Ras had sent us two horses as a parting gift, a beautiful gray racer, which was a delight to ride, and a sturdy chestnut, and while I was still breathless with appreciation of so royal a gift, the *ballambarassi* arrived with several mysterious parcels.

"They are from Waizeru Menen," he said. "Just in memory of your visit."

I opened the most intriguing bundle and found an exquisite Abyssinian dress of softly flowered brocade, embroidered at the edge, like all court robes, with purple, blue, and gold. There was also a *chamma,* spun out of moonbeams by fairy spiders, and barred with peacock blue and green, woven or embroidered, I couldn't tell, but incredibly fine. Another parcel contained a black satin cloak, short, with a peaked hood, and a pair of trousers, also of black satin, very narrow at the ankle, where they were thickly embroidered. I could hardly wait to express my thanks before turning the *ballambarrasi* out of the room in order to try on my new treasures, but he stopped me, laughing, as I almost pushed him to the door.

"There is more," he said. "Wait!" and, from a little basket, he produced a necklace entirely made of old carved gold crosses. It was a delightful example of the native jeweler's art and the finishing touch to the dress.

"It's too lovely!" I said, "I adore it, but you simply must go, so that I can begin to dress up."

The gentle face with the big brown eyes flashed into merriment.

"So you are a woman after all," said the *ballambarassi*, "I thought you were much too fierce to care about silks!" and he shut the door before I could ask for explanation.

Our last two days in Addis Ababa must surely have consisted of more than the usual amount of hours, for we rode an incredible number of miles on mules loaned by the Regent, who generously considers himself the host of any strangers visiting his country, and we hunted pictures with grim determination. The Saturday market provided a varied bag, for there must be ten to fifteen thousand people buying and selling in every street square, and in the great field beyond the usual markets. It would be impossible to describe the variety of goods sold, for they range from livestock, goats, sheep, oxen, horses, mules, donkeys, the grain and hay they eat, the red-covered saddles and bridles they wear, to grass parasols, monster clay pots and baskets nearly as large as a house, or cloaks, capes and *chammas,* civet wax, skins, shields, swords, herbs, spices, kohl, incense, jewelry, charms, and all forms of produce. There are European goods, too, in rows and rows of little booths, and, beyond them, sheepskins, gourds, raw cotton, the cut shrub that is put into *tedj,* honey in leather bags, new made rope, fish that looks rather exhausted, sugar cane, and always lines of wizened old women selling mysterious ground-up trifles heaped on grass platters, condiments perhaps, or those nameless flavorings for which Gabra Gorgis, the cook, was always demanding piastres. When the markets failed us, we scoured the hillsides for industries, photographed the pottery workers and the brewers of *tedj,* who light a fire of green leaves in the mouths of their jars before pouring honey and water into the smoky depths, the silversmiths and scabbard makers, and even the hard-worked mothers of families, who smilingly consented to bake wafer-thin bread in ovens that looked like two clay plates, or grind grain into flour between a couple of stones, under the eye of Jones' camera.

"Well, are you satisfied?" I asked Jones as our second relay of mules crawled homeward in the sunset. Our first appointment had taken the place of breakfast, and lunch, if we had eaten it, had made no impression on me. My lips were stiff with dust, everything else caked with it. A donkey had kicked me in the market and I was sore. . . .

## Concerning Women*

Among the primitive people who originally inhabited the highlands of Ethiopia, paternity was of no value. Marriage was but a pact ensuring community of labor and of interests. The children born of such a union belonged to the mother and were known each by his or her personal name with no reference to their parents. The woman, providing she did her share of the work, was free to establish any relations she chose, and her children legitimate or otherwise, inherited only from her. The family did not exist, except as a matriarchate, so that the possessions of a brother would descend on his death to his sister's children because they were of the same maternal blood, not to the offspring of his wife who, in turn, would inherit from her people. These aborigines were associated in groups according to their work, free men and women without any difference of class, for they were all equally poor. They lived by hunting and agriculture with no idea of commerce until the Semites came from Arabia and intermarried with the negroid women. The problem of paternity became soluble by the paler skin, the result of such unions and the matriarchate gave way before the conqueror's conception of family. The liberty of the woman, hitherto unbounded, began to suffer restrictions, but, with memories of her old freedom, she refused to accept more than temporary union with the strangers. Thus began the legalized respected concubinage which exists to this day and which, originally, was an improvement on the unrestrained polygamy existing among a people who lived and gave birth as carelessly as animals. With the dawn of Christianity in the fourth century the strength of family was reinforced, but the patriarchate, in which the father was sole lord of his women, his children, his lands and his beasts, gave way to a feudal system based on force. After fifteen centuries the struggle between these two fundamentally divergent principles endures, but it is possible that the pressure of European influence with its doctrine of individual responsibility and equality, may prove equally disastrous to both.

Throughout the changing fortunes of Ethiopia the peasant woman remained in the anomalous position of a beast of burden with a complete system of civic and material rights. Moslem girls work until they are of marriageable age and after they are old, but during the years when they can bear sons to their race, they rarely leave the house. But to the Abyssinian woman falls the hardest of the communal tasks throughout a life which prematurely ages and destroys her. She is the hewer of wood and drawer of water, and as the villages are always distant from either, she

---

*Jean Rosita Forbes' ethnographic statements on women are not always accurate. [Editor]

toils for miles with incredibly heavy weights on her back. In Abyssinia each form of labor is exclusively masculine or feminine. For instance, no male being, even on the verge of starvation, could be induced to grind grain into flour between the mighty stones employed by his mother or wife. The woman prepares all forms of food and drinks, but she would not dream of killing the smallest bird or beast for the kitchen. In the fields she may help in the reaping, but she may not sow the grain or drive a plough or the earth would become sterile! In her own sphere she has need to be an artist, since each detail of household life is complicated by custom. A chicken, before being offered at a feast must be divided into twelve parts, each suited to a guest of different rank. For an unimportant person to take a wing would be unpardonable and to help himself to the skin an offence to the mistress of the house whose portion it is. In the same way each section of ox or sheep is destined to special use. The shoulders may only be used for soup, the head, feet, and intestines are the perquisites of the slaves, the ribs are offered to chiefs or the slayers of lions!

It is the woman who weaves the many colored baskets of straw, who brews *tedj* and beer, moulds the great terra cotta jars which contain them, and spins thread from the cotton fluff, but she cannot weave, which industry is confined to the male members of certain families and districts. Embroidery and sewing is also the work of men.

In life as well as in work, the sexes are separated by tradition. At banquets and other ceremonies, the master of the house entertains the male guests in one hut or tented yard, while his wife presides over a separate feast for the women. In churches a sheet is often suspended between the different portions reserved exclusively for men and women. In public the two sexes appear as nearly unconscious of each other as possible, unless they are relations meeting or parting. No affection is shown in public between husband and wife. It would be scandalous for one to kiss the other or even lay an affectionate hand on shoulder or arm, yet kisses are the most common form of greeting in Abyssinia. Between relations of either sex, the kiss is full on the mouth and repeated quickly many times. Between intimate friends the manner of the embrace is the same, but it is numerically reduced or increased according to the intimacy which exists. Acquaintances kiss each other on the right cheek, clergy are saluted on the right shoulder, a chief on the foot or knee, while a dependent greeting a great lady kisses his own hand between each sentence.

Yet, if a husband returns from hunting or from war, his wife must not go to the door to meet him. She must wait inside the house and make pretense of being absorbed in her usual occupations. If she is of inferior rank, she may, when they are alone, bow to kiss his knee, but, if his equal, she must welcome him without even holding out a hand, to all appearance still immersed in her work.

To woman is largely entrusted the hospitality which is one of the fundamentals of Abyssinian life. Its conception dates from those prehistoric days when all means of existence were the common property of the groups which shared their labor and its fruition. It may be abused by needy minor officials, eclipsed where foreigners are concerned by a passion for gain, but I think it is never refused to the poor man, be he friend or stranger, who asks it in the name of Mary. The headman of each village is responsible for the payment of "dergo," the government hospitality accorded to important travelers, whether native or foreign. The amount is theoretically fixed by the rank of the recipient, but I imagine it also varies according to the generosity of the district and the industry of its women, who have to bake the *anjera*, brew the *talla* or *tedj*, mix the potent sauces and condiments, cut the firewood, draw the water (most necessary of all gifts) forage for eggs and, in the case of a prominent personage, cook a dinner of a dozen gargantuan courses, while the men content themselves with driving in a few beasts and supplying grain and grass.

This is the public hospitality levied as a tax by the central Government and by each provincial Ras or Dejezmatch. Private hospitality is often entrusted by a village to certain administrants chosen from among the most respected inhabitants. These hold their honored office for a term varying from months to years. They regulate the provision of food and fodder according to the means of each household, and distribute it, not only to strangers and travelers, but to any of the community who are in need. When a chief visits the districts this master of the ceremonies is obliged to make a special call on the local resources to feed servants and soldiers, but ordinarily his chief duty is to supply sustenance in cases of illness, child-birth, mourning, or any other eventuality which may deprive a family of its manual labor. In every occurrence of family life, the hospitality and coöperation of the village are assured. For instance, when a child is born, not only is all food provided by neighbors during the period of the mother's illness, but the household tasks are divided among them and they perform gratuitously the duties of midwife and nurse.

In the case of a marriage this reassured coöperation is even more apparent. Every one who is invited to a wedding is obliged to send a gift of money or livestock to the father of the bride. Its value must not be less than a dollar [Maria Theresa thalers were then in circulation as currency], but very often it is twenty or thirty times as much. As all such offerings either constitute or augment the *dot*, "it simplifies the problems of the father who would secure husbands for several daughters. It also encourages him to keep on the friendliest relations with his neighbors. The same gifts are made in the case of funerals in order that the bereaved family may be able to feed the numerous mourners, but they are really a form of loan to be repaid in kind when there is a marriage or a death in the household of the donor.

Apparently any number of calls may be made on the gratitude of a recipient, for, if he has received an ox as a wedding gift to his only child from a friend who is blessed with four daughters, he must return an ox of the same weight at the marriage of each of these. If on the day of feast an invited guest does not bring or send an offering suited to his position, he can be called before the local headman and fined up to twelve dollars.

As soon as a married couple arrive at a suitable age they are entitled to a portion of the family land, sufficiently large for its products to support them. This is chosen by arbiters appointed by the district, within whose bounds the husband has a right to cut sufficient wood for the construction of his house. Friends and relations carry this material to the appointed site. The bride, helped by the matrons of the village, prepares food and drink and, with no further recompense for their labors, the whole neighborhood combines to build in one day, the dwelling which will also be stable and barn for the new family.

Thus from birth to death, the life of an Abyssinian villager, his tenure of the land and the assistance which he, in turn, must contribute to the general welfare, is as communal as the *tukel* he shares with livestock and fowls. Such patriarchal simplicity should develop an exemplary family life, but marriage forms, divorce, concubinage and slavery militate against it.

Marriage in Abyssinia may be the simplest and least binding of pacts or the most complicated or legal and religious contract. Legitimate unions between freeborn and slave are regarded as disgraceful, especially in the case of a lady who espouses a serf. In such a case the woman would be reduced to the grade of her husband. Sometimes liberated slaves marry free men or women, but always subject to general disapproval. There are certain trades which do not marry outside their own ranks, possibly because they are suspected of necromancy or other evil powers. Of such are the jewelers and smiths, the players of violin, flute and lute. Should one of these artificers or musicians wed farmer or merchant, her children would be dishonored as having inherited the taint in the mother's blood.

An engagement in Abyssinia has as much solemnity as a marriage and, when the suitor has been accepted by the bride's father, he must produce at least one guarantor who is financially responsible for the completion of what is generally a diplomatic or commercial transaction. There are four kinds of marriages. The religious form, which is rarely adopted except by the clergy and by a few of the great families, is supposed to be indissoluble except for certain causes enumerated in the Fetha Negast, such as:

1. If husband and wife agree to become monk and nun.
2. If one or other cannot have children.
3. If either is unfaithful, but such deliquency on the part of the husband has to be sufficiently public to cause scandal.
4. If either attempts the life of the other.
5. For epilepsy contracted before marriage and previously ignored by the other party.
6. If either becomes a leper or suffers from elephantiasis.
7. If either publicly and falsely accuses the other of infidelity.
8. If either is condemned to a long term of imprisonment.

In practice, with the consent of the *abouna* and the circulation of numerous Maria Theresa dollars, divorce after a religious marriage is possible, except for priests. In their case a difficulty sometimes arises if they have contracted marriages with minors, arranged by parents or guardians. Religious law demands the consent of both parties, so if the wife has been married as a child, she can, on attaining her majority obtain a divorce, should she desire it, on the ground that she was not responsible for the actions of her guardians. The husband has no alternative but to remain celebate or leave the priesthood.

The Fetha Negast is stringent in the limitations it imposes on marriage. A woman divorced for infidelity can only remarry after performing a penance. Marriage is forbidden to dames of over sixty and a widow cannot take another husband until she has mourned the first ten months. A father can force a dissolute son or daughter into matrimony and the virtuous maiden of twenty-five can insist on a husband and *dot* being provided for her. A second marriage is not approved and a third is considered so disgraceful that the offender is only admitted to communion three times a year. Man and maid may be wedded by letter or proxy, but a second marriage must be accompanied by a prayer for pardon and a fourth is never recognized and its children are considered illegitimate.

The Fetha Negast, most intricate of legal, social, medical and religious codes, forbids marriage to lepers, eunuchs, madmen, and sufferers from elephantiasis. Blood relations to the seventh generation may not marry nor may guardian and ward, foster brother and sister, or such spiritual relatives as godfather and godchild or godfather and sister or mother or godchild. The descendants of spiritual connections are forbidden to unite until after the twelfth generation. It also ordains that neither a child's parents nor its godparents may cohabit on the day of its baptism.

If the religious marriage is as rare as it is unpopular in Abyssinia, perhaps because the women remember their primeval freedom and will not ally themselves for a lifetime to any one man, at least the priests are invited to bless the civil marriage *(bercha)* which is the most popular form among families of any position. Sometimes an engagement is ratified before a priest, in which case the couple exchange rings, with hands joined on the cross. The day on which an engagement is announced must be chosen with the utmost care and, generally, an ancient Abyssinian cabal is consulted. In this the qualities and possibilities of each day of the year are noted, as:

Jan.  2nd.  Don't leave your house. Misfortune may happen.
Jan.  5th.  Keep well your soul and body. This day is dangerous.
Jan.  6th.  Go where you will without fear.
Jan.  11th.  Don't go on a journey. Your enemies will conquer you.
Jan.  13th.  Festival of the angels. Pray and they will assist you.
Jan.  16th.  The best of days. Who is ill will be cured. etc.
Jan.  17th.  Don't walk near water, etc.
Jan.  21st.  Do anything you like.
Jan.  26th.  Eat and drink with your friends. It is a day of friendship.

Few possess complete knowledge of this creed and the priests frown upon it, but any one who can repeat the whole cabal, cleric or layman alike, is ensured of a competence and eager to increase it!

The engagement is considered binding when it has been explicitly announced by the father or guardian of the bride in presence of the bridegroom's parents and guarantors, and confirmed by an oath in the name of the Negus. On this occasion the bridegroom hands over a sum of money and certain presents for his fiancée such as clothes and ornaments, oil, scent, and incense. From this moment the guarantor becomes the *deux ex machina* of the family to be. He has made himself responsible that the rights of the bride shall be respected, that she shall be suitably fed and housed and not ill-treated. Therefore all conjugal disputes are referred to him and he acts as guide, philosopher, and friend, as well as a sort of insurance for the bridegroom's solvency. If the marriage pact is infringed, the wife's father can force the guarantor to pay three dollars every three days until his son-in-law arranges matters to his satisfaction. The husband must eventually refund to his guarantor double the sum disbursed on account of his misdemeanors.

A banquet signals the ratification of the fiançailles, and on this and similar subsequent occasions the bride's father can claim a number of beasts and sacks of grain from the bridegroom's family, but in return he must make a present of money which is subtracted from the amount of the promised *dot*. Sometimes a dance follows the banquet, but the men and women sit on different sides of the yard and, while dancing, they do not touch each other. At first the man rotates round his partner while she pivots like a top. Then they posture opposite each other with undulations which would be serpentine but for the thickness and multiplicity of their garments. The monotony at last gives way to a restrained violence reminiscent of a war dance.

The civil marriage is announced at a banquet, where men and women eat in different courts. There are more dances and much firing of rifles, while some responsible person makes a list of all the gifts brought by the guests. After this the bride, so muffled in cloak, *chamma* and muslin veil that nothing of her can be seen, is led into the men's yard and seated on a bench, while her father enumerates the amount of her *dot* in money or beasts and the entire list of household goods he is giving her. He then asks if her father-in-law agrees to accept such a *dot* and upon receiving an affirmative answer, he can, if he wishes, ask for a new guarantor. Unless otherwise previously agreed and indicated before witnesses at this moment of the marriage feast, all the possessions of the young couple are considered to be the common property of both. In case of divorce they are equally divided by three arbiters in the presence of the guarantors and the members of both families. So rigidly is the equality insisted on that carpet stuffs, and even clothing are apt to be cut in two and, if there is but one kettle, it is quite possible that the husband may find himself with the pot and the wife with the lid!

Sometimes after the marriage the husband has to take his wife on a formal visit to her parents that they may see she has not been ill-treated.

A third form of marriage, neither religious nor civil, but conditional, is in use among families who wish to be certain of an heir, without incurring the expenses of repeated weddings. This experimental marriage does not generally last more than two years without being regularized by the civil ceremony *(berche)*, but such ratification takes place with as little display as possible.

The fourth form *(dumoz)* is really a legalized concubinage. It is arranged for an indeterminate period and for fixed terms, and the pact is as solemnly ratified as it is in the case of *bercha*. The "husband" agrees before witnesses to live in faithfulness and unity with the woman of his choice, to give her food and clothing and to pay her a certain sum annually or monthly. A guarantor makes himself responsible for the fulfillment of such agreement and often a priest blesses the temporary pact, which can be terminated at will without publicity. Sometimes *dumoz* is changed into *bercha* when the lovers are old and united by human or financial interests in the shape of children or the accumulation of the sum due to the temporary wife!

There is still another category of respectable Abyssinian women, the *sabaiti nassen,* concubines of chiefs and important personages, well housed and paid and enjoying as much consideration as the legitimate wives, or the helpmeets of the very poor who have nothing to contribute to a common purse, so live esteemed and honored with their lovers, till a turn of fortune pushes them either into civil marriage or the arms of another. The prostitutes are of a class apart, but they enjoy more consideration in Abyssinia, which throughout the ages has been accustomed to the moral or immoral freedom of her women, than in another land. Often, after they have earned a *dot,* they marry, live honestly, and leave no stain on the escutcheon of their children. Only in the religious and civil marriages is community of property acknowledged.

The causes for a religious divorce have already been quoted. In the case of *bercha,* the reasons may be much more frivolous, a caprice on the part of the woman, the omission of some household duties, her neglect of parents-in-law, the husband's refusal to give his wife a present, or the birth of a still-born child which brings bad luck to the whole clan. Family policy may change and an alliance in another direction be advisable. A blood feud may arise and, since marriage is not so much the affair of bride and groom, as a pact made between their parents, it is these who arrange the divorce. If husband and wife separate, each, at the time of the divorce, has the right to forbid the remarriage of the other with one given person who must be named before witnesses. If the man wants the divorce, he merely sends his wife back to her father's house and asks the latter to fix a day for the division of goods. If it is the woman or her family, she returns on some pretext to her father, who obliges the husband's guarantor to pay a daily forfeit until his son-in-law fixes the day for the breaking up of the household, which must be done in the presence of at least three arbiters. Very often, while this is pending, the wife returns to cook for her husband and generally look after his comfort! If a woman divorced for no grave fault, or a widow, does not wish to remarry, she has the right of maintenance from her ex-husband or his family, as represented by a certain amount of land which she can cultivate.

The Fetha Negast ordains that a man must have attained the age of twenty, a girl of twelve before they can marry, but this only applies to the religious ceremony, which is so little used that even the Empress, four times wedded, with at least two ex-husbands living, had recourse to the church only on the last occasion, when she espoused Ras Gooksa. There is no age limit for the civil marriage, but children are seldom wedded until they are seven. Such an affair is merely a friendly agreement among the parents, between whose huts the wife divides her time, so that she may learn to know her groom without forgetting her own family. At twelve she goes to live with her husband who, if he is a minor, still shares the parental roof. His father administers the *dot* until the young couple have a house of their own.

As long as the two children thus married are of the same age, the custom has its advantages for, brought up side by side, they have every chance of caring for each other and no reason for contracting the precocious irregular unions facilitated by a life careless, unguarded, and day-long in fields and woods. Often, however, middle-aged men take a child to wife, or boys marry women twice or three times their age. There are girls of twelve to fifteen who, because of their parents' quarrels and ambitions, have been legitimately married several times. They may even have given their children, generally diseased or still-born, to a succession of such bridegrooms. Their constitutions are never robust, for the altitude and insufficient nutriment tend to weaken the mountain stock. They are broken by this premature childbirth, yet, to support the babies who live, they must exhaust what strength remains to them by labor on farm or in forest. The birth-rate is not high in Abyssinia, probably because of the physical toil to which the women are devoted. A family of more than three or four is rare, infant mortality is very high, and terrible inherited diseases are common.

Circumcision is performed on the boys and clitoridectomy on the girls, possibly to curb an excessive sexual sensibility unsuited to the hard life of the peasants. At one time the Coptic church forbade the latter operation, but, owing to a certain malformation of Abyssinian women, which caused the men to look beyond their borders for wives, the ban was removed. In some places the former ceremony, though carried out in a primitive and rather barbarous way by the members of a local family who are supposed to be hereditary specialists, is the occasion for a feast to which friends and priests are invited. After this the child is left to nature, unless its screams suggest the necessity of an emetic mixed with red pepper! Its first teeth are sometimes pulled out to strengthen the second crop, and its education begins at the cabalistic age of four years and four days. It does not amount to much, for the average Abyssinian knows only the family genealogy and portions of the sacred books. He uses a paid scribe for the writing he despises and employs a seal with his name cut on it, or a thumb mark, by way of signature. A youth's arrival at the age of puberty and his consequent acquisition of civil rights is announced by a feast at which he is supported by four companions a little older than himself, who protect him from the evil eye and generally minister to his needs. After this he wears his *chamma* as a man, not cloakwise opening at the side, and, if the family wealth is sufficient, he buys a peaked cape of stuff or silk according to his station.

In old Abyssinia the sumptuary laws were very strict and none but the great might carry an umbrella. Now the little grass parasols, pagoda shaped, or flat like the Japanese, can be bought for half a dollar in the market towns, so they are flaunted alike by peasant and citizen, but the European form is still more or less reserved for noble or priest, especialy in the north. Red is the color of the Negus and once the red striped *chamma* was forbidden to the plebeian. Like the umbrella, this has been ceded, but only princesses may wear trousers of scarlet and only the Emperor or the archpriests carry a gold fringed parasol of the royal hue.

Great ladies are distinguished by the embroidery at neck and wrists of their "shirts," longer than those of the men and tighter sleeved, by their gold ornaments, by their black silk capes edged and fringed with gold, and by the thickly embroidered trousers which, when traveling, just peep out from under the all-enveloping black woolen capes, surmounted by various white mufflings and a felt hat. Silk and embroidery are forbidden to the plebeian, however rich he may be, as are certain forms of harness, saddle cloths and equipment, so there is a general desire to be able to boast connection, however distant, with a great family.

Genealogies are considered of the greatest importance, not only as a matter of personal pride, but as proof of land tenure, of relationship, of blood feuds, of the possibility of hereditary illness. They are essential in the case of an an engagement, because of the ban on marriages between the most distant relations, whether by blood or some spiritual connection. The law, of course, pays no heed to these religious rules, but they are rarely broken, for the culprits would immediately be excommunicated. The material consequences of such condemnation would be as serious as the disgrace, for the couple would be excluded from the village commonwealth and none of the faithful would maintain any relations with them, either personal or commercial.

To be deserted by its own special father-confessor, who must always be shared by husband and wife, would be a disaster for any household, for he is inextricably involved in its hopes, fears, and superstitions, its quarrels and reconciliations, its prosperity and adversity.

If husband and wife discover some distant and hitherto unknown relationship between them, even after years of marriage, their union is dissolved, but it does not affect the children, who, legitimate or illegitimate, have the same rights. Born of slave or princess, they are equally entitled to inherit, except in Tigre where the priests have most power and consequently a certain precedence is given to the children of religious wedlock.

Domestic slavery in Abyssinia is of course different to the general conception of the word. In earlier days, Ethiopian law recognized the buying of slaves from pagan neighbors or their capture in war, but any

Abyssinian who thus acquired a servant was obliged to have him or her religiously educated and within forty days baptized. Once a Christian, the slave could not legally be sold. Theoretically he or she became one of the family, too valuable a possession to ill-treat, but, in fact, the old law winked at slave traffic and slave markets. Menelik started its reform and to-day the difficulty of obtaining new slaves, even by the most secret and expensive ways, is so great that the Northern chiefs have started breeding them in their own houses from slave parents!

Every slave has the right of appeal in court and proof of ill-usage gives instant freedom. It has long been customary for a man to give dowries to his bondwomen or to slave girls he had freed, but the former can only be married with the consent of their lord and generally only to henchmen of the same household, since the children of such a union are the property of the master and part of the inheritance left to his heirs. It has been a common occurrence for a landowner or merchant to free his favorite slaves, men or women, at his death, and to leave them certain property, beasts, money, or goods, but never land, which is sacred to the family. On account of this custom, few slaves would welcome their immediate freedom, for, without money, fields, or merchandise, with a surfeit of hired manual labor in the towns and the communal system in the country, no existence would be possible for them.

Ras Rafari's edict ordering that all slaves should be freed at the death of their masters, has added to the problems of the police in Addis Ababa, for, yearly, it turns loose a number of ignorant people without provision, who find the career of thief the only one open to them.

How far the arrogant Northerners manage to evade compliance with this law is difficult to say, but it is probable that, in most cases, any effort in this direction would be supported by the slaves who, for the most part, have the mentality of a child or a good-natured animal. No difference is made between the slave man and the servant. Their work, food and clothes are the same and, in humble households, all three are identical with those of the master.

The lot of the woman slave is complicated by the question of concubinage. If a bondwoman bears a child to her lord, automatically she is free and, on the death of the master of the house, custom has always permitted his concubines to claim their freedom should they desire it. It was also habitual for a slave girl who had lived with her owner to acquire the privileges of a daughter. She could neither be sold, given away, nor married (if a major), without her consent and she was entitled to maintenance both from her master and his heirs.

By Islamic law the rights of slaves are as rigorously protected as those of women and children, but in Ethiopia the family is patriarchal enough for the head of it to be able to dispossess any child he chooses, though he cannot alienate the land from all his stock. Should he die intestate, by traditional law which runs in Shoa, the slave-born children inherit equally with the free but three reliable witnesses are required to guarantee the paternity of the first.

There is no effective illegitimacy in Abyssinia, because the traditional law not only thus honors the guaranteed word of a slave, but accepts unconditionally the declaration of any free woman, wife, concubine, or prostitute. By her simple oath she can attribute the paternity of her children to any man and he is obliged to support them, but if she has once committed perjury, her word is valueless.

Even children of a slave man and woman have the right to maintenance at the expense of their parents' master, but they can neither own nor bequeath any form of property. According to his station in life, master, husband or father is legally responsible for the supoort of the household and, even in the most irregular and temporary union, he must supply mother and child with food, until the latter is three years old. The amount of food due to wife or mistress is fixed by tradition and, in the case of a chief's lady, each portion is doubled! The woman also has the right to demand from husband or lover at child-birth and the baptism of her offspring, certain presents such as scent, oil, and stuffs, and certain foods such as fats, spices, and spirits.

In case of divorce the children of a legitimate marriage, either religous or civil, are, like other household possessions, divided between husband and wife. Each is responsible for the support of his or her section of the family. If there are an uneven number, the odd child is given to the mother, but the father has to supply its nourishment for alternate months. When it is time for the daughters to marry both contribute according to their means to the *dot*.

There remains the question of inheritance. In this the woman's rights are limited, if she be maid, to maintenance and a sufficient *dot* to secure her a husband, unless she is the sole representative of the family. Sometimes, however, the heirs prefer to divide the paternal live stock and goods with their unmarried sisters rather than assume the eventual heavier responsibilities of the *dot*. This never applies to land or houses which are the unalienable property of the male. The land may be granted by the crown (to whom theoretically it all belongs) to great chiefs in perpetuity, to governors, officers and courtiers, even to great ladies, for long or short periods, but, under the changing feudal lords, the peasant remains secure in his tenure, so long as he pays the three taxes, a levy on grain and livestock, a proportion of his weekly labor, and a share of "dergo", the public hospitality. The earth he cultivates is his sole means of support and of those of his race who follow him. He realizes, therefore, that he has but a life interest in it, and that he must pass it on intact. To grant right of inheritance to a woman would be to alienate the essential possession of the stock, to jeopardize the existence of future generations. According to tradition the land must always be ready to supply the needs of the whole family. Temporarily it is ruled or administered by the head, but fundamentally it is the possession of the race. From it they wrench the hard living and spare nutriment which, added to the insenate length and number of fasts, the dirt, extreme of climate, and hereditary diseases, reduced their physical and muscular development.

This communality of family land insures a means of existence to all males who are willing to work, for the country is sparsely populated for its size, land is abundant, and each stock has its own recognized area. Unfortunately it limits production, because each household is a self-supporting, self-sufficient unit, working just hard enough to cope with its own needs. It does not produce anything extra unless perhaps a little grain to barter at a distant market, and it does nothing to improve the land, since it will not be able to take advantage of the fruits of such extra labor. The Abyssinian is improvident by nature and, if the wood on his land were not as much family property as the earth itself, he would cut down every tree and leave his heirs without the possibility of constructing a hut or making a fire.

There are districts where the only possible fuel is dung and, in such places, it is the women's duty to collect it, dry it in the sun, pound and mould it into flat cakes, and always keep one small fire alight. In one village we passed there was a communal fire, which each woman in turn had to serve for a certain number of hours, that light and heat might always be at the service of a community which possessed neither matches nor sun glass.

If the woman has no right of inheritance in the family land, she is as maid, or wife, living in the house of father or husband, entitled to a small portion which she can cultivate herself to supply her hairdressing money! The young girl only plaits the edges of her hair, winding these tresses round her temples and leaving the crown fuzzy. With every year the garland of plaits grows wider until there is only a small circle of fluff in the centre, which disappears at the consummation of marriage or her majority.

The grown woman strains her hair into innumerable fine ridges running from forehead to nape and, the more skillful the dresser, the more tortured appears the skin between them. According to whether the harvest is good or bad, to whether she has worked hard in her allotment or not, the peasant can afford one or two such coiffures a month. It takes the whole day, from dawn to sunset, to achieve a masterpiece of the most fashionable

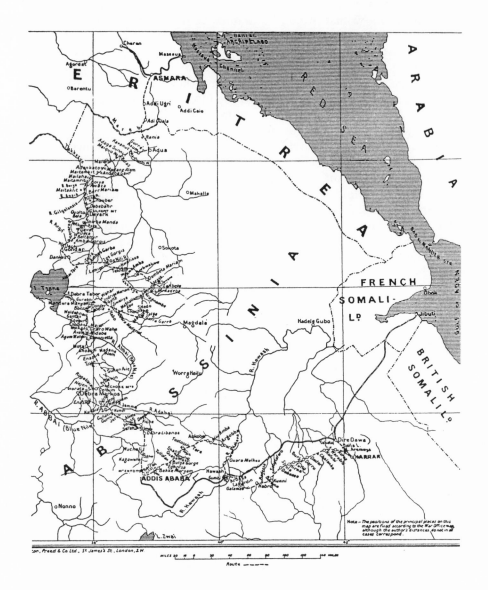

kind, in which the plaits are so thin that they look like fine cord nettled across the head and the scalp is left so sore that the lightest touch is painful till growth relieves the tension on each hair. The artist who performs this miracle with woolly fuzziness, generally in an extreme state of dirt, is paid a dollar for each dressing, and the object of her ministration is obliged to sleep on a wooden neck-rest until she can bear the contact of a hard leather pillow on her taunt stretched skin. The size of the plaits varies according to the taste or wealth of the wearer, but it is always the field which supplies the means to produce them. Sometimes this particular piece of "combing land" may be bequeathed from mother to daughter, and it is by the gift of such a perpetual means of hairdressing that chieftains reward their favorites!

The Abyssinian woman in times of deep mourning is supposed to tear out her web of fine tresses by the roots, but I think nowadays, though one occasionally sees a bleeding head among the most frantic mourners, knife, glass or a razor completes the work begun by hand. Dirty clothes are also a sign of mourning, and a bereaved wife or mother will follow the bier, beating herself so hard with a cord that blood drip from her breasts or temples.

It is generally conceded in Ethiopia that a woman's first judge is her husband, so nobody can proceed against her judicially without having previously consulted her spouse, who has the choice of publicly supporting her in court by which he assumes full financial responsibility, or, should he deem her guilty, of paying for her delinquencies. These are nearly always vocal, and consist of perjury libel, false accusation, or slander. It is very rare that a woman commits any graver offence, since the blood feuds which justify all forms of murder, are carried out by the men, and crimes of passion hardly exist in a country where so much license is permitted. She may, of course, run into debt, or steal, but there is no state prosecution in Abyssinia, so the husband can stifle publicity if he chooses, with those all-powerful Maria Theresa dollars. A woman is punished for infidelity by divorce with the loss of her *dot,* a man more often by a fine, for whose payment the guarantor is responsible. If a husband beat his wife, the guarantor has to pay, and here there is direct conflict between two admitted rights, for a man is allowed to punish his wife, and the woman to claim damages. Consequently, in an ill-tempered household, the man continues to beat, and the woman to pile up a fortune!

Crimes of violence committed on a woman are punished by fines based on the price of blood. If this is, say 120 dollars, sixty would be levied for an offence against an unmarried girl, forty for the same offence against a married woman, less in the case of a widow, and perhaps only a twentieth part of the price of blood if the victim were a courtesan. To prove such offence only the oath of the woman is necessary.

In Abyssinia only rebels and habitual thieves are punished by mutilation, flogging or imprisonment. All other crimes are settled on the basis that a man's life is worth so much, his honor so much less, and everything he possesses can be replaced for a varying sum. In fact price has superseded value. The guarantor takes the place of correctional justice and, in his vigilance, he is assisted by all his family who consider that they share his responsibility. Nothing is private in a life which entails so much community of interests that everyone is his neighbor's policeman. If blood money is not accepted, murder is more often punished by vendetta than by public justice, and the death of a woman imposes the same duty on her relations as that of a man, but it is her father and brothers who must revenge her, not her husband, and it is to them that blood money must be paid. It is the race which claims payment for its blood, not the husband for a home destroyer.

Undoubtedly the women of Ethiopia enjoy a greater measure of respect than is granted to their neighbors. Their word is honored as in no other country in the world, since it is accepted without witness or guarantee. The same deference is extended to their persons, for if, in a discussion or quarrel, a man seizes a married woman's arm, even if he rests a hand on her shoulder, she can claim his punishment. It is sufficient for a stranger to touch a woman against her will, or to make any illicit suggestion to her, to menace her with the mildest form of violence, for her to claim a pecuniary recompense. In all such cases judgment is granted on the unsupported testimony of the woman.

In Abyssinia the peasant woman takes no part in public life, but the great lady can administer lands granted her for life tenure by her husband or the Negus. She administers justice, receives and pays taxes, dispenses hospitality, apportions the farms and, in case of war, while assigning the actual command of her troops to the officers of her choice, she is quite capable of directing operations from the vicinity of the battlefield. Greetings or letters from any man, whatever his station, to such a woman would be full of exaggerated compliments, in which scriptural passages would be cited in praise of her beauty and virtue, even if both were obviously defective. Compliments are essential to conversation between the sexes of whatever position, providing they are not married, but deference depends on position. The peasant woman may have her civil and family rights, but, overworked and undernourished, nature is harder on her than man and, before she is forty, she is too exhausted physically, mentally, and often morally, to claim them. The lady with no other labor than the bearing of two or three children and the supervision of many slaves, secluded, sedentary, with few calls on mind or body, expects and is granted consideration. Both are amazingly free as far as the disposal of their persons is concerned, but the labor of the one, the property of the other, belongs to the husband. Money is the alpha and omega of Abyssinia, and through the traditional law of inheritance, in its only definite, enduring form,—land—it is in the hands of the men.

*Christianborg Castle*

# H. H. Princess Marie Louise*
# (Gold Coast, 1925)

Louise Augusta Marie Christiana Helena was born at Windsor Castle, the youngest child of Queen Victoria's third daughter. She enjoyed a happy childhood in England and, at the urging of her cousin, William II of Germany, married Prince Aribert of Antalt. Unfortunately, it was a bad marriage. After nine childless years Marie Louise obtained an annulment, and never remarried. Instead she devoted her considerable energies to charity and to world travel.

Described by contemporaries as "standing above average height and with imposing features" she was an artist of some renown, specializing in design. As the last British princess to be referred to as "Highness," Marie Louise appears not to have been carried away with her status as a royal. She lived a rather simple life with her sister, Helena Victoria, to whom she wrote *Letters from the Gold Coast* during a tour to that British colony in the early 1920s.

Marie Louise arrived off the coast of today's Ghana while her cousin, David (later, and briefly, Edward VIII), was in residence at Christianborg Castle. Located near Accra, the Castle was then the official residence of the colonial governor. Since it was bad form for two royals to be visiting the same area at once, and because David was then Prince of Wales, Marie Louise was forced to sit idly on her ship until he could be persuaded to depart. In the meantime, Marie Louise began the series of letters with lovely descriptions of the tropical sun setting into the Atlantic Ocean, and with thoughts on the ties that bound this Princess with Ghana's past. Her mother, Princess Helena, married Prince Christian of Schleswig-Holstein, whose ancestry stretched back into the Denmark of slave trade; and the Danes were builders of the castle David then occupied. Her brother, Christian, had taken part in the Asante campaign that marked the final submission of that part of West Africa to British rule.

In her letters Marie Louise appeared extremely well read on the traditions and history of the people she traveled among, often citing long passages from early authorities in order to provide background for her

*H. H. Marie Louise (Windsor), *Letters from the Gold Coast,* London: Methuen & Co., 1926, 11–24, 26–39, 79–97, 230–234.

sister at home: ". . . Wa is of great interest, and I assume that you will wish to hear something of its history. . . ." On folklore, Marie Louise sent along songs and stories that characterized Asante tradition, including a few references to Ananse, the spider, who "dwells in the moon, and you can see him quite easily when she is full, if you look long enough." Throughout much of her stay, the Princess is accompanied by her lady-in-waiting, Alice, whose husband Captain Puckridge served as a kind of aide-de-camp to the party. When they traversed beyond Accra, the colonial governor Guggisberg, and his wife, Decima, accompanied them. All are referred to with warmth and sensitivity. These notables were attended to by a retinue of servants: drivers, cooks, domestics, and porters. Some forty trucks were pressed into service to convey the luggage, cooking utensils, bathtubs, and necessities required to convey the entourage into the rural areas they visited.

As a European royal where succession is conventionally confined to the oldest son of the monarch, the Princess is fascinated by the importance the Queen Mother in Asante plays as "descent is exclusively through the female line." [Citing Rattray, whom she met on this trip] ". . . under this system of matrilineal descent the Queen-Mother would far outrival the importance of men as regards position and power, were it not for her inferior physique which prohibits her from fighting alongside of her people in battles . . . but the poorest woman of royal blood is the potential mother of a King. . . . Keeping in mind this curious fact that the son of the King can never inherit, you can realize how puzzling it must have been for the people to understand that David was the heir to the 'stool'. . . . I, as the daughter of the daughter of the 'Great White Queen' would have been far simpler to explain."

Marie Louise, the artist, paints vivid pictures of her encounters, and, in the process, reveals a sense of humor. "The ladies [in one of the provinces] must have gone to great expense for the occasion, for they were extravagantly attired in bunches of freshly gathered leaves. Sometimes they neglect to renew their dresses and their leafy costumes present a very bedraggled appearance, but today, in honor of this great gathering, they had apparently stripped all the available bushes in the neighborhood to provide themselves with Ascot toilettes. Even so, no one could honestly accuse them of being over-dressed."

On the discomforts of travel, Marie Louise was notably stoic. At one point the party stopped for lunch only to discover that the lorry (truck) had been waylaid elsewhere. Unknown to the group as a whole, the resourceful Lady Guggisberg had packed a "chop" box and announced "the welcome and astonishing news that she could provide lunch. . . . a cold guinea-fowl, a tin of canned peaches and two bottles of soda water.

There were no plates, no knives, no forks, and, of course no napkins . . . a calabash of water was produced in which we washed our fingers at intervals between courses. . . . I grasped my portion of food thankfully with both hands. The bird was carved with a pocket-knife."

And, Marie Louise is compassionate.

> Unless one has lived on the Coast, one cannot possibly realize how splendid these Englishwomen are. Their lives are not easy; they are sometimes very lonely; the "boys" can often be a great trial . . . and food is a serious difficulty. . . . Above all the trials, is that of the climate. Yet these women are cheery and full of courage that they make light of their many difficulties . . . I am convinced we do not sufficiently recognize the magnificent and unselfish part played by the women in these distant and little-known outposts of the Empire. . . .

As to the African colony she visited, Marie Louise was notably attentive to customs, but not judgmental.

> I ought to mention here that no stranger can acquire land on the Coast. The laws of land tenure are as complicated as those that govern inheritance: fifty years being the longest lease granted. If you want to know more about this intricate question, please read the twenty-fifth chapter of Leviticus, because the laws given by Moses to the children of Israel are precisely the same as those that are in force in West Africa today. . . .

We meet the Princess Marie Louise on her arrival at Government House, Accra, travel with her briefly to some nearby sites, and then move into the Northern Territories where she visits a French station across the border.

## *Letters from the Gold Coast*

Government House, Accra.
*April 15.*

We have arrived! But how am I ever to describe the wonder and beauty of our surroundings, the strange old castle built on a rock jutting right out into the sea, with the surf thundering up to one's very windows, the dazzling whiteness of the walls and the vivid brilliance of the flowering trees in full bloom in the courtyard! I live in a dream of enchantment, and it is almost impossible to know where to begin to tell you of all I have seen and done since the day I landed on the Gold Coast.

The first thing I must describe is the actual landing. Decima [Lady Guggisberg, wife of the Colonial governor] and Captain Doherty, the Governor's A.D.C., came on board at 7 a.m., and after I had taken leave of all my kind friends and fellow-passengers of the past fortnight I was placed in the famous "Mammy-chair," which is exactly like a chair on a merry-go-round, and is swung over the side of the ship by crane into the surf-boat. The crew of our surf-boat consisted of ten "boys" who paddled and a steersman who stood at the stern of the boat. Please don't be misled by the word "boy" and imagine that it applies only to children or boys in the strict sense of the word—a "boy" in Africa, like a stable "lad" at home, can be any age from sixteen to sixty, and the word is always applied to your servants or employees whatever capacity they may fill. All manual labourers are "boys."

The paddlers sit sideways on the gunwale of the boat with one foot in a leathern loop, and the paddle resembles a Neptune's trident. As soon as we got under way, our crew began to sing, one starting the story and the remainder chanting the chorus. The story is usually about the passengers and how much "dash" the crew expects to receive. (The word "dash" is derived from the Portuguese "das me" which has degenerated into "dash men" and is the usual expression for giving a present or "tip." "I dash you . . ." means "I give you . . ") The chorus is chanted in a curious rhythm to which they keep time with their paddling. We had a splendid surf, in other words a fairly calm sea, just sufficient to run us up on the beach without any difficulty.

The Governor met me and at once presented all the officials and ladies who had assembled for my arrival. Driving off with the Governor, a wonderful and unforgettable sight met my astonished gaze as we turned into the main street. Both sides of the road were lined with an assembly of the most imposing and impressive character I have ever looked upon. It was the Chiefs and their followers gathered together in all their barbaric splendour to give me greeting. We dismounted from our car and the Governor presented each Chief, the Chiefs in their turn presenting their sub-chiefs and high officials.

It requires a far more vivid power of description than I possess to give you an adequate idea of the splendid and dignified appearance of a West African chief. His cloth or robe is a wonderful blend of many colours: a veritable Joseph's coat! It consists of a multitude of small pieces of woven material, each piece being about five inches long, by two and a half broad, all of a different pattern and design, sewn together in long strips into one harmonious whole. To the uninitiated stranger these cloths may appear to be merely specimens of very clever and beautiful native weaving; but the small squares have a special significance, as the different designs denote the social rank or family, as well as special incidents of interest or importance in the wearer's life. One might describe them as a résumé of the family history.

The cloth is draped over the left shoulder, leaving the right arm and shoulder bare, and hangs down in heavy folds resembling a Roman toga. When an African, be he chief or otherwise, speaks to one of high or royal rank, he bares his left shoulder, removes his crown or fillet from his head and takes off his sandals. A chief's ornaments, anklets, rings and bracelets, are very beautiful and of pure Ashanti gold, strange and rare in design and of the best native workmanship. The bracelets are sometimes so heavy that the arms of the wearers have to be supported by their pages. Heavy chains of the same precious metal adorn their necks.

Each chief sits under his state umbrella, surrounded by his sub-chiefs, court officials and followers. Some of these umbrellas measure ten feet across; they are usually made of velvet or brocade with heavy fringes of gold and are the most practical institution in this land of sun.

After the ceremony of presentations was concluded, we returned to our cars and motored to Government House.

Accra itself is just an ordinary tropical town, with a picturesque native quarter and, in strong contrast, ugly modern buildings and stores with corrugated-iron roofs and some very fine Government offices. The European residential quarter consists of very charming bungalows and gardens, a mass of flowering trees, the glorious flamboyant cassia, frangipangi and crotons. Some people try to grow English flowers, but here as everywhere in the tropics, you have to contend with white ants, the deadly enemy of all vegetable life. All ants wherever found, whether in an English pine wood or in the torrid zone, have, as every one knows, the most complicated and rational systems of government; but the African white ant possesses the distinction of being by far the most destructive of the species. . . .

This castle [Christianborg] is really a lovely old building, with high walls and bastions and a courtyard in the centre, in which are widespreading trees, casting a welcome shade, while their crimson blossoms form a vivid contrast to the dazzling whiteness of the surrounding walls. The castle is built on a mass of rock stretching right out into the sea, against which the surf dashes up with a ceaseless and deafening roar.

My rooms are delightful: a huge sitting-room, with comfortable leather-covered arm-chairs, a big sofa, tables, and a large electric fan in the ceiling—this room opening on to a wide veranda overlooking the court-yard, with broad steps leading down to it; and a bedroom, which is the other half of the sitting-room, the partition dividing them having been removed. A sort of inside veranda runs round two sides of the bedroom, and all the windows, of which there are at least a dozen, look down into the sea. Oh! it is so beautiful that I am adoring every minute, but the heat is intense. . . .

*Later.* I have just returned from a wonderful drive to Achimota with the Governor.

Achimota I ought to describe as the centre round which revolves the whole of his schemes, his plans, his thoughts and his ambitions for the future of the Gold Coast. To describe it merely as a college is inaccurate; it is more in the nature of a university in embryo, and is the first of its kind in West Africa, founded solely for the training and education of the young African in his own country.

The whole question of our past system of education for these alien races is one so open to discussion (and perhaps criticism) that I should not dare to express an opinion, even if I were in the position to do so. But in the course of my many travels, the doubt has sometimes arisen in my mind whether in olden days the introduction of our European civilization and education has always been conducted on the wisest lines. . . .

We British always consider ourselves a practical and common-sense people, but in spite of realizing and rather priding ourselves on our distinctive national characteristics as opposed to those of other races, we were apt in the far-off days of our early colonization, to introduce our peculiarly British form of civilization, and even education, on primitive lands without sufficiently considering the traditions and beliefs which had hitherto governed them, or how capable the inhabitants might be of absorbing what was to them a wholly foreign system.

We have learnt much since those early days. Those who have the arduous task of administration and government fully realize the importance and vital necessity of training these people step by step and providing them with a practical and technical education as well as the higher branches of learning. . . .

Hitherto the young African desirous and keen for higher education has had to seek his training overseas, in surroundings alien to those amongst which he must ultimately live and work, thus exposing himself to the danger of growing out of touch with his own race during the most important period of his intellectual development.

Achimota will provide all the opportunities and facilities for acquiring what would be necessary to him were he studying in England, but with the added advantage that his college and university training is taking place in his own country instead of four thousand miles away. . . .

The site of the College is magnificent, standing two hundred feet above the sea-level, about eight miles out from Accra, and covering an area of four square miles. A great feature is a number of avenues of every variety of tree radiating from the main building. . . .

*April 19.*

All our plans are altered—instead of leaving tomorrow for Kumasi as originally intended, we remain here till next Monday. The Governor has influenza; he developed it on the very day I arrived, and though already he is much better, the doctor will not allow him to start on our trek until he is quite convalescent.

To-day is Sunday; I went to church at seven and again at 9.30. The church is not very large and it is quite the hottest and worst ventilated building I have ever been in, the heat during the services being indescribable. I have been told a very amusing but rather ill-natured bit of gossip as to the reason of its stuffiness. Two churches were designed, one for the tropics and one for the very coldest part of Northern Canada, but by some disastrous mistake the plans got mixed up, with the result that the one specially planned to keep the worshippers warm and to exclude every draught or breath of air has been erected in West Africa, and the tropical church with all the ventilation possible now stands amidst the snows and ice of the Arctic regions. It makes a very good story even if it is not according to fact. . . .

The [new] Hospital, which took three years to build, cost over £220,000. I have no hesitation in saying that it is one of the finest, most modern and elaborately equipped hospitals I have ever visited. I wish that many of our patients in England could be nursed under such medically ideal conditions as are the sick African men and women at Accra. The plan on which it is built is that of separate blocks connected by long colonnades. The one for out-patients contains a large dispensary, roomy and well-fitted waiting-rooms, and a small emergency theatre for minor operations. On the first floor are the ophthalmic and X-ray rooms, as well as an extensive dental department, reached by means of an electric lift.

Next comes the Administration block, with its carefully thought-out plan of record offices, lecture rooms and laboratories for the use and instruction of dispensers and sanitary inspectors.

The two large wings, comprising four wards, lie each behind this last block, and are again joined by these long and airy colonnades; a wide, shady veranda has been built at the end of each ward suitable for open-air treatment, and the two operating theatres with all the indispensable sterilizing and anaesthetizing rooms would fill the soul of a London surgeon with green envy.

Of course there is a perfect labyrinth of kitchens, laundries, disinfector-houses, and store-rooms, medical and domestic, as well as the necessary workshops and engine-rooms. The whole is lit by electric light and it possesses the most perfect water and sanitary arrangements—in fact, it is a model hospital. . . .

*April 25.*

There has been so much to do and see during the past week that I have had no time to write to you since last Sunday. The mail for home leaves to-day, and from my windows I can see the "Aba" surrounded by a whole fleet of surf-boats, busy taking in her cargo. She arrived early this morning from Lagos and leaves to-night for Sekondi.

It is impossible to realize that I have been here only twelve days, for I have become so absorbed in the many and varied subjects affecting the welfare of this wonderful Colony that I feel as if I had been living on the Coast for years.

Needless to say, I have been visiting and inspecting all the schools and many of the other Government buildings; I will not weary you with a detailed lecture on each one, but try and give you just a brief outline of the events of different days.

Last Monday we motored out to the Government Sisal Plantation. I do not suppose that you have very much knowledge of, or interest in, sisal; nor had I, till I came here and saw this huge experimental plantation of 1,000 acres. . . . Government is now trying to develop this new industry in the hope that it will prove to some extent an alternative source of revenue should the cocoa crop show signs of failing.

There is a further advantage, namely, that sisal can be grown on what has hitherto been very unproductive and poor land on the plains of Accra. I can best describe sisal as first cousin in appearance to the aloe. Its leaves are known to reach a height of five feet, and, like its cousin the aloe and the New Zealand flax, at the end of the fourth or fifth year of its growth it produces a long pole-like stem. So much for its looks. This apparently uninteresting plant, which seems to thrive and flourish best wherever the soil is poorest, produces the article known as hemp from which ropes, big and small, are made.

When once this is a thorough-going concern and the plantation has repaid the initial outlay, Government, I believe, will hand it over to the chiefs, providing, of course, that the African has proved himself qualified to carry it on. If this plantation succeeds, which it has every appearance of doing, others of the same kind will be started.

Amongst my many tours of inspection I visited not only the very important Government Schools for boys and girls, but also the most excellent Technical School. It was started some years ago in order to give carpenters and metal-workers a sound, practical training. It has now developed into an important residential school run on the Boy Scout principles, with a resident house-master.

I am glad to say that great attention is being paid to the physical training of the pupils in the different schools, and I have been most agreeably surprised to see how admirably they carry out their drill and exercises.

We have been having mild tornadoes most days, but up to now they have been very considerate as regards the hour of their arrival and have never seriously interfered with any of our plans. Except on Friday! The Governor had to make a very important speech that morning at the Legislative Council, to submit a proposal to raise a loan of four million pounds for the country. The proceedings were to be conducted with full pomp and state, with escort and guard of honour; and as he thought it would interest me, he asked me to be present. Decima, Alice and I were to leave the Castle at 9.30, well in advance of him, so as not to clash with his official arrival. The tornado broke just as we were sitting down to breakfast, and the rain came down in such deluges that it was out of the question for the ladies to move from the house.

Escort, guard of honour, everything, in fact, had to be put off, and the proceedings were shorn of all their splendour. I was much disappointed.

Of course the storm stopped just as H.E. [the governor] returned to the Castle—too provoking!

In the afternoon we went out to the European Hospital, a very modest and unpretentious-looking building. . . .

Of an evening we sit on the bastion looking out to sea and watch the stars shining like myriads of fairy lamps in the sky. We talk of home and England and try to realize that this is West Africa.

Kumasi, Ashanti.

*April 27.*

It has just struck 6 (a.m.). I have been up and dressed since 5. My modest amount of baggage has been taken downstairs, and from my window I can see the long line of lorries all loaded up and preparing to start.

Quite late last night I heard that there was just a chance that letters might catch an intermediate mail home if posted to-day, and as there is a whole long hour to wait for breakfast I cannot do better than spend it in writing to you. The last morning at Accra was very busy, every moment being taken up with sorting and packing our things: our luggage or loads had all to be ready by three o'clock in the afternoon. My baggage consists of a camp bed, a tin bath (in which all the "last things" are packed), table, chair, three small tin boxes containing my clothes, a dressing-case, and the small brown bag with its precious contents of cigarettes, face lotion, clean handkerchiefs, and soap. Alice and I spent most of the last morning sticking labels on to all our loads. We shall each have a lorry to convey our belongings—each lorry is lettered and all our baggage must have the corresponding letter. I am "F" and Alice is "I." In case the roads prove to be impassable and our motor transport breaks down, everything will have to be carried, so all has to be portioned out into 60 lb. head loads. As you can imagine, the heat and the gum combined rendered our labours extraordinarily sticky—everything stuck excepting the labels; but eventually our work was accomplished, and an army of prisoners with a warder in attendance appeared to carry our baggage down to the lorries.

The courtyard presented a strange appearance—piles of luggage and stores of all sorts and descriptions; wherever one stepped one tripped up over a tin box or a bath; but by four o'clock all the lorries were loaded up and on their way to the station.

With their departure peace and quiet descended once more on the Castle and its occupants, Alice and I went across to Commander Whitfield's quarters to have tea with him on his little balcony overlooking the sea; he has, alas, just resigned his appointment as A.D.C. to the Governor, owing to ill-health, and is returning home by the next mail; Captain Doherty has replaced him on the Staff. Then a farewell walk round the garden, a final "look round" our rooms to see that nothing had been left behind, and shortly before seven we motored down to the station. Here a large number of officials and friends had assembled to bid us farewell and "good luck," and accompanied by all their good wishes we climbed into the train and started on the first stage of this marvellous tour.

I believe I have quite forgotten to mention the names of our party on the trek. There are—

The Governor and Decima,

Alice and myself,

Commander Hemans, Private Secretary,

Captain Doherty, A.D.C.,

Captain Puckridge (who, I am glad to say, the Governor has now attached to me for the whole of this tour),

Dr. Le Fanu, brother of the one I met at the European Hospital at Accra, and

Captain Doole, Transport Officer.

We shall gather up successive Provincial and District Commissioners in our party as we pass through their respective districts, so with all our "boys," orderlies, cooks and motor-drivers, not to omit that important person the washerman, we shall be a large party.

My "boy" Malam is excellent; he calls me "Sah" to my face, but talks of me as "the big Missis"; Alice is "the small Missis," and Annie "small, small Missis," or, "big Missis's mammy." He is fearfully upset in his mind over my bath essences, and he came to Annie to ask why "Big Missis" turned bath-water green and why his hands smelt. This means that my "Omy" tinges the water, and when he cleans the bath his hands smell of all kinds of delicious and unknown scents.

I had also a little African maid, named Jessie, really very pretty, but a little minx. She was to have gone with me, but I decided not to take her as she would have been too much of a responsibility.

The night journey to Kumasi was wonderfully comfortable; my coach was the last one on the train. It consisted of a huge saloon furnished with three big arm-chairs, a table, a sort of cupboard and side-table combined, which served as my dressing-table, and my own camp-bed.

Captain Puckridge had spent most of the afternoon in superintending the stowing away of my loads and making all the preparations for my comfort, with the result that when I got into my coach I found not only my camp-bed put up and my bath ready, but everything I needed for the night unpacked and laid out just as if I had been in my own room at home. I had quite a spacious bathroom next to my saloon: adjoining it a small kitchen and pantry and a sleeping place for my "boy"—in fact nothing could have been more comfortable or convenient. Alice and Annie had each their own coach just beyond mine.

About three stations out of Accra our train stopped for an hour to enable us to have our dinner in peace and quiet.

We did not sit up very long after dinner, as we were all tired and anxious to get to bed. I woke very early, and went out on to the little platform at the end of my coach and there I sat watching the dawn break over the forest.

How can my poor pen ever do justice to the indescribable beauty of that dawn, or give you even the faintest idea of the strange mixture of memo-ries and emotions that crowded in upon me.

Consider my feelings.

It was just thirty years ago that Christle was passing through this same scene, gazing, as I am, on this strange, mysterious forest, but oh, how utterly different our two journeys! He came on duty as a soldier and one of an armed force penetrating into a hostile land, for there was then war between England and Ashanti; I, his sister, come to the same country thirty years later, welcomed as an honoured guest with every token of loyalty and friendship by the chiefs and their people. He wearily, and often sick with fever, marched on foot from Cape Coast, cutting his way through the impenetrable depths of the Ashanti forest, held up almost at every step by a tangle of century-old undergrowth. I also travel through the forest, but in a saloon carriage attached to the Governor's train, in perfect comfort. My journey of 192 miles from Accra takes twelve hours; Christle could make only forced marches of six miles a day, and it was twenty days before he reached Kumasi. . . .

We were due to arrive at Kumasi at seven, but owing to a breakdown on the line had to wait for over an hour at Juaso. Here Alice wandered into my coach, to share our early morning tea. We were both rather silent, not because there was nothing to talk about, but because, the spell of the forest being upon us, there was too much.

My first impression of Kumasi was a strange one. We passed by the great market, full of busy native life; on the upper road I could already distinguish in the distance the outline of many state umbrellas and a vast crowd of people. All along the line and perched on the top of each small tree sat masses of hideous bare-necked vultures, flapping their huge wings and uttering hoarse cries as they flopped down on to the ground to carry on their useful but revolting work of scavenging. . . .

The Seriki of the Zongo presented me with a wonderful necklace of large oblong ivory beads, the centre ones decorated with gold bands beautifully engraved, the necklace being of course of native work-manship. . . .

All the cocoa plantations are owned and cultivated by the chiefs and local farmers, the European trader merely buying the crop. This is quite a different system from that in the West Indies, where the plantations are the property of the European planters.

Hitherto one of the great difficulties on the Coast has been to impress upon the native the vital importance of keeping the land clean under the cocoa trees, and of destroying the old pods instead of allowing them to lie and rot on the ground, for decaying vegetation is the bitterest enemy to the young delicate pods; besides, it breeds every description of insect pest.

The Government Agricultural Department is doing admirable work in teaching the farmers how to cultivate and tend the trees on more practical as well as on more scientific lines, and is also instructing them in the varied and many cocoa diseases, their prevention and cure. From now on, the centre for all this training will be Cadbury Hall.

I spent a long time examining endless specimens of cocoa pests as well as a collection of most repulsive-looking bugs and beetles in bottles; after having quite an interesting little lecture on tropical agriculture, and being laden with many beautiful flowers (including sprays of absurdly large gardenias), we continued our drive. . . .

On our return to the Residency we found the Governor entertaining a large tennis-party. It was already so dark we could scarcely distinguish one another, but it was delicious sitting out in the cool dusk.

I am being repeatedly summoned to breakfast; therefore, good-bye. Goodness knows what hair-raising adventures I may have to tell you next time I write.

Tamale.
*May 2.*

We have arrived in the Northern Territories, but, oh, such an upset of plans! H.E. is ill again. We were greeted with this disappointing news this morning when we assembled for breakfast. The Doctor is rather worried about him and has advised some days' complete rest; perhaps the fatigue of driving the heavy Lanchester for so many hours on end in such intense heat was not wise, considering that he was only just convalescent from influenza. He showed signs of strain already at Palbe and was in considerable pain, which made me rather anxious; I promptly offered every kind of remedy (you know I never move without an emergency chemists's shop in my bag), all of which were gratefully accepted, but I fear did little good. However, H.E. gallantly continued the journey to Tamale, but now he has been obliged to give in. . . .

I must now go back and tell you of our first two days' trek from Kumasi to Tamale. The first day's run was 145 miles straight through to Yeji, where we spent the night. We left Kumasi at eight o'clock in the morning, having taken a very sad farewell of Annie, who has returned to Accra to await my return to the Coast in seven weeks' time. We were indeed a formidable procession; six motors, consisting of the Governor's Lanchester, a Crossley, a Buick, a Standard and two Trojans (noisy but useful cars which go by the names of "Tweedledum" and "Tweedledee"), and sixteen lorries. . . .

Ouagadougou,
La Haute Volta,
L'Afrique Occidentale.
*May 11.*

This imposing address will tell you that we have arrived in French territory. I am so bewildered and mentally out of breath through all I have done and seen during the past twelve hours that I fear I shall have great difficulty in giving you a clear description of our trek from Navarongo and the various incidents of our arrival and reception at Ouagadougou. . . .

I ought to have mentioned that the great agitation of the past two days has been the question of what we ladies were going to wear on our arrival at Ouagadougou, for you see that clothes retain their importance even in "far bush." I was very firm and decided in my views on the subject, and declared that nothing would induce me to motor a hundred miles in the blazing African sun dressed in party clothes, thin stockings and smart shoes. I had made up my mind to appear in "bush kit," i.e. short skirt, shirt and high boots. I am glad to say that my practical common sense gained the day—at least, so I imagined, until Decima issued forth from her hut after lunch at Nobili clad in a Paris creation of spotless white drill. I think she regretted it, for never have I experienced a more trying journey, nor such heat. The sun alone was sufficiently fierce to satisfy the demands of the most ardent of sun-worshippers, and we had to endure a burning hot wind laden with fine sand which lashed our faces to ribbons. I was painfully aware of rivulets of ochre-coloured mud trickling down my cheeks, but tried to comfort myself with the knowledge that every one was as hot or even hotter than I was, for H.E. and all the Staff had to be in uniform in honour of the French.

Our first halt had been at the frontier, a distance of ten miles from Navarongo. We were met by M. Michel (Commandant du Cercle Ière classe), M. Pouverau, whose official position would correspond to a District Commissioner in our service, and M. Albert Hesling, son of the Governor of Ouagadougou. After the necessary presentations and introductions, much bowing and exchanging of compliments, we continued our journey to Nobili, a further run of thirty miles, where, thank goodness, we were to lunch and rest. The whole journey from Navarongo to Ouagadougou is one hundred and ten miles.

On arrival at Nobili there were more presentations, and then, after inspecting the Guard of Honour and all the ex-service men, we walked across to the Rest House compound. It was of a fair size and consisted of about a dozen little "swish" huts, each one surrounded by a low wall, and in the centre of the compound a specially constructed "bush hut" for our "chop." Arm-in-arm with Monsieur Michel, and followed by all the

French officials, I was conducted to my hut. I assure you it was an achievement to crawl into it without bumping my head, for it had only one very low narrow opening, and which served the double purpose of window and door, and was quite dark inside, but deliciously cool and restful after the fierce glare of the sun. In her charming and gentle manner Alice expressed her doubts as to how we could possibly see to "tidy up" with no light, and no furniture—just four bare mud walls—and where and how were we to spread out our few necessary *objets de toilette?* I suggested using the narrow space between the hut and its surrounding wall as our dressing-room, since the grass roof sloping down made it quite sunproof, and the flat top of the wall would do admirably as a dressing-table. . . .

We halted about five miles from Ouagadougou. I cannot tell you the relief it was to get out of the car and stretch our stiff limbs, and as at this particular spot Providence had kindly provided a few stunted trees, we tried to remove some of the dust from our burning faces under their so-called shade and to prepare for the arrival of M. Hesling, the Governor of La Haute Volta. These trees were our rendezvous with M. Hesling. We were rather in advance of our time, but even so I was still busily occupied with my face lotion and powder when he arrived, long before I was prepared for the official meeting. Everything therefore had to be hurriedly stuffed into my bag, to enable me to advance with becoming dignity to greet the French Governor.

M. Michel stepped forward and presented the Governor to me. I, in my turn, presented Alice and Captain Puckridge. H.E. introduced Decima and presented his Staff. M. Hesling, in his turn, presented the French Staff. In fact, there were so many presentations and counter-presentations, bowings and exchange of compliments as well as inquiries as how "Madame la Princesse" had survived the heat of the journey, that my poor brain whirled, especially as all this time we were standing frizzling in the sun. . . .

At length we arrived at our journey's end and entered Ouagadougou, but I fear I shall utterly fail to give you any idea of what our entry was really like; it is almost impossible to describe the scene, with its picturesque and barbaric touches.

The town is extraordinary, and certainly the French have wrought a miracle. Five years ago Ouagadougou was nothing but a native village surrounded by virgin bush and scrub; now it is a large and beautifully planned town with imposing Government and other public buildings, schools, hospitals, barracks, and a large aerodrome. (Ouagadougou is intended to be one of the most important French air stations in this part of Africa; one might describe it as the junction between their Northern and West African colonies.) Broad boulevards have been laid out with avenues of trees and public gardens; in fact, it is a typical Continental town in the heart of Africa. The most remarkable feature of the place is the fact that it is constructed entirely of mud, but the Governor tells me that in a few years it will be rebuilt in stone and cement. . . .

After the first breathless moments I resigned myself to the heat, dust and noise, and proceeded to enjoy the scene most thoroughly. The streets were beautifully decorated, with hundreds and hundreds of flags (Tricolour and Union Jack), garlands, streamers and banners, with charming words of welcome and goodwill. Thousands of natives of every description and tribe lined the route. At length we reached the big square in front of the Residency and here we left our cars and inspected the Guard of Honour. When that was over, M. Hesling offered me his arm, and, surrounded by the whole French Staff and all the officials, I walked across to the Residency. . . .

I am now resting on my veranda. Our lorries have arrived, and Malam is busy arranging my things. The wonderful piece of rope has already been fixed across the corner of the room and my clothes hung up. The orderly is boiling water for my bath, so all is well.

I don't think I ever told you of the disaster that occurred to one of our household at Tamale. The day before we left for Zuaragu one of our steward "boys" developed chicken-pox, and as Alice's "boy," John, had been sharing the same hut with the invalid, the doctor advised leaving him behind in quarantine. This meant that Alice would have been left helpless and maid-less—a very serious consideration in the wilds—had not Major Walker-Leigh come to the rescue and offered one of his "boys." Alice accepted with gratitude, and he has proved quite excellent. The only difficulty is that we cannot quite make up our minds as to his name. Of course he has one, but neither Alice nor I can remember it. She sometimes calls him Zani, more often Ali. Since either seems to answer the purpose, he reminds us of the gentleman in "The Hunting of the Snark" who "would answer to Hi or to any loud cry." As I write I can hear Alice appealing alternately to Zani and to Ali to help her in the mysteries of her toilette.

We are all sharing the same quarters, a very imposing mud building with a broad flight of steps leading up on to a wide veranda. Alice's and my rooms are at one end, Decima and H.E. occupying the opposite end, while the large centre room dividing us is used as a joint sitting and "chop" room. All the rooms open on to another veranda at the back.

I have a whole suite of apartments: a large room with an enormous bed in it, as a second equally large room in which I could dress were it not being used as a right-of-way by the "boys" and orderlies, and then a very dark room at the far end, which, as it contains a big round tin pan, I conclude is my "salle de bain." Malam, scorning the tin pan, has ostentatiously unpacked my own bath; he also informs me, "Big bed bad," and has therefore put up my camp-bed on the veranda. I fear he regards everything outside his own country with deep suspicion. I hope that this rather heartless disregard for their furniture will not strike our kind hosts as rude or ungrateful, but I do agree about the bed, and I am sure it would be impossible to sleep in this heat on a thick soft mattress, with masses of equally soft pillows.

The sun is just setting, a ball of fire in a sky of pure opalescent green. Soon will come a brief moment of wonderful twilight, gone before one can realize its indescribable beauty, and then with sudden swiftness will descend the velvety darkness of the African night.

As my lanterns do not give very much light, I will therefore stop.

*May 12.*

Oh, my dear, what a time we have had! I am absolutely breathless with all I have been through since 5.30 this morning, but I will try and give you some idea of what has occurred since I concluded the first part of this letter. Last night we dined at the Residency. It was quite unofficial—*un petit diner intime*—just our own party. . . . Having mentioned, in the course of conversation to M. Hesling, that I had been riding a good deal in the Northern Territories, he suggested that I should ride this morning, but a chorus of protests arose from all present. The idea that I should ride was declared an impossibility and far too risky, every horse in the town being pronounced a dangerous animal and unfit for a lady to mount. M. Bailly, however, the only one who did not think that I should *me suicider* if I were to mount one of these ferocious beasts, encouraged me; so it was arranged, not without many gloomy forebodings on the part of the rest of the company, that I should ride this morning at six o'clock, attended by M. Albert, Captain Le Roy, and Captain Puckridge.

It was a strange and very strenuous performance, this ride of mine at Ougadougou. To begin with, horses and escort arrived half an hour late, the sun being well up and beating down upon us without mercy. My horse looked all right and seemed harmless, but, oh, his mouth! I can compare it only to one of cast iron or reinforced concrete; also my saddle was full of unexpected lumps and creases, which proved rather painful as the ride proceeded. We trotted gaily down the boulevard and into the open country and when clear of the town, I perceived I was expected to go *au grand galop*. This I flatly refused to do, since the road was the hardest that man or beast had ever trodden, and very dusty. Not a tree was to be seen for miles and the sun was blazing in my eyes. Eventually, however, we reached a strip of virgin bush through which some paths had been cut, for patriotic reasons named the "Bois de Boulogne," and here we halted to recover breath and mop our streaming faces: I shudder to think what my appearance must have been like, especially if it resembled that of my companions.

It was rather an attractive strip of bush, and we trotted along peacefully in the shade by the edge of a small pond-like lake. During the rainy season this rises and overflows the bank, washing away the paths and converting everything into a seething mass of water. It is almost impossible to imagine the contrast of scene in dry and wet weather. After two hours we returned home, and, though you may not believe it, in spite of the slight discomforts of saddle, heat and dust and my pulling horse, I thoroughly enjoyed my ride. I hope that my companions did likewise, but fear for Captain Puckridge, because his pony, which closely resembled a pedigree shorthorn bull, had pulled to such an extent (he had only a snaffle) that his arm was numb for hours. . . .

Our next call was on Madame Michel, where we found the rest of our party sitting about in various stages of exhaustion and heat, but oceans of iced drinks and mountains of delicious little cakes restored our strength and energy, and at eleven we were on our way to the large open square near the War Memorial to watch more curious and varied active dancing.

One of the dances, called the "Harvest Dance," is performed with slight variations all over West Africa. The participants, who chant as they dance round and round in a circle, beat time with short wooden staves that produce a strange rhythmic accompaniment. Their costumes are as varied as their steps. Some wear nothing at all; others, elaborate loin-cloths with the tails of leopards or other wild animals fastened on behind. Their heads are decorated with fillets and strings of cowrie shells or beads hanging down in festoons. Next in interest were the "ju-ju" men, who reminded me of a Jack-in-the-green, except that, instead of leaves, they were clothed in grass and what looked like long strands of tow. On their heads they had strange wooden masks, some of a gigantic size, supposed to represent different animals, and symbolizing some illness or peculiarity of the beast. They had no concerted dance, but bounded and careered about separately, whirling round and round, leaping into the air, and then, whether from intention or sheer exhaustion, throwing themselves suddenly on the ground. All the time a wild drumming and beating of tom-toms was keeping up a strange accompaniment, with the loud blowing of horns and the usual so-called musical instruments in addition. There was an endless series of dances, all very much the same with regard to rhythm and noise, but each with its own significance. . . .

Nobili.
*May 13.*

We are halting here for breakfast on our way home to Navarongo, and I am trying to add a last chapter to my letter from French Territory.

Our departure this morning from Ougadougou was attended with the same state and ceremony as that which had greeted our arrival, M. Hesling accompanying us to that little clump of stunted trees where we had met and made friends three days previously. M. Michel, M. Albert and M. Pouvereau took leave of us here at Nobili.

Can you believe that we had to endure another tornado last night, or, more correctly speaking, in the early hours of this morning! I had been in bed for about an hour when it began, and as I was sleeping on the veranda, everything had to be dragged inside at a moment's notice, and not only my bed, but my chair, table, and in fact all that I possessed. I stood and surveyed the wreck, very sleepy, very tired, the rain beating in through totally inadequate wooden shutters, and that awful and continuous crash of thunder over my head.

It was about three in the morning and I was to be up at five and our loads packed and off before six. It was not worth while to have my bed put up inside, so I sat, a huddled lump of damp misery, in the centre of that enormous French bed and wondered why I had ever come to West Africa. Alice was full of sympathy, but as she had not established herself on the veranda as I had done, she was safe and dry under her mosquito nets.

I must not omit to tell you of the wonderful conclusion to the events of yesterday. After all the excitement of the thunderbolt and dust storm had subsided, Alice and Decima went out for a drive, while I remained at home, wrote to you and packed. At 7.30 we went to the Residency for dinner, reception and a dance. I assure you it was far from easy to dress for an official evening function by the light of two hurricane lanterns: Malam held one over my head while I endeavoured to do my hair and pin on my orders. However the result, he assured me, was good and that "Big Missis look smart.". . .

In the middle of dinner we heard the sound of drums and bugles in the far distance, and on my asking what it meant, M. Hesling said it was *La Retraite aux Flambeaux* which was being carried out in our honour. We all hastily left the table and went out on to the veranda. My dear, it was the most marvellous and surprising sight you can imagine. A tattoo at home is beautiful, but here, with the added romance of its strange setting, the beauty of an African night, the wild, barbaric crowds, the splendid and picturesque native troops, the flare of hundreds and hundreds of torches, the sound of the bugles and the roll of the drums—it was one of the most stirring and impressive scenes imaginable. The entire population took part in this tribute of welcome, to prove their friendship to France's great ally. The tears came to my eyes when the band played "God save the King." Remember I was in the heart of Africa, and home seemed very far away.

To return to our dinner seemed something in the nature of an anti-climax.

Later we danced under the stars, to the light of the moon and torches.

Tumu.
*May 14.*

Just a few lines to continue my daily story. We reached this camp to-day at noon, having left Navarongo early this morning.

I must tell you of the cruel disappointment that awaiting me on my arrival there yesterday from Ougadougou. Do you remember a mail was due when we left on that great expedition, but failed to reach us before our departure? We knew it would and must be there, however, to greet us on our return, and the thought of all the letters from home which were waiting for us helped to make the motor-run of one hundreds and more miles pass like magic.

As we drew up at H.E.'s bungalow, I saw the mail bags lying on the veranda and I begged the Private Secretary to open them at once, for he had suggested we should lunch first, but how *could* we stop for food or drink when an unopened mail-bag lay at our feet? I stood breathless with excitement as the seals were broken and the contents of the three bags poured out on to the floor, but there was not one single letter for me. Every one else had a large budget from home except myself—not even a bill or a newspaper, just nothing at all! Do you remember that extraordinary play "White Cargo"? It is a cruel libel on the Coast and utterly false and untrue, except in one scene where there is an incident of heart-breaking pathos when the long-expected mail arrives and the old drunken doctor discovers that it has brought him nothing. I felt just like the old doctor as I walked away across the burning space back to my own hut.

None of our lorries having arrived, there was not even a chair for me to sit down on, so I perched disconsolate on the sill of the window and thought and thought over West Africa and the strange desolate feeling of no mail from home. I know that this absence of letters from home has taught me more of what the loneliness of life on the Coast means than anything else, because it has been my own personal experience. . . .

R.M.S. Aba,
Off the Gold Coast.

*June 21.*

I am back once more on board the *Aba*. I have seen and experienced so much during these past weeks that I can scarcely realize that only two short months have elapsed since the morning when, with the aid of "mammy-chair" and surf-boat, I landed on the Gold Coast.

It is rather absurd that I should be sitting here in my pretty and familiar cabin writing to you when we are carrying the homeward mail. But my daily letters to you have become such a habit that I feel I should be doing my tour an injustice if I did not write down the events of my last hours on the Coast while their impression is still so vividly in my mind.

Let me go back to the end of our last day at Accra. The rain continued all day, and we were in despair. How about the State Ball? All Decima's lovely plans for transforming the courtyard and bastions into the most perfect "sitting-out" places had to be abandoned, and we had terrible fears as to whether anyone would be able to get through the floods to us at all. However, the "Sky God" was kind, and towards seven o'clock the rain ceased, too late, of course, to think about illuminations, but in time to save our guests from being drowned on their way to the party.

The evening began with an official dinner at which all the Members of the Legislative Council and heads of Departments were present. After the King's health had been drunk, the Governor proposed my health, and in a very kind speech bade me farewell in the name of the Gold Coast.

He reviewed our tour in a most amusing as well as interesting manner, and pointed out that we had really accomplished a remarkable journey. We had travelled two thousand five hundred miles, of which only three hundred and sixty were by rail, all the rest being done by motor. Not so very long ago this trek would have taken at least six months: we did it in seven weeks.

It was really a beautiful ball, and I was glad to have the opportunity of seeing all the friends I have met during my stay at Accra, and of thanking them for the unfailing kindness they have shown to me, in helping to make my visit one of such real enjoyment.

The next morning it was fine, though cloudy and rather stormy. What would the surf be like? This was the question that agitated most of the party at breakfast. The *Aba* came in about ten o'clock, and at 10.30 we left the Castle. The Governor drove me down to the beach, and I was quite overwhelmed to find so many friends assembled to see me off.

At length the last farewells were over and I stepped into the surf-boat. It was a very perilous proceeding, as the narrow plank I had to walk along to reach it was well under water, with the waves dashing over it. Decima, Alice and Annie followed, and we were just pushing off when, much to my surprise, Captain Puckridge jumped in.

It had been arranged for him to come off separately with all our loads, and not till we were safe on board did he tell me the reason for this sudden decision on his part. While I was busy saying good-bye he saw no fewer than seven boats upset, and considering it positively dangerous for us four women to face the terrific surf alone, he had instantly decided to abandon the loads to their fate and come with us.

I am not going to attempt to describe what that surf or that passage to the *Aba* was like. But I have the doubtful consolation of knowing that it was the worst surf during the last twenty years. Thus, at the very moment of my departure, I have gone through another typical "Coast" experience.

Captain Johnston Hughes received me with obvious pleasure when I scrambled out of the mammy-chair on to the deck. It was delightful to have such a warm welcome. Even my stewardess (Miss Perry) and my stewards met me with beaming faces.

If only this voyage did not entail leaving the Coast there would be nothing to cloud my happiness, for shall I not be with you again in a fortnight?

We lay off Accra till night. There were heavy and sudden rainstorms during the day, but the evening was fine, and we sat on deck and looked towards the twinkling lights of Christianborg and talked and talked of these wonderful past weeks.

We got into Sekondi early this morning, when Captain Puckridge took leave of us, and transferred the arduous duty of looking after me to Captain Peake.

Captain Puckridge has been simply splendid throughout this tour. It has been an enormous help to me to have some one so capable and so thoughtful attached to me. He took every worry and care off my shoulders, and, as I said in my first letter from the ship, I could not have wanted two more charming and delightful companions than him and dear Alice.

It is still raining. It began last night and has continued all day without ceasing. I never even saw Sekondi, for although we lay off the town for six hours, it was completely blotted out by the rain. Just as a matter of curiosity, I am copying out the last day's rainfall at Accra since our arrival from Cape Coast:

| | | | | | | | |
|---|---|---|---|---|---|---|---|
| 9 a.m. | 13th June | – 9 a.m. | 14th | ................. | 4.86 | inches |
| " | 18th " | – " | 19th | ................. | 4.12 | " |
| " | 19th " | – " | 20th | ................. | 2.73 | " |
| Week 9 a.m. | 14th | – 9 a.m. | 20th | ................. | 16.5 | " |
| 1st–19th June | | | | ................. | 21.53 | " |

Even now, though each throb of the engines, each swish of the waves against the side of the ship, tells me that I am on my homeward way, I cannot realize I have actually left West Africa.

It is a marvellous country. What is its spell? I cannot tell you, nor wherein lies its strange and unfathomable charm. It lays its hand upon you, and, having once felt its compelling touch, you never can forget it or be wholly free from it.

In spite of the heat and rain, in spite of loneliness and hardships, I might say in spite of every discomfort and drawback (and the Coast offers you many), you love it.

*May Mott-Smith*

# MAY MOTT-SMITH*
# (West Africa, 1920s)

May Mott-Smith was another intrepid traveler to the African continent. Her nationality was American but May was born in the territory of Hawaii, and carried with her all of the colonial attitudes of her solidly upperclass background. An artist of some renown, Mott-Smith was also a well-known travel writer. In order to follow the path of fifteenth-century explorer, Vasco de Gama, Mott-Smith traveled from West Africa to South Africa and Rhodesia, before she moved on to Portuguese Mozambique, and over to the island of Zanzibar.

In Sierra Leone, Mott-Smith found the heat oppressive and photographs of the locals difficult to take: ". . . [the Muslims] had no use for the 'white mammy' with the black box and its glass eye. . . . Even with the most stealthy tactics I found it impossible to get photos unawares." The artist's eye was always at work. She was captivated by the natural and diverse beauty of the landscape as she made her way around the coast of the African continent. Stopping at Grand Bassam in the Ivory Coast, she noted the "big-leaved, bitter almond trees, palms and umbrella trees in gorgeous red bloom." Arriving in Sekondi, on the Gold Coast, "between us and the shore the sunlight glittered in trembling spatters on the surface of the seas. Sea, boats, light—all in motion. . . ."

In the excerpt that follows, Mott-Smith is in Nigeria, where Anna Hinderer first labored in her mission nearly seventy years earlier. The changes are many. Europeans can be found in considerable numbers in all the major towns, including Ibadan, which had grown from a missionary outpost to a prosperous settlement. Contrary to Mary Gaunt's findings at the turn of the century, Mott-Smith meets numerous white women in her travels through Nigeria (and elsewhere in Africa in the late 1920s). Racial lines are still tightly drawn; and Mott-Smith echoes Gaunt in attitude and imperiousness. Here, white women resembled some of their male counterparts—openly flaunting their prejudices in their published writings. Perhaps these women addressed the issue of race fearlessly because their men preached the doctrine of inferiority at home and in the pulpit. How-

*May, Mott-Smith, *Africa from Port to Port*, New York: D. Van Nostrand Company, 1930, 174–192, 194–208.

ever, they frequently practiced racial "intermingling" with local African women.

In Lagos, Mott-Smith picked up the old refrain of cannibalism. As Mary Kingsley before her, she only heard about it from those who had heard about it from someone else. But in Nigeria, it is not only the African who comes under attack: "I want to . . . expatiate a bit upon the Britisher's naive ideas about plumbing, both in his home country and his colonies. . . . He is so unaware of his backwardness in sanitation that it seems positively cruel to wake him up."

When she reached South Africa, Mott-Smith noted that Boers "cannot refrain from vituperation. . . ." "The business of South Africa is almost entirely in the hands of the Jews . . . [upon whom she makes no further comment] but in the matter of racial intermixture "[the] mixture of blood of Kaffir, Malay, Zulu, Portuguese or Indian, with English and Dutch, even among the better families is appalling. . . . many families of social superiority were found to be tainted with the tar brush."

Mott-Smith veered off the by-now-beaten-track to Madagascar, where she visited Tamatave on the coast but was unable to travel inland to the capital because plague was rumored to be rampant. Madagascar was an outpost of the French empire and Mott-Smith noted that the island was "treated at the home office like a poor relation and looks it." On to Mauritius, a paradise on earth by most any account; but during Mott-Smith's stay "the rain came in frequent squalls or just continued disappointingly in a long, drizzling downpour. . . . Glowering days were mine" she recalled, before finally reaching "The Garden Isle of Reunion." She eventually retraced her steps to Zanzibar and the East African coast of "overrated Kenya."

In Kenya Mott-Smith experienced difficulties that landed her in the care of "an oily person in a fez" who, for a fee, helped her through the trying red tape. Noting that "Ali Baba and his forty thieves have nothing on the technique of the baggage rustlers of Mombasa. . . . Here they presuppose the entering voyager is an imbecile." In fact, survival was the name of the game for the porters, many of whom had fled outposts like Lamu in the north where the economy was in severe depression; or were displaced men from the west whose lands had been usurped by the ever increasing numbers of white settlers.

As her journey drew to a close, Mott-Smith steamed up the coast into the Red Sea, visited Italian Somaliland briefly, and then headed for Port Said in Egypt. "I was leaving Africa—the continent which for so many months had been the scene of my trials, my interest, my hopes and so often my despair. Would I ever come back? Of course I would! Everyone goes back to Africa, in heart, at least, if not in reality."

## Nigeria

At Abutemeta, across the lagoon on the mainland from Lagos, is the railway, the station, the shops, and beyond at Apapa are the docks and railway yards. Adjacent to the old terminus is a community of bungalows in a reservation that has the air of a private park. Here the officials of the railway have their residences. In less attractive surroundings at Iddo the junior and lesser officials are housed. In fact some of the housing accommodations here are so primitive that some of the men are given allowance, the same as the bush house rebate, on their pay.

On my first visit to Abutemeta I was bidden to luncheon at the home of the railway official and his wife who had so amiably helped me on my arrival in Lagos. Her house was similar to several of the neighboring bungalows. It was of modern design, two stories of cement with a garden and a built-in garage. Although she had been installed but six days she had already hung up some new, cheerful colored curtains, had spread out her personal knick-knacks—cushions, covers, silver and china ware.

In answer to my praise she assured me all was not as serene as appeared. My hostess had just found a tsetse fly in her living room. Besides the tsetse fly she had discovered her precious Scotch Kairn suffering from worms, and in addition during her sojourn in Port Harcourt the woman who had occupied the house in her absence had dug up and carted off her best and rarest variety of cannas. But to cap the climax that very day "Small Boy"—the impudent young black who was most untrained and could hardly understand English at all—had turned Bolshevik. His small vocabulary, however, had adequately served him to make her understand his demand for higher wages. More money he must have or he would leave her flat. However these domestic tragedies did not seem to have affected her very good looks or to have interfered with the repast, which was excellent.

Lunch finished and the usual siesta indulged in I was taken to Apapa to see the new docks, warehouses and railway yards. Apapa up to that time had cost the British government over three millions of pounds and was going to cost it as much again before completed.

The newly made road from the old to the new terminal had a way of disappearing over night, or of buckling up into impossible lumps. Already a long canal had been dug to drain the swamp through which it ran—a deep groove of orange-colored earth clean cut through the tangle of green. The wedge-shaped banks were quite a distance apart, as cleanly sliced as if a giant scoop had made a groove in a piece of cheese. Yet this whole V-shaped water channel had been excavated by hand. Hundreds of black boys had carried away the baskets of earth on their heads. Man power on the West Coast is cheaper than mechanical aid. A machine means supervision by a white man and a white man's salary in the budget more than offsets a large gang of natives.

Our motor car negotiated the road that day all right although the way was perilously spongy at times. A conduit line, resting on low posts paralleling the road, was so askew in places that it looked as if some mammoth animal had been playfully kicking it out of line. A few days later, when I wanted to revisit Apapa to take pictures, there had been another one of those periodical road slumps, and the way had to be negotiated in a motorcycle side car. In the deep spot all sorts of things had been slung to fill in quickly—scrap iron, cement blocks, poles, boards and even an old auto tonneau. From a few flat cars near at hand a swarm of black boys were trailing back and forth with baskets of sand on their heads.

I remember that one of the things which most displeased Sir Graeme Thompson in the play "White Cargo", as being an untrue representation of conditions on the West Coast, was the entrance on the stage of a steamer captain in bare feet. A British official, no matter how lowly, would never do that. After seeing Apapa it is hard to credit any of the scenes depicted in this drama with authenticity. Certainly times have changed. Now the large mail steamers can discharge passengers upon vast cement docks. A de luxe train, "the boat express" awaits those who go up-country. The first class (there is a second and a third class) have compartments of two berths each. It is a three-day journey to Kano. There are electric fans, washing cabinets and lavatories, darkened glass in the windows to keep out the glare, and a dining car.

Cargo ships can unload and load at the same time alongside the concrete and iron warehouses. Outgoing cargo is carried through the second story and incoming goes via the first floor from and to freight cars in a yard with eight or nine rows of railroad tracks and switches.

The railroad shops are a few miles inland, built in the modern unity style of construction—fireproof, light and airy—to which new units can constantly be added. To my surprise I found machines here of the very latest design. Steam engines were being completely dismantled and put together again. In the foundry most creditable castings were being turned out. In the carpenter and paint shop were being rebuilt old cars or entire new cars were being made. Even furniture and fittings were executed from the raw material. I saw finished chairs which would grace any grande dame's drawing room—all native made. In fact, in the whole plant there were only a few white overseers, not more than one or two to a department, while all the rest of the operatives were Africans.

Lagos abounds in contrasts of luxury and squalor. There are golf clubs, tennis courts, country clubs. At the latter on certain days members fore-gather at tables on the lawn in the late afternoon and early evening, and to the music of a band dance on the turf. The greensward of the tennis club is of a marvelously fine texture.

At Ecoy, a suburb on the mainland just across a narrow canal, are many recently built bungalows; some of simple and others of most expensive proportions. Yet in one of these, because the construction (home-designed in England) was so poorly adapted to the needs of the country a woman one day during her siesta when her bed was too near the window had a sunstroke, or a "touch of the sun" as they call it out there, because the inadequate overhang of the roof allowed the sun to come in and shine on her back.

On the Marina in Lagos, under a blossomming frangipani tree, I often took tea with the nursing sisters of the African hospital. New buildings will soon replace these where the natives even now receive more efficient care. At King's College near the race track is a campus surrounded by splendid stone dormitories and classrooms where the African may ap-pease his mental cravings at the feet of excellently trained head masters.

Yet I never went along Victoria Street that I did not want to close my eyes. I would look across the harbor at the marvels of modern Apapa—and then directly about me at the filth and crowded hovels. How could a people who had accomplished such a fine task across there let such another condition exist here. There are some in Lagos who pray every day that a chance fire may happen to clean up Victoria Street. Yet what a charity it would be if only some one might forestall the act of God.

On the water front is an open air laundry. Women with babies strapped to their backs bend over hogsheads of water. The newcomer to the Coast is always warned about where and how to get his clothes washed. Dobey itch as an affliction is not fatal, but it appears in the form of a pestilent rash which makes the sufferer feel as if he were teeming with every kind of itch known to humanity. It comes from impure water in cleaning clothes. One does not die of it, but at some stages death seems preferable.

Every one suffers from prickly heat—some more, some less. I was told that those who suffered most from it rarely came down with fever. I know my own body looked like a complete map of the constellations done in red—and I never had fever. Not that this proves anything.

There is no fresh milk in Lagos. An "iron-cow" at the dairy caters to the daily needs of the Europeans. Diminutive goats appease the wants of the natives. Eggs are scarce and small. Chickens are the size of pigeons. Chicken-raising is left to the natives who know nothing about it. Combined with inadequate shelter, dampness and no feeding, the poor mother hen rarely saves more than three chicks from the brood, and often not more than one. Yet one fond wife in Ecoy, because her husband like eggs, has built a small but good chicken run, and through intelligent care and feeding, raises eggs and chickens of normal size. She has had disasters, of course. Unaccountable losses of birds of fine stock, and so forth; but who in chicken raising the world over is not accustomed to poultry cataclysms! I must also hasten to add that she has one advantage because she is not of the government people—but is a trader's wife. She can return year after year to the same place and is not shunted about from one domicile to another as are those who serve their country.

With the government employee, however, she shares one common irritation—that is the billeted guest. As I have said before, there is no accommodation on the West Coast for the visiting stranger. There are no hotels either for the traveler, the trader or for the government official. No place for any one except at the homes of friends or at the home of a resident representative of his firm or of his country. Therefore any day a local agent must be prepared to share his bed and board with some visitor. Sometimes it it literally his bed unless the one who must depend upon his hospitality is put up in the dining room. There are few bungalows with guest rooms. This is all right if the stranger is of a congenial temperament to his host. It is a lonesome country at best and life for the gregarious person is hard, but one can imagine in such an atmosphere of imposed care and close association how antipathies and prejudices become magnified and how quickly they grow.

The situation is complicated rather than softened by the presence of a wife. In a land where so much of the food supply is dependent on cold storage stuff from ships, an extra mouth to feed, if one is caught when the larder is bare, becomes an embarrassment. Not that I heard any murmurs or complaints about this problem from those who are there. It is a duty and they perform it with a smile.

It was my privilege to see something of the home life of the people of Lagos. Not only of the propserous but also of the very modest resident. Besides that, I was a guest at the home of some black people, of two particulary—one was the leading lawyer and the other the most prominent merchant of the town.

I first had an opportunity of gauging Mr. Ajassa's apt wit on the occasion of the ceremony attending the retirement of a white judge. I came late to the Court House. The program was in full swing and Mr. Ajassa was on the up-tide of his discourse. I wanted very much to take pictures but the majesty of the British law always has scared me. I was so afraid of unconsciously transgressing or of hurting some one's feelings I dared nothing. To be a woman alone in Lagos was bad enough—but to stir up the old British Lion in a colony was far too much of a hazard even for me. Yet afterwards I found they were all disappointed I had not made an exposure while the ceremony was on. I sat on the back bench, camera in hand, most wistful—not daring and they not asking.

The court room might have been anywhere in England, the English *do* transplant themselves so thoroughly, except that two boys whisked a punkah over the judge's dais. In front of him grouped, leaning and lolling a bit, was a cluster of African lawyers. Their very much worn wigs were far from the color of driven snow and in some cases were too small for their round wooly pates. The climate had played havoc with many of their black silk robes—or perhaps the industrious cockroach was responsible for some of the rents and holes. I know a beautiful heavy silk dress of mine, the day before, had been the target of this pest's appetite. Garments of much frailer fabrics weathered the whole trip. Such are the many inconsequentialities of the tropics. . . .

# Lagos and Abeokouta

To an American accustomed to having the social status of the negro, and his contact with the white race, so rigidly defined in his own country, the conditions prevailing both in the French and British colonies of West Africa were at first somewhat startling. Prejudices had to be instantly readjusted.

Yet even with the situation of equality cultivated so sedulously there is considerable stress and strain felt on both sides in the admixture socially of the white and the black. The burden as usual falls on the woman—on the educated negress. The black man constantly meets the white man in business. At least ninety per cent of all the jobs of trade and government are held by Africans. But the woman, after she leaves school can rarely continue any social contact with another white woman. Occasionally she may meet a white man. I know of a case where a brother sometimes brought his sister of an evening to the bachelor quarters in Lagos of some white men with whom he negotiated business. There are young negro women in Lagos, of well-to-do parents, who drive their own motor cars. They dress in quite the latest fashion and have been educated in England. In Britain they may have been received socially, but not now in Lagos. It is not uncommon in London to see a white woman with a negro or vice versa.

On certain occasions at Government House the Africans are invited with the Europeans. A bid for either black or white man to one of these functions is a command. A valid excuse must be given for inattendance. But as one promiment negro merchant confided to me, it was never a soirée of joy for any one of them. This trying to fraternize didn't fool him. He knew, and they knew, just how far to go—which wasn't very far. At the reception, after the first intermingled greetings were made, he and his wife would have to walk around and around until tired out, wishing mightily all the time they could go home. But the invitation had stipulated certain hours for the affair and it would be *lèse-majesté* to leave before the specified time.

I did not hear of one case of a white man marrying a black woman. . . The Britishers were quite unanimous in saying that no minister on the Coast if called upon to do so would ever perform a marriage ceremony between a white man and a negro woman, not even with a half-caste person. However, at least eighty per cent of the men who go out to the Coast cohabit with the native women. Some men openly live with their dark mistresses. There must be some appeal. Men return time after time on each of their tours to the same woman. In one case there was such an attachment that when the wife of the white man was coming out to join him, the night before her arrival the negress and the white man spent the hours together in tears—a genuine agony on both sides at the thought of separation.

These black women are clean in their personal habits. They demand little and are almost always good-natured. Those who have relations with a white man are not highly regarded by their own kind. It is only since the European came that the African woman has taken up the profession of the courtesan. She has learned to walk the streets—not to ensnare those of her own color who would beat her—but to lie in wait for the white.

My eerie perch on the balcony of the Bonanza was made sleepless many a night by the Anne-Fanny motor cars which would line up in front of the gin parlor. They would chug-chug their engines to attract the attention of those within until I was fairly ready to scream. I watched women in the shadow of these cars loitering, peeping, waiting, for some half-drunk person to start on his way home.

Once I saw two men go across the road to a motor cycle which was parked across the way. A black girl had been waiting beside it. I heard the men quarrelling over her. Finally one jumped into the side seat, pulled the girl down on his knees, and with arms locked, fervently kissing her, waited for the other man to start the engine. Finally the three disappeared down the street.

The Bonanza was opposite the tennis courts and gardens which belonged to Glover Hall. The building was on the corner—a sort of public clubhouse which could be hired by anyone. From my balcony I could see under the back porches and into the hall. One stifling night the music from a band over there kept me awake. Finally I went out on my own balcony for a breath of air. What I saw made me run back and get my opera glasses to be sure my eyes were not deceiving me. Negro men were dancing with white women! Black hands were on pale backs! Some months later on my way to Madagascar, when I told this to a British officer from Mauritius, he said it couldn't possibly be so! It was inconceivable that any of his country women—even in the colonies—would ever do such a thing. But there was the evidence of my own eyes. I noticed when the dancers sauntered out on the porch that the little group of white women clustered together away from their darker sisters.

There are about seven white women in Lagos married to negros. What their life is can only be conjectured. They are pariahs to both races. Usually the woman was some hard working girl from England who had been won by tales of the riches and princely importance at home of her dusky suitor. Too late she learned the real conditions.

In the afternoons after four o'clock the two tennis courts back of Glover Hall were filled with players. One day some English clerks would hire the place. On another it would be negroes, dressed in the height of sport fashions. Their observance of the phases and the courtesies of the game was punctilious, an exceedingly British accent larded on the swagger of the dark race. Even so the negroes more often than not played a much better set than the whites.

The sick husband of the household I was expected to visit recovered and helped me to many avenues of information. One day he made an appointment for me to meet Mr. Pearse at his home. Mr. Pearse was one of the outstanding figures of the rich negro merchants of Lagos. He sent me helpful books and other literature of the West Coast.

One day Mr. F—— and his wife took me to Elephant House, an important-looking edifice near the water front. We were shown at once to the top story to get a view of Lagos. Nearly the whole of this floor was given over to a sort of social hall—billiard and music-room in one. There was a huge orchestrion of German origin. The sausage-like music-rolls it swallowed were the size of a small satchel. Time and weather had not improved the mechanism. Even a slight diminuendo was not in its capacity. Going always at full blast, it made conversation almost impossible. After some futile attempts we sipped our warm champagne in silence. I for one was quite fascinated by the little baby grandchild who was brought in—a wee, black mite. I had never held one in my arms before.

It was arranged that I should visit the Alake of Abeokouta. This potentate holds sway over some dozens of square miles in the Yorrabu [Yoruba] country, up-country above Lagos, over the Egba tribe, a people who have had a rather turbulent history. They have conquered and been conquered by neighboring tribes and at one time were even besieged and subjugated by the King of Dahomey. There is now an authentic record of a line of kings or Alakes since the early part of the last century. The tenure of their rulers seems always to have been of short duration. . . . One of their last Alakes—as is the present one—was not a lineal descendant of the old rulers, but was chosen by a council of chiefs.

The principality of the Egbas is one of the few semi-independent communities left in Nigeria since the British occupation. That is, the Alake administrates his state independently but is subject to supervision from the British mandate of Lagos. For his stewardship he draws two thousand pounds a month. Even the Sultan of Zanzibar does not enjoy a more affluent allowance.

The missionaries came to Abeokouta in 1846. With them came Samuel

Crowther—a black lad who had escaped from slavery and who afterwards became a bishop of the Anglican Church. He was the first colored prelate to administer the sacrament and to baptize children in the cathedral of Liverpool. He translated the Bible into the Yorrabu language.

On the day appointed for us to go to see the Alake, Mrs. F—— called for me in her automobile. We picked up Mr. Pearse, who had arranged the audience. That morning and the preceding day there had been two violent tornadoes. I feared we would not start as a motor car going over the same route the day before had skidded and the occupants had been quite badly hurt. In fact, one was the very same doctor whom I saw hiking to the beach.

I confess that even my travel-hardened nerves were constantly set on edge by our own lightning rate of travel. Much of the road was on a high embankment curving through the bush. The top was barely wide enough for one motor car. The recent heavy rains had washed away the outer dressing of laterite, which is decomposed granite used to solidify the road bed. The banks shelved down steeply on either side. In spite of the slippery road, the negro chauffeur took all the curves at top speed. Mrs. F—— from the back seat would feebly admonish him to go "Softly— softly!" The word "softly" is of elastic interpretation. If one is being helped to too much ground nut stew, or an excess of whiskey is being poured out—"softly—softly" stops the flow. It alters the noisy shutting of a blind or regulates the pace of someone carrying a precious burden.

There was not much variation of landscape. There never is in the bush. The country about Abeokouta is high and open. Peculiarly shaped crags, sombre groups of rocks appeared here and there. In some of these were caves in which the natives in the earlier days once lived.

On arriving, Mr. Pearse went off to see the Alake to arrange the details of the meeting. . . .

The Palace and the Ju-ju house stretched along the back line of the square court yard. The former was a two-story, gray-shingled frame house of simple design. The Ju-ju temple was a long low building. An overhanging roof shadowed the open front. Weird symbols, groestque animals and figures were carved on the supports and painted in gaudy colors. I wanted to stop and look at them but the boy hastened us on.

We entered the main door of the Palace and followed the servant up a flight of stairs which led to a balcony from which some rooms opened. When he got to the last three steps our cicerone stopped and very deliberately shuffled his feet and cleared his throat. This was a signal to Mr. Pearse who, having had lunch with the Alake, was discussing affairs of state over some "schnapps" in an inner room. We heard chairs hurriedly pushed back. As Mr. Pearse hastened out to greet us I caught sight of a tall figure disappearing behind a frosted glass door. The drawing room adjoined this dining room. Windows between them, frosted half way up, augmented the light. While Mr. Pearse was bidding us welcome I was watching an active shadow behind one of those panes. Now and again a reaching motion would send a long skinny arm up above the frosted pane, and I could see real flesh poking through folds of yellow drapery.

I took the opportunity to ask Mr. Pearse if he would ask the Alake to pose for me. Our interpreter rolled his eyes and looked very doubtful. That was a request I must make myself, the inference being that I alone must be responsible for the royal displeasure in case the request was denied.

At this juncture his majesty appeared. His six feet six inches were resplendent in flowing folds of canary-colored brocade, embroidered here and there in a soft jade green. It was a fabric one's fingers itched to touch. His crown was less satisfying, an affair of stage jewels, a mixture of a bishop's mitre and a duke's coronet. Imitation or not, he had probably paid a good price for it. On a table in the room I had espied some other crowns. They were much more interesting—all done in small cream-colored glass beads with strange elongated animals moulded in the round straddling across the head bands. Each halo, Mr. Pearse explained, was used on some one or other particular occasion for which its design had a special significance.

For a moment I had a fleeting urge to ask the Alake to try them all on for me but I did not dare. Besides, His Highness was distinctly fluttered. He shook hands in democratic fashion and then sat down. His nervousness showed in the way he pressed his hands together and as he spoke his voice slipped way up into a trembling falsetto, while an intermittent high-pitched laugh revealed far-spaced and much filed-down teeth. On several of his fingers he had native made gold rings of most unusual shapes. I wanted to ask him about them too but had to keep my mind on the photograph.

In a few minutes he got used to us and the tremor left his voice. A very tiny black girl came in with glasses and a bottle of champagne. While Mr. Pearse was negotiating the cork the Alake showed Mrs. F—— and myself the press notices of his predecessor's visit to London and the Bible presented to him by Queen Victoria. In a short time he had not only consented to sit for a photograph but had commanded a slave to bring in two ostrich eggs. They had been laid by the imperial birds and were sucked by His Majesty himself. On these with a fountain pen he inscribed our names and his own title.

Now began the serious business of posing. We went out on the glass-enclosed balcony for better light. Just as I was about to shoot a time exposure the Alake recalled he had neglected to bring along his sceptre.

We all rushed back to the drawing room to help hunt for it. Mrs. F——
picked up a feather-duster looking affair. I pooh-poohed it and was trying
to restrain her from presenting it to him when the Alake himself on the
opposite side of the room picked up a similar tufted wand with perhaps a
few more highly colored Ju-ju symbols on the handle. With it, his crown
and his robe, his great stature, and now a solemnly benign expression, he
looked quite regal.

The exposure taken, I ventured to ask the Alake about the men we had
seen downstairs when we had nearly gone in the wrong door. I had had a
glimpse of the crowd of somewhat grizzled, half-naked men wrapped in
toga-like draperies of deep rich tones, squatting or half-lying on the floor.
The modern touch in this primitive tableau was that of bottles of beer with
gaudy labels standing around on the floor.

These were his ministers of state, the Alake informed me. "May I take
their pictures?" I asked. "Certainly," he said, "we will go right down." In
her haste Mrs. F——, forgetting the presence of royalty, started to descend
the stairs in front of him. The frown encompassing his visage she must
have felt right through the back of her neck, because before she had gone a
couple of steps she turned in an embarrassment of belated remembrance
and excused herself. Then, bless her heart, with a gesture of apology she
kept right on going ahead of him.

The Alake, when we got to the bottom, now preceded us to the doorway
of the council chamber. It was evident that those within were not at once
aware of his presence. He peeped around at us like a small boy, as much as
to say "Wait and watch the fun." With a swish-swish of his sceptre he
tapped on the door lintel and sing-songed a phrase or two. There was an
immediate turmoil. The ministers prostrated themselves on the floor, or
crawling on their bellies, voicing loud protestations, they wriggled along
and kissed his feet. Still waving his sceptre he looked around at us with a
satisfied infantile smirk of delight. The expression in his eyes so plainly
said, "See what a big toad am I!"

During the fealty demonstration bottles had been knocked over and
others hastily gathered up. I followed the Alake into the dark interior, but
as the ministers gathered around, I protested to him that there was not
enough light, the picture must be taken outside. Orders were given and we
all repaired to the courtyard. There was much confusion. The Alake
wished to sit under a royal umbrella. In the meantime a Ju-ju man,
gorgeous in colored robes, had appeared outside the temple with some of
his satellites, and beat a drum continuously, meanwhile dancing and
jigging. I took some shots at him unawares while the ministers, like
temperamental mummers lining up, were edging each other off the front
center stage. I didn't help matters much when I asked them to make the

circle around the Alake even a little smaller. However the Alake quieted his followers, ending discussion with curt imperial suggestions as to which one should stand forward, the other back. These old fellows, now on their feet, one shoulder bare, their draperies gracefully swinging, looked more than ever like ancient Romans. I longed for a color camera. The hues of their robes, their dark skins, the canary trappings of the Alake, were all so gorgeous. One imperial umbrella, the Alake now decided, was not enough for the importance of the occasion. Some slaves scurried off and came back with another gold-fringed one. The Alake, disdainful of the sun, then sat between them. . . .

# *The Mahogany Hunt*

The belt of mahogany trees lies rather far inland in Nigeria—more so than on the rest of the Coast. From Lagos it is necessary to go back country fifty or sixty miles into the interior before finding a monarch of the forest. The giant trees are felled by the natives during the early months of the year, in the dry season. They then haul the logs to the nearest creek bed and wait for the tornado season to fill up the stream so the tree trunks can be floated down the tortuous lanes and so on to the wider tributaries and thus on to Lagos.

The white dealers on the Coast contract with the black for so many logs to be delivered before the cutting begins. This is where the trouble starts, for the negro is an adept when it comes to short changing the European. If the proper amount of timber does not arrive at flood tide then some one has to be sent up into the bush to investigate.

I got wind of one of these expeditions and decided that I wanted to go along. At first when I suggested the idea it was deemed impossible. No white woman had ever done it. In fact very few white men had stood the strain of the long trek in the bush on foot. Part of the discouragement proffered was that it would be necessary to go some of the way on a bicycle. At least it would save time. That was all right, I insisted, I knew how to ride a bicycle. How long ago I had learned I did not divulge, or what an age it was since I had put foot on a pedal. I was determined to do away with all obstacles. Insistence finally won out. However all plans were nearly upset the day before we were to start. One of the two Englishmen who were going on the expedition got laid up with a touch of fever. The other one happily decided to start out anyway, with the native interpreter. So I begged to go along just the same, stressing the argument that I would be of so little trouble neither of them would know I was in the party.

I borrowed some shorts from the tallest man in Lagos. These abbreviated, khaki knickers on a male person leave the knees bare. But in my wise calculation the trousers loaned to me came down almost to my shin-bones. To keep out wild animals and insects I gathered them under my knees with a garter. The long shirt, with nicely tailored pockets, which I let hang outside, loose like a blouse, reached nearly to my knees. Fortunately I had high, thick hunting boots of my own. My white helmet, green lined, and my bright rose-colored scarf, a protection for my spine, completed the costume.

I do not insert this description of my clothes in a spirit of vanity. During the trip I went into villages where no white woman had ever been seen. I regretted I was not a greater credit, at least in matter of dress, to my sex. It was something of a responsibility to be the first mannikin on view in a jungle fashion show. However an advantage accrues to those who may follow after me. They won't find it much trouble to raise the standard of style already created by my feeble representation in Miss Black Dame's mind.

On the day appointed we started off in a motor car at six in the morning. On the back of the machine was strapped a bicycle which had been procured for me. Two other wheels for the two men would be hired at the native village of Otta, forty miles inward.

The blacks love bicycles. They ride them with bare toes. It was astonishing to find in communities way up in the bush there would be at least one lad who owned one. In some most remote places there were even repair shops where as many as a dozen wheels could be seen propped up against surrounding palm trees awaiting attention.

Otta was quite a sizeable village. It was a junction for many trails leading out into the bush. The native-fashioned houses were of mud with grass roofs. Several open-faced stores displayed European wares.

As we drove into the village our automobile pressed too near a post. It caught the out-lapping end of my bicycle and crumpled one wheel into a futuristic pattern—that was the end of that! Luckily three bicycles were found in the village for hire, but of course they were all men's bicycles.

Our motor car was left in the care of a worthy black citizen, while a native boy with the "chop" box on his head was sent on foot in advance of us. Now came the moment when I must show my skill on my iron steed. I was a bit daunted at the unexpected complication of having to mount a "he-male" bicycle. I had never been on one before. How in the world, I quavered to myself, was I going at a moment's notice to master the technique of deftly swinging one leg over the wheel and hop on the saddle. With the two men steadying my steed I climbed on while they ran alongside to start me off. The ground of the village square was hard, so in spite of much inward shaking, and a wobbling front wheel, a little run around of practice put some confidence in me—and the hope that I would grow steadier by experience.

I started off in the lead on the path indicated. Once on my way I dared not stop. There was no way for me to get off my bicycle, but to fall off. The thought so dithered me that my front wheel wobbled more perilously than ever and developed a most disquieting tendency of running off side at any little object. The road, as we got out of the village, narrowed down to a primitive path. It wasn't long before I just couldn't help running into a tree. To cover my confusion, when the men hurried to pick me up I suggested that the saddle of my wheel was a little high—a little high! my heavens, it seemed as if I had dropped from the Eiffel Tower—no less!

The seat was adjusted and I was started off again. The meandering lane through the bush had now become criss-crossed with roots alternating with mud bogs. The pedals were my misery. When they locked I would loose my foot out of the clip and nearly tumble off trying to get my toe back in it again. In the pre-historic era of my early biking days we didn't have any such intricate contraptions. One just kept one's feet going around all the time.

The very sight of an oncoming native with a bulky head burden—although he nimbly dodged me—made me land in another tumble. This wasn't such a bad spill, but it seemed to worry the two men. I feebly suggested there was something wrong with the pedals. To my relief they really did find the chain a bit long or something, so it was altered.

Davis—the interpreter—was now made to take the lead to warn any oncoming pedestrians, and also to point out to me any special obstructions in the path. By now I wanted to tumble off all the time, longed to feel real earth, even if it was mud, under my feet instead of a wheel which skidded sickeningly in the ooze. It was not long before I had my wish. My painful concentration on the immediate foreground prevented me from noticing Davis (he was a short way ahead) when he slowed up to point out an extra large bulging root across the path. The Englishman behind me evidently was wool-gathering. Besides, he couldn't see around me anyway. Before any of us could think I had run into Davis, the Englishman had jammed his wheel into mine and we all fell in a heap.

My knees were knocking when I got up. I was in despair. I couldn't go on this way any more. There were five more miles that we would make on the wheels. I said I would walk the rest of the distance. This was favorably received. Davis was sent on ahead to get to the creek as soon as possible, where he could leave his own wheel in the care of someone and return to get mine. In the meantime we would keep coming on foot and push the bicycles. After those long five miles I am quite aware of why the Britishers call them *push*-bikes. The sun beating down on the tree-tops made the jungle stiflingly hot. In places the tangled undergrowth thinned out, or there was a clearing of cut trees. Even so, with much shade and the sun filtering through only in spots, the damp heat was exhausting. Davis coming back to meet us and relieve me of my wheel was a most welcome sight. . . .

The canoes were more primitive, heavy and clumsy than any I had seen before, but ours was generously large and easily accommodated the three wheels, ourselves, and two natives who did the poling. We floated silently and smoothly along this watery pathway, with the trees meeting overhead. All the world was one monotone of green. The quiet was soon broken by sounds ahead, voices and the splashing of water. We drifted into a more open space and way ahead of us saw the mud houses of a village. Near the bank lined up thigh deep alongside of a mahogany log were women laving, beating and wringing out cotton garments.

A tremendous chatter greeted us as we approached. Suddenly it died to utter silence. One or two women broke away and ran up the bank. Some just stood—rooted—staring—spellbound. I was the first white woman they had ever seen! The children recovered first and ran in and out around us, getting underfoot as the bicycles were unloaded. The children were naked, but the women wore Sunday cloths around their hips even as they stood in the water.

We were guided to the house of the tailor. Inquiries were started as to the whereabouts of the logging pirate we had come to see. The orange-colored ground around the mud walls of the houses was packed down hard. In the clearing was not even a spear of green, although the heavy tangle of the bush was just beyond, cut as if with a knife. The village covered about an acre.

The house of the tailor had a grass-thatched lean-to in front of it. Under this we sat waiting for the native log contractor. He did not materialize. In his stead a black-bearded person appeared with the long muzzle of a queer looking firearm over his shoulder. He was the contractor's "carpenter". He would take us to his boss who was up another creek getting out the logs. By "carpenter" he meant he was the one who cut down the trees. The natives have no large saws to fell the trees but chip away at the great trunks with small axes. After felling, they dig pits under the prostrate trunks and hand strip, and sometimes shape up the logs. We had come across one or two of these pits on the way up, where the chip-covered ground attested to the patient, slow, hand labor.

Following our new guide, we now went to the canoe. The barrel of his old muzzle loader had so many kinks and curves in it I am sure he could have shot anything around the corner, almost around two corners. Smeared over the stock and near the trigger was some dark red, semi-translucent stuff in which were embedded small shells and other fetish trinkets. This he told our interpreter was good Ju-ju "to make the meat come."

This time we had only one man to pole because one man in the bow armed with a machete had to cut away overhanging branches. The stream was swift and narrow. Sometimes the curves were so sharp we could not get around them with one turn but had to go back and fill, like a big motor car wedging into a small parking space. The stream grew narrower, the overhanging bush thicker and thicker. It was soon evident that our canoe was too long to make the journey, so reluctantly we backed down stream again to Iju.

There we once more repaired to the house of the tailor. He had brought out a standard sewing machine and was busy stitching up long lengths of the flowing garments which are worn by the Hauserman.

It was time for chop. The capable Davis produced out of the box a tablecloth, knives and forks, meat pie, bread and butter, canned fruit, soda, beer and gin. All of Iju watched us eat. The little children especially went off into gales of laughter as we consumed our food.

Some of the little girls were very scrawny and undeveloped while others, eight or nine years old, looked very mature. Davis with a little cajolery was led to demonstrate that if he was not afraid to let me take his own picture why would not some of the little girls pose alone for a photograph? Davis felt very important in this matter. The Englishman told me that the black helper was making great capital out of this expedition and was bragging about escorting a lady journalist who was going to put his picture in the paper.

Davis was a widower, a lad not much over twenty. He was preparing to buy another bride. In fact he would soon have the price. Of course they would be married in church very properly, just as he and his first wife had been. When Davis first came to the Englishmen he received a pound a month. Besides being valet, laundryman and messenger, he had horned in on office duties. He soon proved to be such a dependable clerk managing outside work so well—assembling the logs when they arrived in Lagos and getting them dispatched on various cargo boats—that he was now drawing down the princely income of three pounds ten. It was now but a matter of a short time, even with the present high price of wives, when he would have enough to purchase the lady of his choice.

Chop done, our hunter man appeared again to guide us up to "the big tree". This was a most exhausting hike of about five or six miles because it was undertaken between one and two o'clock in the afternoon when the sun beats down the hardest. Much of the way ahead had to be cut for us. At other times we would traverse a clearing where the cottonwood trees lay prone on the ground. We had to crawl up and over one after another of these recumbent monarchs. A long series of these high hurdles wellnigh finished me. In the clearings between the fallen trees yams had already been planted in little earth hills by some hopeful farmer.

At last, when even the Englishman was growing sceptical about ever arriving at the big tree, we suddenly came upon two of them, one already fallen and the trunk of the other a third of the way hacked through. Their huge bulk dwarfed all of the other growth around them. They seemed so majestic, like some great wounded things, that I had the illusion we ought to talk in whispers. From the bed of chips about the base came the pleasant smell of resin. The Englishman inspected the work and the two men, after a little consultation, started back. We dared not linger for we must take a side trip to a clearing where the contractor lived, in hopes of finding him there. We were quite four miles from Iju from where we must still push on to Otta and arrive at least by dusk—a matter of a twelve-mile hike.

The contractor's village was a small patch of waving corn tassels. The growth was up and over our heads. But our man was not there. As natives go, he was rich, and bragged of having some forty wives. A dozen or so of them came running out to meet us. They stood still, puzzled, when they caught sight of me. Davis interrupted their trance-like stares by suggesting they get something for me to sit on. After much hunting about, for they had never seen a chair, a small box-like affair of bamboo was provided and placed under the low-thatched eaves of a hut. The women waited about in groups, looking me all over. For some of them my appearance was apparently too much. As they talked me over, they giggled and stared and stared and giggled again. Although naked above the waist they wore Sunday cloths about their loins, kerchiefs on their heads and—*European earrings!*

I was sitting outside their husband's quarters. Inside the mud structure all was very neat and tidy. There was actually a bed with some coverings but hardly any other furniture, certainly no chairs.

The first time the women had ever seen a white man was when the two Englishmen had come to this place on a former trip. The two men on that expedition were going further up country so they had to stay here over night. The contractor, as a mark of hospitality and to show how honored he felt at their visit "dashed" each of the two white men with one of his wives. It was with difficulty that the visitors convinced all concerned that having perfectly good spouses at home they must refrain from his proffered hospitality.

The wives did not know what a camera was. At least they did not seem afraid of it but stood still in a wondering sort of way while in my efforts to get good shots of them I walked about, sometimes towards them, at other times viewing them from a distance. They were getting almost too interested when they were distracted by the arrival of a native woman with a child on her back. On her head was a basket tray piled high with all sorts of cheap gew-gaws' such as one finds in the five-and-ten-cent stores. This explained the earrings. She must have walked the seventeen miles from Otta.

Their mother's attention now diverted, the children clustered about me. In order to keep them far enough away to take snapshots I threw, now and then, some African pennies in the air for which they scrambled like any small fry the world over. When I stopped their mothers extracted from the pickaninnies most of their winnings. We soon departed. All of them followed us well out of the place, laughing, hallooing, gesticulating, crying out a native sort of godspeed. In that village, if my personal appearance was not admired, at least my beneficence will not be forgotten. I wondered how many more earrings the woman pedlar would sell and what friend husband would say when he saw his well-bedecked harem. . . .

It was now late in the afternoon. We must hasten. Our bicycles were again stacked in the canoe. We floated slowly along the silent, tree-roofed channel. The swish of the poles lifting out of the water was the only sharp sound. The hush, the heat, the slanting rays of sun filtering through the green barrier, the glinting of light spots upon the long sweeping and dangling ropes of parasitic vines, the shut-in-ness of it all, the monotone of green—these helped an illusion that this was an unreal world, a painted scene, the gigantic stage setting of a Wagnerian opera or an act in a Reinhart phantasy.

Even the appearance of a native woman coming through the water did not dispel the fantasy. Her clothes, in a neat bundle, were balanced on her head; her baby, head lolling backwards, was almost on her shoulders for the woman was nearly breast deep in the water. She was proceeding slowly. I could divine from the motions of her body that she was gingerly placing her bare toes in the slime and rocks on the bottom, fearful of losing her balance. Behind her, the water almost to his chin, a boy followed timorously, skinny arms stretched waveringly towards her, reaching for, but never quite touching, his mother.

As we neared the end of the creek a man came surging through the water, hurrying to Iju. His garment was rolled up tight and balanced on his head. The water swished and rippled from his hasty pace. I do not remember hearing any birds or seeing any other living thing.

After we left the canoe, it was a steady climb through the forest. The path was very muddy and criss-crossed with numberless roots which made treacherous, stubbly bumps even for walking. The sun was not yet low enough to make it safe to take off our helmets. Even in the jungle one must be cautious. By now I was terribly tired but would not admit it to the two men. My flagging spirit was revived by little swarms of butterflies which darted out at my approach and winged up the path ahead of me. I adore butterflies. These were of those rare varieties for which the collector pines. There they were fluttering, capering in front of me, cajoling my laggard limbs to give chase.

A huge tree lying across our path was an excuse for a short rest. Just as we were about to move on, two weeny little black girls, quite naked, came down towards us. On their heads were basket trays wider than the children were tall, filled with palm kernels. The obstructing log halted them. It was too high for them to climb over it with the burdens on their heads and they didn't have strength enough in their slender little arms to lift the baskets over the high obstruction. The Englishman with helpful intent, quickly aware of their dilemma as the little girls paused, swiftly lifted one child up, head load and all. Everything went well until he, leaning way over the log, tried to deposit her on the ground on the other side. One little degree of tilting too much sent the basket flying, scattering the kernels all over the place.

Profiting by this disaster he took the basket off the other child's head and held it while she pulled herself over the great round trunk. The wee mites began silently gathering up the kernels. They did not even speak to each other, but would indicate by gestures where was an an overlooked group of kernels. Perhaps the catastrophe and consequences of it had rendered them dumb because soon their better attuned ears heard the pat-pat of bare feet on the path. Shortly two women appeared, each almost hidden under a bulky load of greens. We were just in the act of giving the little ones some pennies. The women scolded the tiny tots and tried to take away the coins from the children. In sign language we protested vigorously. Grumbling and muttering the women continued on their way, leaving the girls to shift for themselves.

The scattered kernels were now all assembled. The two small figures stood opposite each other with one tray on the ground between them. Both girls with little grunts, for it was terribly heavy for their skinny little arms, succeeded in raising the basket about shoulder high. Then one, still holding the container, ducked shoulders and head under it, and straightened up very gradually and warily. This burdened one in turn now aided her companion. That was some trick with a heavy load on her own head. Gingerly she began to squat, with careful attention to the balancing of her tray, and helped lift the other basket shoulder high, while her vis-à-vis repeated the maneuver of getting her head under the tray. The little faces were solemn with the effort. Such a strain for tiny bodies! Settling their loads with little hands upraised to help the balance, they turned and without a word or a backward look marched down the path.

It was dusk when we reached the outskirts of Otta. The village seemed to have grown in size since morning—it took us such a time to get to the main square. I just made the grade; one step more and I would have fallen flat. I dropped in a heap on the seat of the motor car. While the men were busy with preparations I was glad the shadowy light and a protecting elbow over my face made it impossible for them to see that I indulged in a few quiet tears. Every muscle pained like a boil. After a few minutes of rest and a tot of proffered gin and soda, I felt better and was a little ashamed of my weakness.

The villagers began to crowd around, the ring ever enlarging. There surely must have been two or three hundred of them packed in a close ring by the car, so near I could touch them with my elbow. Silent for the most part they stared and stared, that steady, bland gaze of the absorbed dullard. In the semi-light the phalanx of dark faces so close looked a bit uncanny and got on my nerves. I could appreciate the phobia confessed to me by a young bank clerk in Lagos—that after months and months of nothing else he got so the sight of black fingers constantly reaching under the wicket for coins nearly drove him frantic.

The forty miles motor ride back to Lagos blew away my "crise de nerves". We arrived about ten o'clock. After a warm bath at the company's bungalow (the first and only time I ever got hot water in Lagos) and a good dinner, I danced for a couple of hours in spite of the strenuous day. . . .

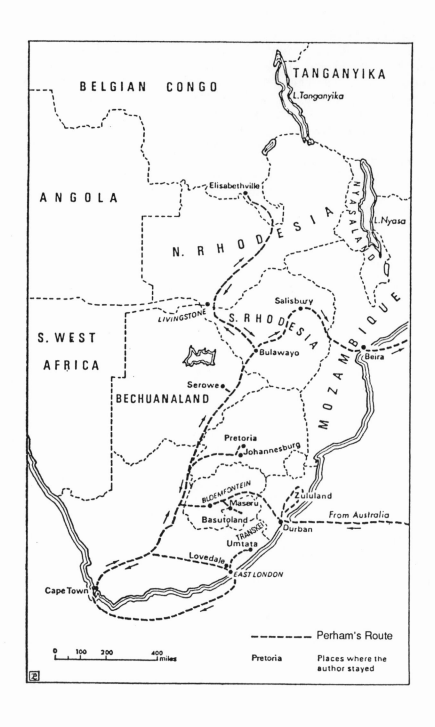

BELGIAN CONGO

TANGANYIKA

L. Tanganyika

ANGOLA

Elisabethville

N. RHODESIA

NYASALAND

L. Nyasa

S. WEST

AFRICA

LIVINGSTONE

S. RHODIESIA

Salisbury

MOZAMBIQUE

Bulawayo

Beira

BECHUANALAND

Serowe

Pretoria

Johannesburg

BLOEMFONTEIN

Maseru

Zululand

Basutoland

From Australia

TRANSKEI

Durban

Umtata

Lovedale

EAST LONDON

Cape Town

0   100   200   400 miles

– – – – –   Perham's Route

Pretoria   Places where the
author stayed

# MARGERY PERHAM*
# (Southern Africa, 1929)

Dame Margery Perham began life in Harrogate where her father was a prosperous businessman. The youngest of seven children but one of only two girls, Perham's early stated goal in life was to become "a big-game hunter in Africa." She read Kipling (whose works should have "turned me against hunting"). And the romantic Rider Haggard whose books "gave me the Africa I dreamed about." But "what hope could there be for a child, a female child at that, and at the turn of the century, of getting to Africa, least of all of becoming a hunter?"

Perham got to Africa, not as a great white hunter, but as a result of a nervous breakdown. Her schooling was inconsistent in her youth, going in and out of boarding schools at the whim of her much-traveled mother. Finally, however, Perham settled into an Anglican boarding school, where she was personally unhappy (she missed her older brother, Edgar), but where she excelled in her studies. At the encouragement of the head-mistress, Perham studied for and passed the entrance examination for Oxford, just as World War I began to draw away male scholars. Although Margery and her beloved Edgar overlapped one year at Oxford, the war took him away to die in France.

Perham was anxious to volunteer for war work, but was encouraged to finish Oxford before "I managed to get out with the army lecturing on Salisbury Plain and in northern France." When the war ended, Perham was faced with a decision as to what she would do with her life. "I definitely did *not* want to teach," she wrote, yet because of the "flood of men" returning to university, Perham accepted a post at Sheffield. It was not a happy time in her life: "I was alone in a strange grimy city. I was not welcomed at the University. I was the first woman appointed to the academic staff."

There were no facilities for women at Sheffield, and no intentions of mixing gender among the faculty. Perham was assigned a small, dark, and cold "commons room" (hers alone). She took cheap quarters in the city because her parents were retiring and she was "determined to be indepen-

---

*Margery Perham, *African Apprenticeship: An Autographical Journey in Southern Africa in 1929,* New York: Africana Publishers, 1974, 20–53, 86–95, 124–126, 191–203. Reprinted with permission.

*Margery Perham*

dent." Although Perham makes no mention of Edgar beyond noting his death in France, it is possible that she had not allowed herself to mourn this most loved of her siblings. With her parents away on the Channel Islands, and finding herself mostly ignored by faculty peers at Sheffield, Perham became ill and depressed.

Her doctor ordered a year of rest. Fate intervened, too, in the form of her older sister, who was then living in British Somaliland. Having gone to East Africa to become a missionary, Perham's sister met and married a businessman instead. They became pioneer settlers on the Juba River in "wild, hardly tamed Somali country." The invitation to come and stay in East Africa fulfilled in part Perham's childhood dream; but, the reality was far different as during her preparations for departure, she realized "[I] was about to commit myself to that black continent across the water. . . ." The early recognition of what she referred to as "racial fear" passed "and I have never felt it again, not on the Somali frontier or later in any situation or danger or isolation in any part of Africa. Even . . . at night alone in the African slums of Durban."

Perham's adventures in Somalia were notable principally because she was with family who had good connections with the local administration. She enjoyed her stay—part of that first experience in Africa is included below. Now recuperated, Perham returned to Sheffield where she became the first woman to receive a Rhodes Trust Traveling Fellowship and set off to study the "race problem" that eventually landed Perham in South Africa, where we pick her up in the final selection from her memoir.

The romance of Africa, which Rider Haggard pictured in novel form, was briefly that of Margery Perham when she and the handsome Assistant Commissioner of Maseru toured parts of Basutoland together. From there she visited both black and white South Africa: the political arena, courts, colleges, and private homes. She met white professors, black labor leaders, and the inevitable missionaries. And, no matter where she went, or whom she was querying, we recognize the piercing quality of her intellect as she probed beneath the surface of this racially divided land.

Receiving the female equivalent of knighthood towards the end of her life, Perham was something of a role model to the many academic women who followed her in increasing numbers, especially to those with an interest in Africa. To these women, Perham was full of grit and determination (although some men found her crusty). She represented a bridge between the old pseudo-scientific racist notions of Africa inferiority and the more egalitarian attitudes prevalent today.

## *Prologue*

We disembarked at Aden and my first experience of tropical heat was to have it thrown back at me like a blow from this place of solid rock. We stayed at a dingy hotel in the middle of the town—hellishly hot. I looked out from a rickety balcony on to the crowds seething below—Yemenis and Arabs of many other kinds, Somalis, Jews, Indians—also of many kinds—and Negroes—all dark, brown to black, alien, unknown, unknowable. Next day we were to cross the Gulf of Aden to Berbera to live almost alone and far inland among a population of dark people. I had an overwhelming spasm of recoil, of something more than physical fear. I referred to this in one of my Reith Lectures—a revulsion against the thought that I—how can I express it?—I, so white, so vulnerable, so sensitive, so complex, was about to commit myself to that black continent across the water; one, almost alone, among tens of thousands of strange, dark, fierce, uncomprehending people, and live away on that far frontier, utterly cut off from my own race. It was more like a nightmare than a natural revulsion. I suppose it was racial fear. It passed and I have never felt it again, not on the Somali frontier or later in any situation of danger or isolation in any part of Africa. Even, when alone in remote almost unadministered pagan areas in northern Nigeria, or at night alone in the African slums of Durban.

We boarded the dingy little Indian-owned cattle boat which fed foodless Aden from Somali flocks and herds. It was now on its empty run. We disembarked at Berbera, the headquarters of the Protectorate—a few white bungalows in some irrigated greenery with the native town a discreet distance up-shore. A shock awaited us. The Mad Mullah had been defeated but some of the tribes into which the Somalis were divided—there was no unity—were giving trouble. And this was down in the south along the Abyssinian frontier—my brother-in-law's district. He was in danger—I forget now whether the trouble this time was an attempt to register the too-numerous firearms, or the first taxation in this newly occupied district. Whatever it was, the Governor told us no women were to go there and we had better turn round and go home. Here was a stunning disappointment! We pleaded for a little delay. And got it. So we kicked our heels in the pitiless heat of Berbera, riding on the shore or sailing the shark-infested sea or dining in or out with the handful of officials.

At last the situation cleared—Major Rayne came up to Berbera and persuaded the Governor to let us go back. After all it was upon my brother-in-law's judgement that our safety depended. I have already mentioned his faith in Somalis as soldiers. He knew them well and had then just written a book about them and the recent final expedition in which he had taken part. It made no difference to his affection for them that Somalis had more than once tried to murder him and in one attempt killed his colleague beside him. So, backing his D.C.'s judgement, the Governor let us go. First across the burning coastal plain, then 5,000 feet up the terrifying masses of rock which led to the plateau—past Sheikh, the Governor's little hot-season retreat. On again through a sandy waste, dotted with thorn trees, rocks, ant-hills and spiky aloes. We met Somalis, very few, travelling with the mats and poles of their huts strapped on their camels. Sometimes through dim aisles of the thorn trees there would be a scurry of buck or an ugly wart-hog trundling off. And always birds, doves of many kinds and sizes. Now, for me in England, the voice of doves always recalls Africa—a harsh setting for such a gentle sound. There were other birds—why are they so numerous in semi-desert lands?—storks, vultures, hoopoes, hornbills, carrion crows and the glorious jays with feathers of a dozen iridescent blues.

At last, after threading a route of nearly two hundred miles and seeing buildings only at Sheikh, we reached Hargeisa. It is still a magic word to me. Yet there wasn't much to see—sand, thorn-trees, aloes, a few stony hills, a *tug* or dry water-course. On the other side of this *tug* from our bungalow the Camel Corps were living in tents, two Somali companies and half-a-dozen British officers.

You might well ask how such a place could give me 'the time of my life'. Yet it did. Whatever my later travels in more beautiful and dramatic parts of the continent, this was my *first* Africa. The people—few enough of them—were at once fierce and beautiful. I think the people of Africa's north-east are, by our own standards, the most beautiful in the world—slim, upright, with dry polished skins, dark hawkish eyes, fine-cut features and proud carriage. They are hard people in a hard land. I used to watch them in my brother-in-law's court litigating tenaciously for compensation after inter-tribal fights—100 camels for a man, 50 for a woman. But they could be loyal to Europeans they respected. Even gentle. We made friends with the Somali leader who had backed the British against the Mullah, Haji Musa Farah. He once expounded to me the habits of the weaver birds who were making their nests in a tree over his tent. He treated his ponies like children. We bought a lovely grey from him, which we called Griselda, marvellous on trek and over the jumps and a real member of the family.

Why was I so gloriously happy in Hargeisa? There was little enough to do. We had to stay indoors during the heat of the day. But there were books to read, letters to write, and a menagerie to play with, young buck, cheetahs, two young lions and an irreconcilable little leopard. There were tennis, riding and steeple-chasing. There were the Camel Corps officers across the river-bed to be dined with in their mess tent. Or they would come across to drinks or dinner with us. There were buck and guinea-fowl to shoot for the pot. No rule against shooting sitting birds! I once shot seven with one shot—they were all bunched together and rather young. I felt like Herod. Above all there were the nights. I slept in the open on the roof. We had a breed of very large hyenas there and at night they came snooping round. They could bite off half the face of a sleeping man. Their extraordinary howl punctuated my dreams. And if the moon was up I could see them slinking around the bungalow like grey ghosts.

The rains broke late that year. I saw the misery this meant for man and beast in this desiccated land—and the satisfaction to the vultures! Then the first huge drops fell. The shrivelled land drank them in and gave out a strange, acrid, never-to-be-forgotten smell. The first soupy water came fingering down the dry river-bed followed by a torrent full of branches and dead creatures. One night the river rose high enough to cut us off from the Camel Corps and dinner. I had to mount a camel and tuck my long dress—of course we dressed for dinner!—round my waist.

Among many memories of Hargeisa three events stand out. One was the day we found a document stuck on a tree near our house. It was a call to the Somali soldiers in the Camel Corps to cut all white throats and go with their weapons across the border into Abyssinian Somaliland and join those fighting for the deposed Muslim emperor, Lij Yasu, against the Christian contender, Haile Selassie. Obviously our throats were *not* cut: the Somali soldiers remained loyal. Lij Yasu's star sank while that of Haile Selassie rose to shine for nearly half a century and is still shining.

It may have been in some relation to this threat that the military authorities decided to add an Indian Company to the two Somali ones, and this led to my second thrill—the right word I think. The newly arrived Indians needed training in Somali bush warfare. It happened that just before we arrived, many of the Mullah's soldiers had been captured and it was difficult to know what to do with them. So some of them were drafted into the Camel Corps. They were now told to take off their uniforms, put on their dervish clothes and play-act the part of the enemy. The officer in charge of them was rather a special friend of mine and he said I could go with them. I am sure he must have got into trouble afterwards. But could anything have been more gloriously exciting than galloping around with this wild-looking troop, ambushing the enemy in a narrow rocky defile and later dashing madly around them like Red Indians as they formed up, and almost breaking a British square?

The third thrill was the best. Major Rayne had to beat the bounds of his newly reconquered district up to the Abyssinian frontier. I was allowed to go with him. This meant setting off into the blue with a string of camels, ponies, and mules, a handful of Somali police looking splendid in their uniforms, and a few cooks and orderlies. We would keep up the pace by shifting from one kind of mount to another—camel, lofty and romantic but liable to let you get swept off by a branch of a tree if you got sleepy and you had a long way to fall—mule, tireless but rather dull—pony, handsome and sensitive. I remember caressing my pony's neck—crisp, chestnut hairs, burnished in the sunlight—in gratitude for his gallant responsiveness in spite of the blazing heat. It was generally a matter of going single file, weaving our way through the universal thorn trees.

The sun decided our routine. The cook and orderlies got up in the dark and set off with the baggage camels. We rose just as there was the first low hint of light through the trees and jogged along generally in that strange silence which the mystery of an African dawn seems to impose. We would catch up the advance guard for our breakfast. We would rest in the midday heat. Perhaps we shot something for the pot—a buck for the men, birds for ourselves. But we also had a little flock of sheep with us, the hardy Somali fat-tailed sheep. I thought this was rather horrible. They well knew the dangers of the bush and panted along after the baggage train in order to keep up with us and preserve their lives—only, one by one, to lose them to the knife as they reached camp.

We carried wonderful tents. They had been made for King Edward VII's great Indian Durbar and later distributed to appropriate colonies. They were large, with a decorated blue lining, two rooms in each, blue druggets on the floor and a lavatory bathroom leading out. Only there was no water! We could be sure only of what little we carried for drinking. I remember stopping at a so-called well in a dry river-bed—just a very deep hole with a man at the bottom scraping up what looked like cocoa—yet I drank it.

Night was the zenith of adventure. I slept on a camp-bed in the open with large fires on each side of me to scare potential carnivores—lions, hyenas or leopards. The police built a high *zareba* of thorn branches round our camp. They would sing themselves gutterally to sleep. Then that miracle of the tropical night of stars! If the moon was up the sand turned the colour of milk. These nights utterly fulfilled the heart's desire of my childhood for adventure in Africa.

The adventure *could* have ended there. One night some trekking Somalis asked if they could build their *zareba* alongside ours for extra protection. They did. But just before dawn lions came and chose to jump *their* defences rather than ours and seize a man. The racket that broke out caused them to drop him but he was dead. My brother-in-law said we must go after them. So in the first light we started out on our ponies to follow the tracks. We followed them nearly all day. Late in the afternoon the lions must have got tired of being hunted and began to slow up. We dismounted. My brother-in-law became separated from me by a bit of thick bush. One of the lions stepped out of this. I reached to my bearer for my gun but he had silently stolen away. It was just as well, for if I *had* fired I should probably have done no more than wound the lion and this might have ended in serious trouble for me or someone else. Fortunately the lion made a noise—neither a roar, a growl, or a grunt, but something between all three. Major Rayne was, of course, a very experienced hunter and knew the meaning of this particular utterance of the lion. He therefore fired in the air and the lion, not relishing enemies behind and in front, sheered off into the bush. Not much of an incident to any experienced hunters but, for me, the climax of adventure.

But the whole trek was to me, in the full sense of the word, thrilling. What especially appealed to me was that on our very blank map the word 'Unexplored' was printed right across the area we were traversing. At some points there was no way of knowing for certain whether we were in British Somaliland or Abyssinia. As it was all just Somaliland and unad-ministered on the Abyssinian side it was only by geodetic survey that we knew where we were. As far as I knew no Europeans had ever followed our route, yet when, from time to time, we met a few Somali nomads filing through the bush with their camels they hardly turned their eyes to look at us—strangely snubbing encounters!

My Somali trip came to an end. I had to leave Hargeisa, pass again through that grim thorny wilderness, and across the oven-hot plain to reach Berbera. I had still one more very minor adventure. The little Indian cattle-ship was loaded with animals for the return journey and I had to walk among and on top of its living cargoes destined to nourish foodless Aden, in order to reach my cabin. Worse than that, the Scottish captain—his post was hardly an élitist one—was reeling drunk. I was the only passenger and he followed me around with a glass of whisky in one hand and photograph in the other with the ceaseless refrain—'Have a drink! Look at my wife!' He was clearly quite unable to take the right line out of the harbour. . . .

But that was the last adventure—at least in this particular 'time of my life'.

It will be obvious to anyone that the reason why this harsh corner of Africa was Heaven to me was that it provided the perfect stage in which to play the romantic role of which I had dreamed as a child. I delighted even in the costume needed then for the part I was playing—the high leather boots, the breeches—the short circular khaki skirt, the becoming double terai hat—long since discarded as an unnecessary protection; above all the rifle over the shoulder and the pistol under the pillow. . . .

## *Arrival in South Africa*

The long voyage, four weeks without sight of land between Western Australia and South Africa, is nearly over. I can look back upon my travels from England to America and on to Hawaii; the Samoan Islands (both America's and New Zealand's); Fiji; New Zealand and then across Australia. I have had time to brood over the coloured races which, pursuing the purpose of this long journey, I have surveyed, rather than studied—Amerindians, American Negroes, Hawaians, Samoans, Fijians, Maoris and Australian aborigines. The last were too far away from civilized Australia to be visited so I could do no more than test Australian opinion about them, too often either blandly ignorant or even contemptuous and derogatory. And now—tomorrow indeed—I shall see the continent I mean to make my main study, and to which on this long journey, I shall be giving most of my time.

This morning I woke up at 5 a.m. being suddenly aware that the ship was slowing down. I knew that this would be an important day for me. I had seen no land since we left Western Australia two weeks ago and after the long emptiness of the sea it was with a sense of shock that, looking out of my porthole, I saw great blocks of concrete sliding past almost perilously close to us. Then, squatting on the concrete, I saw black men with fishing-rods—the first Negroes I had seen since I left America. Behind them was a low green hill. And what a new value the green of earth offers after weeks at sea! The hill was capped by a lighthouse and in front of this the disreputable-looking flotilla and implements of what I later learned was a whaling station.

I dressed hurriedly and went on deck. The ship was making her way across a great dull enclosed sheet of water, with docks and a town smudging the coast at one point—Durban! So this was Africa! Except for those black fishermen there was nothing so far to suggest it. Dull skies, dull colours, dull town, not a scrap of foliage or an architectural feature to distinguish it from a port in America, England or Europe. I thought of the only other part of Africa upon which I had landed, the almost empty white-hot desert coast of Somaliland with its few thousand slender, handsome, fierce Hamitic nomads.

When we had breakfasted I went up on deck. I found we were now berthed and that the wharf was alive with black men, Zulus, I assumed. How like, and yet unlike, the Negroes of America! Two or three centuries of life in that country have set a stamp upon the faces of Africans. Gone is the unrestrained expressiveness and merriment. Not that the men I was now watching showed no dignity but it was something brought with them from their tribal life and—so I speculated—deeply threatened by their inclusion within a world they cannot yet understand or influence. These men were dressed almost entirely in black coal sacks, which hung, toga-like, from their shoulders, and every sort of battered, borrowed headgear was stuck on their heads, down to an officer's cap of which not much more than the wire frame was left. Beneath the coal-blackened jute, legs and arms sometimes flashed with copper wire; ears were weighed with lumps of wood and tin; some woolly heads were shaved in strange designs. Even to my ignorant eye the men were of different tribes, mostly Zulu, but—I later learned—Basuto, Pondo, Fingo as well. They looked up at us impudently, their faces nearly fell apart with their continuous laughter and every now and then they hurled themselves into a battling whirl of limbs over some small largesse from the decks. The people on the boat laughed and commented:

'Look at the niggers!' 'Aren't they priceless?' 'Throw them a penny and see them fight for it.'

I went below after a bit and sat in my cabin. I felt faint but the cause was mental rather than physical. Whether my mind had become softened with three weeks' isolation from the puzzling world, I don't know. But the sight of the Kaffirs on the docks was like a stunning blow. I seemed to feel the immensity of the problem they represented and the absurdity of my attempting to understand it. How could any humane relationship be established between the people on the wharf and ourselves, the people on the decks? And this was only a sample, only the first corner of the continent which I could visualize spreading west and north, the whole terrifying map, with its enormous distances, its oppressions and cruelties, its voiceless, primitive people, its senseless political divisions. I wanted to lock myself in my cabin, hide under the blankets. Understand this? Study it? Report on it? I felt I dared not face this ridiculous enterprise, could hardly dare to step off the ship on the docks, in order to begin it.

But Africa now came right on to the ship. The black faces, bleared with coal dust, unfamiliar, grinning, were passing, peering into my window, and the shouting, singing, groaning, whining, and thumping of coaling was in full swing. So I went out to keep my appointment with the two or three passengers I knew best, English, German and American. I was foolish enough to marvel that none of them shared my feelings—not that I asked them!—that people stepped so cheerfully for the first time on to the black continent, as if Durban were just like any other port, and the dockers around us like any other dockers.

Certainly the natives showed no such sense of gloom. It would be hard to imagine men who looked on better terms with their world as they seethed on the coal barges, laughing and singing, lay smiling on the wharf, or ran and jumped at dangerous speed with their porters' trolleys.

Two or three of us, including Underberg, a German friend I had made, hired a car and went a long drive for three hours. I thought the town of Durban quite uninteresting: the suburbs had the usual pleasant roads, the houses perhaps a little bigger than in Australia and New Zealand, and made more distinctive by the Dutch influence, for the curving gables and pillared *stoep* are easy to mould in concrete. To anyone fresh from Australia the most striking feature was that all this European life was built on a black foundation. Black errand boys, street sweepers, nurse girls, maids in doorways, gardeners in gardens. Yet this black labour is, I soon learned, rigidly controlled: no native may enter or leave the town without a pass: if he has to stay for his work it must either be on European premises or in the native compound. Entering this he is dipped and his clothes fumigated; the same on leaving.

We stopped by the beach—it was Sunday—and had a good opportunity to study the physique of the bathing and sun-bathing crowds. To me it seemed poor. I saw scores of rather weedy men, pale, with weak blue eyes and dark hair; it almost seemed as though a type had been evolved, at least in the city. They looked very different from the big, beefy, Australians I had lately been visiting.

I dined in town and at night walked along the 'front' which a Blackpool expert, imported for the purpose, had bedizened with coloured lights and littered with band-stands and shelters, all the tawdry bric-à-brac which in Britain so often, and so lamentably, borders the majesty of the sea and amongst which the Zulu rickshaw boys looked very strange objects.

I made contact with one or two of the white 'gaugers' in charge of the dock labour and through them I went to see the manager of one of the biggest of the firms which recruits labour from the reserves and contracts for the work on the docks. He was a hard, stringy Scot, with gimlet eyes and a mouth like a rat-trap, working in an office full of Indian clerks and Zulu foremen. Queues of natives, looking bewildered as cattle in a pen, waited their approach to the big counter behind which he sat. He could speak to them, such words as were needed, in any Bantu language and did so with a voice like a machine gun. It was impossible to tell from his tone whether he were cursing, dismissing or accepting them and equally difficult to interpret their manner as they wavered up to the counter. Some were clearly straight from the bush, others had been there before. He distinguished them, Pondos, Basutos and Zulus, down from their kraals for six or nine months, forty-five shillings a month and their keep in the compound. He explained to me:

'I have been at this for forty years and I can tell you I know my job. My firm can get all the labour it wants because we have a good reputation. They know where they are with us. We are firm but just; we give a boy his rights, no more and no less. I accept only the raw bush native. No mission boy is allowed inside this place, no so-called educated boy. Any suggestion that a boy has had the faintest connection with the I.C.U. [the native Industrial and Commercial Union which, I have since learned, is just struggling into existence] and out he goes! But the I.C.U. has been pretty well dealt with in Durban, I'm glad to say. To his shame, a white man has been mixed up with it.'

'No,' in answer to questions, 'there is no government inspection of our compounds, nor do the government lay down any conditions. Our natives are perfectly happy so long as they don't get interfered with. Yes, breaking of contract is a criminal offence and I always see to it that they get jailed for it or, better, fined, then they have to stay longer to work off the fine.'

Rather unwillingly he agreed to let me look at the compounds. But at this moment a policeman came in. He reported the death of a man who had just been killed. A rope had broken and a basket of coal had fallen on him and he had died almost at once. The policeman described the condition in which he found the body and handed over the man's belt, wallet, etc., all dripping with blood. The manager took them, excused himself from coming with me and shook hands. I withdrew mine to find it stained with the blood of No. 1102. There was nowhere to wash it off so I had to go as I was, carrying the mark. I went with one of the Zulus. We threaded our way through some dirty backquarters until we found the compounds. My companion, questioned about the I.C.U., seemed afraid to speak, except to disavow all connection with it.

The compound, though gloomy and prison-like, was not too bad. My entry caused a good deal of excitement among the men who had just come off night-shift and were lounging about in a state of undress. I looked into everything—the kitchens where huge vats of white 'mealie-meal' were cooking or cooling: the shower-baths through which they must pass on their way in from the docks: the dormitories where two rows of wooden shelves have been polished to ebony by sweat and coal dust and where groups of men were squatting, gambling, or cooking their own food in native cooking-pots. Then I went to the sick-wards, where flu, fever, and bronchitis had turned black men grey, and where they lay on rather dirty grids under tattered blankets. The native pharmacist, however, looked clean and efficient and was very proud of his cupboard of medicines and his long experience. I asked him if he were going to be a doctor. He looked at me in surprise and said: 'How can a native be a doctor?'

Then aboard again *en route* for Capetown. We had had three days with flat, sandy coasts slipping past to the north. On the fourth, in the morning, I stood on deck looking at some very interesting shaped rocks sticking up out of the mist and sea, apparently quite close to the boat. I could hardly believe this was Table Mountain hanging over Capetown and still some thirty miles or more away. We had to run very close before the magnitude of the rocks was indicated by the town at their base coming into view. When I did see the whole thing I was simply amazed. Nothing had prepared me for the grandeur and strangeness of the site. It was, I think, the first time on my journey that the real thing was so far beyond my most brilliant expectations. The mountain looked unreal, like an impressive piece of painted scenery. For me it was the gateway to a continent. I knew that north and north-east of it there stretched a thousand miles of racial problems deeper and more complex than any I had yet surveyed.

*Margery Perham*

## *Capetown*

I spent my first two days here clinging to my ship and wandering round in search of a hotel, finally going down to the docks to see the last of my friends on the S.S. *Demosthenes* and then sitting up all night to read the glorious armful of letters from home which I found waiting for me at the post office. I found myself every now and then looking up to catch my breath in astonishment at the mountain wall rearing up behind the town, so high that not even the tallest buildings in the main street could shut it from view.

I engaged a room in the part called Seapoint where the open sea breaks on the rocks and rows of hotels and pleasant villas cluster along this favourable site like shellfish. The Lion Mountain, as rounded as Table Mountain is square, lies behind, and its couchant, rocky lines against the brilliant South African sky save this suburb from looking commonplace. Also, the architecture is good; simple houses are washed in pale grey or lemon: they have gardens and pergolas brimming over with blossoms, wide pillared verandahs, and often a red-flagged terrace garden climbing up the hill. Household standards can be high for cheap coloured labour makes possible what is denied to the Australasian colonist.

The crowd is motley in Capetown streets. I saw the English in all degrees of acclimatization; brawny, tanned harsh-faced Dutchmen in big hats; Jews of all kinds, white and prosperous-looking Jews or lean, dark Jews from eastern Europe: well-dressed Malays in black or red tarbooshes; Indians; 'Cape coloured' people, only a degree less respectable-looking, and very various in type and tint; and, of course, every kind of African drawn from all parts of the Union and beyond, including bare-legged women balancing pots and bundles on their heads.

One of the first things that strikes the newcomer is the thoroughness with which the new bilingual rule is carried out. Every single public notice of every kind, however long or large, has to be duplicated, and what this means in a big town, in the post office, the railway station, and even in the museum, can be imagined. All blue-books are printed double at huge cost. Even on the Official maps they Dutchify English names—East London becomes Oos London, though why does Johannesburg not become Johnstown? The size needed for the stamps defeated the Afrikaners until they thought of having alternate stamps in Afrikaans and English, getting the balance in their favour by abolishing the king's head. As for the flag, it has to be seen to be believed. Only fanatics, devoid of taste as well as humour, could have reduced the Union Jack to its present minute size within the new stripes.

I had hardly settled into my Seapoint Hotel than I was rung up by a Mrs. Cartwright, sister-in-law of Monsieur Marzorati, the Anglo-German-Italian governor of the Belgian mandated territory of Ruanda-Urundi. I had looked after him and his wife in Oxford and now Mrs. Cartwright insisted upon my staying with her. To fetch me she sent a vast limousine with a white chauffeur and he took me the sixteen miles out of Capetown to Fernwood in Claremont. Here I relaxed into hospitality so luxurious that, in this country, and with my commitment, I felt almost guilty in enjoying it. The house stands in a beautiful garden with a bathing pool. There is plenty of social life and a car at my disposal.

One of my first engagements was a visit to the beautiful racecourse, Kenilworth, for *the* race of the year, the Metropolitan. Here I saw the extraordinary mixture that makes up Capetown society in the enclosure. Incidentally it was my first race meeting ever. There was one horse that to me was quite obviously *not* a racehorse, an enormous, thick-set, grey, which looked almost absurd in the string of twenty slender, silk-skinned aristocrats. So I tried to be very clever and staked on the slenderest and satinest. The grey simply romped home. I saw my first big crowd of natives there, hundreds and hundreds, thronging their own special part. Horseracing seems a taste easily acquired.

The Rhodes Memorial was up the hill behind the house. The area of the Rhodes estate is kept free from all buildings except public ones. This means that the whole steep slope up to the towers of mountain rock is an unbroken forest of pines, mostly the beautiful chalice-shaped stone pine or the lofty *pinus insignis*. This is the outcome, of course, of wise plantation long ago. The result is rich in colour. The sky here is famed for its almost constant and radiant blue which is given its full depth by the dry air while it has not the white glare of the tropics. From its earthy bases the towering crest of rock springs straight up in walls and towers: it loses all grimness from the variety of its colours. Then comes the sheath of pinewoods reaching further up the slopes, green as only southern pines are green. The earth, when it shows itself bare, is almost flaming with colour; where men are levelling a site for the new hospital you can see it, changing in fifty yards from bright sienna to crimson and from crimson to orange and salmon-pink. At rare intervals, in a high creek on the mountain, the dark moss of the pines is streaked with the palest silver-green, the colour of the last, lingering indigenous trees, crowded out as the Bushmen and Hottentots have been crowded out, by alien growths. It is worth a climb to see them. Each soft green leaf is bound in a close silver net which can be rubbed away from it and when the evening sun catches the upheld branches the whole tree does, in truth, turn silver.

I was not quite isolated from history in my luxurious setting. My hosts' place was close to the beautiful old Dutch house Groote Schuur. (The Afrikaners' domestic architecture was one of the few good things they brought to the sub-continent.) This house was restored and modernized by the young architect, Herbert Baker, whom Rhodes selected to work with him, and who later designed impressive public buildings elsewhere in South and East Africa and, in Oxford, Rhodes House, my own place of work. Close by Groote Schuur is the house of Rudd, the man Rhodes sent up to Lobengula's kraal to obtain the concession which led to the foundation of Rhodesia and so to the destruction of this African chief and the loss of his tribe's lands to white settlers.

I think I must just remind you of the general situation in South Africa as I arrive here in its political capital. (Pretoria is, of course, the administrative capital, Bloemfontein the judicial. South Africa is too nationalist in its provinces to agree, like Australia, upon a single capital.) The two unifying Boer generals are now out of action, [Louis S.] Botha by death and [Jan] Smuts by electoral defeat in 1924. General [James] Hertzog, with the help of the Labour Party, is in power and is determined to swing policy in a pro-Boer and anti-African direction. Above all he plans legislation to destroy the remaining limited voting rights of Africans in Cape Province, the last stronghold of those Cape liberals who, during the making of a united South Africa out of the four provinces (Transvaal, Orange Free State, Natal and the Cape) have struggled to save this last relic of racial equality. My object in the Cape is to make contact with the British leaders, both those who worked to achieve the Union which is now taking on such an unfavourable shape for them with their religion of the British Empire, but especially with the Cape liberals who are trying to defend the native franchise. I don't yet know whether I shall be able to meet the Afrikaner leaders.

It was easy enough to meet what I must call the British element. Among them is Sir Drummond Chaplin, once Administrator of Rhodesia, friend and associate of Rhodes, an M.P. and now director of the Rhodesian railways. He asked me to dinner at the palace he has built twenty miles from Capetown, with a mountain behind and the ocean in front, and gardens, terraces, and loggias round a house of which one might dream but never hope to see. There, Lady Chaplin sleeps in a luxurious bedroom crowded with parrots and love-birds and pekinese, the room stinking like a fowl-house with stale feathers and wet bird-sand. I called *en route* at the house of the Archbishop of Capetown to pick up two bishops. One of these was Bishop Paget, whom I knew. When Dean Church left his books to my college, I had been deputed to select what we wanted for the library and Bishop Paget had followed me anxiously round the bookshelves to glean my leavings.

From the Church to the Law in the person of Sir James Rose-Innes who asked me to lunch. He is a great champion of the Cape franchise and represents the Cape-British tradition in native affairs. I did not realize that he was the Chief Justice and lightly engaged him in debate on the subject of the whereabouts of sovereignty in a mandated territory. I rather fancy myself on this issue and brashly tried to make him see sense. I was told only afterwards that he had given judgement in the famous international case about the status of South West Africa. . . .

I was entertained also by Mr. B. K. Long, editor of the leading South African newspaper, the *Cape Times*. He is very much in the limelight at the moment because, backed by his intelligent wife, he has published very strong comments upon the character of a lately deceased millionaire, Mr. J. B. Robinson, with regard to the terms of his will. The scandal has, I think reached the British Press. This multi-millionaire, his fortune having been made in South Africa, is accused of having left nothing to any South African cause. He is reported to have left £1,000 to one daughter on condition that she did not receive money from any other source. His other daughter, Countess Labbia, married to an Italian, is said to have got £3,000,000. Mr. Long said what he thought of this in his paper. And all Capetown is buzzing with it. B. K. Long printed all Countess Labbia's furious letters to his paper and added this note to her final one: "In view of the writer being a lady, I have erased the more abusive expressions."

Next came Professor Eric Walker, author of the best history of South Africa, an extremely handsome giant of some six foot three. He took me over the splendid new buildings of Capetown University. If Berkeley, California, is supposed to be the finest (modern) university building in the world, taken in relation to its site, then it will have to be demoted to second place. Right in the centre of that mountain-slope which I have described, the pine trees have been cut away and three terraces excavated. Along these run low, simple Italianate buildings with soft red-tiled roofs. This, again, is the work of Rhodes' friend, Baker. Inside I found good taste and simplicity. I went to the girls' wing, talked to some of them in their studies, drew them on native questions and found them quite liberal.

Then there was Professor Barnard (the pupil of Professor Radcliffe-Brown, the Sydney professor of anthropology). To him I had been specially recommended. He is a blue-eyed, fair-haired, poetic-looking person. He asked me to lunch to meet the Director of Education in the Cape Province, the last of three generations of pro-native Britishers, who has done an immense amount for native education. It is very hard for all these men to have to work now under a Dutch Nationalist government, especially when they can still remember the happy days of working under an autonomous Cape government, free to follow their own traditions and in close contact with Britain. Doubts about the future hang like a cloud over the Cape British and, I expect, over all liberal-minded British in South Africa.

I could well understand their feelings when at last I made contact with the Boer Government. This was not easy. Twice I had appointments with the Prime Minister, Hertzog, and twice these were cancelled at the last moment. Finally I did have an interview with his Minister for Native Affairs. His hard face and hard voice were intimidating. As I could get no response about the current and repressive native policy I urged him to look ahead, twenty-five, fifty years, with the natives growing in numbers and resentment. This angered him. He said, 'Don't worry your pretty little head about such things', in a voice which made 'pretty' an insult rather than a compliment.

On my last day Mrs. Cartwright took me the seventy-mile drive round the Cape Peninsula. I shall not forget that drive. . . . Nearly the whole of the coast is a natural rock-garden, its steep, tumbling masses of red and brown rock netted with flowers and spicy shrubs. The sands are, in real truth, almost as white as snow, and the sea is all the colours the sea can be when it is sparkling with sunlight, with cloud-shadows above and a changing floor of weed, rock and sand below. You double and circle round the rocky heights of the peninsula: away inland are the smoky-blue, comb-shaped crests of the Hottentots' Holland Mountains and between them and the peninsula the flats, where, clearly, once the seas met to make the Cape an island. Coming back to Capetown you pass the Naval Station at Simonstown, where two little sloops seemed to make up the South African navy; then the famous surfing beach of Muizenburg and the cottage where Rhodes died, so prematurely, before the Boer War was ended. It is a gay place now, generally called Jewsenburg, because on the sands, in the season, the Jewish girls are said to be walked up and down and round and round, to be judged and selected by the Jewish men. At least, so goes the story; but prejudice may have told it, for national prejudices of all kinds are strong here.

One thing I have noticed about the South African light. . . . I have not forgotten how in Somaliland the mountains turned opal and amethyst but here no jewel would make a simile. It is colour from the paint box, as crude and clear as colour can be. I have seen a big turret of rock catching the last shaft of the sun over the curve of the earth and its face was orange and crimson and the shadows purple. Superlatives become stale, I can only say that I stood like an idiot, struck motionless, my brain refusing to credit my eyes.

I snatched odd hours to work at the parliamentary library where I was given a special permit to read and the staff were very good to me and smothered me with "native" literature, all very depressing. In the intervals I rode a lovely ex-racehorse called Fuschia, belonging to my hosts, winding through paths in the pine woods. I bathed in my hosts' swimming pool and played some tennis. There were two beautiful creatures in the house to play with: the daughter, Yolande, and the son, d'Arcy who was having a term off from Oxford. I made contact with the Governor-General, the Earl of Athlone and his attractive wife, Princess Alice. I rode for hours with the highly intelligent Imperial Secretary, Captain Birch-Reynardson, my chief informant on South African affairs, at least as seen from the top.

All this, packed within a fortnight, has been marvellous experience but very exhausting so, not surprisingly, one of my visits has been to the doctor. The unseen Afrikaners, now the real rulers of the country; the vast dark background of the Africans—these are the forces to be understood and I do not see how it is to be done. But tomorrow I leave this lovely curtain-raiser of Capetown. I have chosen to go to the famous missionary school for Africans, Lovedale, founded in 1841, and the new University College of Fort Hare which has lately been founded alongside the school. Here at least I shall meet Africans of a kind, I hope, with whom I can talk freely.

It may be a long time before I can get off my next diary letter.

## *Lovedale and Fort Hare*

I left Capetown at four o'clock on 12 November, seen off by my hostess, she, splendid in a red picture-hat trailing red and white chiffon. To my joy, Professor Barnard, the young and brilliant anthropologist, was on my train.

But the train! Travelling luxury has been in a descending scale since I left America. The gauge here is, I gather, only three feet odd and the equipment is most primitive. There is no gauze to keep out the grime: the berths are hard; lavatories and wash-basins all crude and rather dirty; no hot water; no emergency chain and no locks. All that can be said in defence is that travelling here is fairly cheap. I feel a bit gloomy as I shall have to spend so much time on trains. And this was a main line train to Johannesburg and most of my travels will be on branch lines.

Professor Barnard travelled with me for a day and a half. . . . We met for all meals and morning tea so I got the chance of picking the brains of the man who, Professor Radcliffe-Brown said to me in Sydney, was the only other real anthropologist in the world—and his pupil! No, I think he included Malinowski among the select. . . .

Like his master, he has been unable to establish a regular course in anthropology at the University and can only get it in as a subject among others for B.A. with an advanced course afterwards. But he has succeeded in establishing a summer school to which administrators are sent from Basutoland, the Rhodesias, South-West Africa and the Transkei. Missionaries also attend. In his opinion such a course is more necessary than even the appointment of government anthropologists. . . .

I arrived at Alice the third day in the train. I was met at the station by the Principals of both Lovedale and Fort Hare. They had decided that I should start with the potential university, Fort Hare.

Heavens, what a day! I was up soon after seven, and we had breakfast at seven forty-five. I then went over to prayers with the Principal and sat with one of the staff. The hundred or so students filed in, including the first eight women students. I looked along the lines. The faces were of all types, a few undoubtedly, from their appearance, would support the controversial and superficial view that the African black man had smaller brain capacity than the white. But how far do such appearances count? All the students were dressed in conventional European clothes but nearly all of the suits, though neat, were, upon closer inspection, shiny and even threadbare.

The Bible lesson was very appropriate—how does it go?—'Do good to them that hurt you—pray for them that despitefully use you and persecute you.' I wondered whether Christianity could and would enable these people to exercise the almost unimaginable restraint that will increasingly be demanded of them. One item in this morning's paper contains news of a raid with machine-guns and tear-gas upon natives in Durban—I must try to get there. Another, a new stringent bill against native agitation. A third item reports a strike, quite an orderly one, in which the strikers were surrounded by two or three hundred police and given five minutes in which to decide whether to go to jail or continue work.

The Principal offered an extempore prayer in which he thanked God for the day in which they lived; for the League of Nations and the new hopes of peace and co-operation, above all for the great opportunity that had come to them at Fort Hare. The students filed out to their lectures and I went with the Principal to his study. Here I sat down opposite his desk with pencil and paper and interviewed him.

The Principal, of course, is a Scot, a fairly young, fit, vigorous man, liberal-minded, cultured, Scottishly rugged. He seems sensible and able. I asked him first how the Union Government, so opposed to native education, could have made such an exception to its own policy as to establish anything so dangerous as a native university college. He explained that there had been plans and propaganda by friends of the natives for years before 1916 and that the surrender made by the Government, that is by Botha, was partly political. In the War, the fear of native trouble was intensified, and the establishment of the College was a sop, an amicable gesture. Also, because otherwise they would get higher education in the United States and were, indeed, already beginning to go there. Botha showed great courage by coming down to open Fort Hare himself. Since then it had been supported partly by a grant from the Union Government, partly by endowments from Carnegie, Rockefeller and the Rhodes Trust— the latter for £2,000 only. The students pay £30 a year and more than half of them are on bursaries raised by the natives of the Transkei, Basutoland, and one or two other sources. One is sent every year by a Negro 'Sorority' in the United States. £30 is not much as an all-inclusive fee and the students live a very simple life, their food consisting largely of native 'mealie-pap' and a loaf of bread a day. They live in hostels that have been built by the missionary societies; there is a Presbyterian, a Wesleyan, and an Anglican hostel and one which is central and undenominational.

It must not be imagined that the hundred students are all doing degree work as external students of the University of South Africa. About 75 per cent are working for two years at matriculation; others at an agricultural course; others for a special College Diploma in Arts, a kind of adapted matric course. Others are doing a theological course at their denominational hostels and only join in occasional work at the college. Finally, a

very small minority are doing the three years of the South African University B.A., a mixed pass degree, with exams at the end of each year. So far
about eight men and one woman have taken the degree, the latter being the
first of all South African women—of all African women?—to become a
graduate. The men were mostly medical and went on to get the degree at
Edinburgh where they are all said to be doing good work. The policy of the
College is of course to increase gradually the proportion of degree students. But they are very much at the beginning of things. Only some 20 per
cent of African children go even to the elementary schools and as, until
lately, there has been practically no provision for secondary education,
higher education was almost an impossibility. At present the majority of
students come to Fort Hare from the old-established mission schools of
Lovedale and Healdtown.

The students are of all tribes, mostly Fingoes and Xosas, some Zulus,
Basutos and Tembus, a few coloured, and one or two Indians. Discipline
presents no difficulties; they do not fight and they work only too hard.

The Principal took me round the College. In a corner in the library we
found a graduate, now doing an advanced course in English literature. A
very dark, shy man from Basutoland, it was a little difficult to get him
talking. But he told me that he had not found Anglo-Saxon very difficult—
he had already passed in it—that his favourite period was the eighteenth
century and that in that period his favourite poets were Pope and Addison.
I thought this very surprising, as if a starving beggar had expressed a
preference for truffles and caviare over bread and beef-steak. But he stuck
to his point; the vitality and humanity of the Elizabethans seemed to leave
him cold, as did the romanticism and sentimentality of the nineteenth
century. I wanted to go on talking to him but the Principal dragged me
away to a lecture-room where a huge Irishman was giving senior matric
mathematics. The Bantu excel in maths and yet hate them. They have to
give great time and effort to the subject but they get excellent results. I
went down among them and asked an Indian boy what he was doing. He
explained, and there were shouts of laughter when it became clear that,
being no mathematician, I could not understand his explanation. All the
time I was struck with the cheerful atmosphere the African seems to bring
with him. These people are not cowed; they *seem* free and lusty.

All the same I found occasion to criticize the Principal, to fear that he
was not all pure metal unalloyed. In one class he showed off a little, teased
the men for my supposed benefit. He made them stand up in tribes and
was very jocular with the Zulus because they were so proud of their
fighting record and strength and yet this lot happened to be smaller than
the other students. It was all in fun and the men laughed and yet I imagined
they were laughing to please us and not themselves. He picked out one

small man, put his hand on his wooly hair, twisted his head about and said, 'Look at this representative of the great Zulu nation!' If ever a black man can blush, this man did.

On to the labs, where five men and one girl were cutting up snails and making diagrams. Then to the business and commercial class. Here I was introduced to a huge Nyasaland native, a government clerk in Rhodesia, spending the whole of his holidays at Fort Hare to improve himself. He is the uncle of Clements Kadalie, the notorious 'agitator', who has been head of the I.C.U. and is said to have pocketed some of the funds. This great giant, so black that one realized how little black most of these southern Bantu are, rose from beside the tiny white woman who was teaching him, gazed at us with hostility, whether learned in Nyasaland or from his nephew, I do not know. Questioned by the Principal he told us, unsmiling, that he had lately been to see the sea for the first time.

'And did you like it?'

'Yes, but I do not like the taste of it.'

'But you surely did not drink it?'

'Yes, I did. My nephew Kadalie told me to go and drink the sea because the sea was medicine.'

We found another man in the library, a thin, alert creature, with gentle brown eyes. He was from Johannesburg.

'How are things there now? Are they better in the last few years?'

'Oh yes. Europeans sometimes come into our compounds and locations, a thing which never happened before.'

'Have you any water or light?'

'They have put on a little water but we have no light. We use candles.'

'Do they still push you off the pavement into the gutter?'

'That is becoming difficult. They have brought so many of us into the town that there is no room in the gutter.'

We left the building again, passing the Principal's office, where his secretary, who was an African, was handling all the work and plant of the big office with what seemed to be quiet efficiency. He brought a sheaf of beautifully typed letters for the Principal's signature.

We then went out to run up to a native village to see a bush-school. Five or six miles over appalling tracks in a sturdy Buick brought us to a big village on a hillside. The one square house among the round ones was the school. . . . We told the teacher to carry on. She was a young, loud-voiced, stout African girl. At the top of her voice, in slow, laboured words, she bellowed, with suitable gestures:

'Dees—ees—ma—HAD.'

They screamed the repetition:

'Dees—ees—ma—NAWSE.'

I cathechized Standard III. Quite a decent map hung on the wall and they picked out the main towns of South Africa, darting like lizards to the spots. The reading-book alas! was an English one, wholly unadapted to their use, and dealing mainly with objects and events that would always be foreign to them. It is strange that though we have been in South Africa for a hundred and thirty years we have not been able to produce adequate text-books for the native children, while the Americans have a whole elaborate series for the Philippines—which we borrow for Fiji! In Samoa they have done better than this.

Mr. Ker asked one of the children to read. He read well. Then Mr. Ker held the book upside down, the boy seemed to think something was wrong but, at a second order, continued with the story.

Then we went into a native hut close by. Two women, clean and dressed in flowing garments to the feet, ushered us in. The hut was beautifully clean and neat both inside and out, and the mud walls decorated with a spotted pattern of lime and polished. On the walls hung faded photographs of the family and a picture of Lord Haig. There was an iron bed and mattress, a chair, and a kettle. On the floor was a child of three, covered with flies, its bronze having turned to sickly green. It was gasping out its life in little coughs.

In the afternoon from two to four I worked at the literature of the place, reports, syllabus, etc. At four I went out to review the 'Wayfarers', the Guides. All the women students studying for the degree—and there are only eight—are Guides. But they are not allowed to wear the same uniform as the whites. They wear rather ugly brown cotton faced with orange, with big straw hats. A nice half-Dutch, half-English woman presented them, Miss Maritz. I was told that she had had a great struggle with herself and her friends before she came but that she had 'converted' and it was clear that she was devoted to her students. I was told that she had had a sick girl to sleep in her own room with her. She is leaving now to take up a lectureship in science at Wellington College in order to keep up her standards but she told me that she hoped to come back again to Fort Hare. She was rather apprehensive about my request to be left alone with her girls for fear we should not hit it off and certainly they were shy with the two of us. At last I got her to go. I put them in a circle round me on chairs.

We talked for an hour. It was astonishing how quickly as I talked to them the impression of their ugliness faded and the intelligence and beauty of some of the faces appeared. They were soon most animated and though at first they would answer me in whispers, all at once, so that I could distinguish nothing, they soon improved, and one after another began to speak out and stand out as individuals.

Only one was a 'coloured' girl, and she was different from the rest. The strain of white blood was enough to make her look very different and enough, too, to make her slicker, and more self-conscious. The knowledge of that almost unrecognizable kinship with myself was enough to introduce a slight confusion into our relationship. I felt it, and I am sure she felt it too. With the native girls it was different. They were almost too good to be true, responsive, quick to pick up points, intelligent, courteous, attractive.

I asked them first about their work. They sketched in a hard day with little room for recreation. Were they never tired or bored? No, they liked it all so much. Their favourite subjects? Not history! 'Not as *we* learn it—we are not interested in the war of the Spanish succession. Perhaps, if we did it in more detail.' No, science was the favourite and perhaps it is well that it should be so as it is probably the best corrective to the non-reason that has dominated many concepts of the tribal past. English, too, they like: especially Dickens, Jane Austen and Charlotte Brontë. Two of them smiled at each other in joint appreciation as they said, 'Oh, yes, we *love* Jane Austen.' Miss Austen—and Zululand!

They questioned me eagerly about Oxford and listened with gleaming eyes to what I said of the life and the students. It was clear that dimly, far away, English student life was their ideal. It is upon *that* we shall founder with all our theories of differentiation, of adaptation to native society, etc., upon their passionate determination to accept nothing but that which will give them not only the right but the power to gain equality.

Presently, rather tentatively, I probed more deeply. Did they not find the life here strange? How and why had they come? What would they hope to do? 'There is nothing we should be allowed to do in South Africa, Miss, except teach.' And when they went home to their tribes did they not feel strange—different—from their own people? No, they said, they loved to go back. And what about the customs and ideas they found there? Here at last I got an answer that went to the essential point. One girl, whose keen, clear eyes denied the impression given—to us—by her thick purple mouth, said:

'Yes, we *do* find it difficult. Do you know, Miss, that smelling out witches has not died out at all. Even round here, within five—one—mile, it is going on. They do not often kill the witch now but they lie in wait and beat him or her, burn the house and drive them out. It is when something happens that cannot be explained.'

'But *you* have studied science. *You* know the reasons for what happens.'

'Yes, Miss, but when things happen that we do *not* know the reason for—'

'But you know that there *is* a reason and that you could find it out if you had the knowledge.'

There was a pause.

'Yes, but, Miss, there *are* things that happen that cannot be explained. I am afraid—I know that if I went back and lived among my own people I should believe these things again. I know I should. I feel it.'

'Do you know', said another girl, thrusting her dark face forward in the ring, 'that among my people were two, a man and a woman, married, who had both been educated. They were both teachers. And someone died suddenly and they smelled out the woman as a witch. And in the night the husband cut off her legs, and put knives into her body, and then cut off her head.'

The first girl, who was very wise, said:

'Miss, if the Europeans would only be more sympathetic and *explain* things. When I was at school (a mission school, of course), one of the girls suddenly found some funny little marks on her arms and leg. She thought she was bewitched and she went in great terror to the white head-mistress. But the mistress was annoyed and said, "Don't be silly. That's nothing at all." So the girl went on believing she was bewitched and she died. The Europeans don't seem to understand.'

I wanted so much to go on talking to the girls. They, too, wanted me to stay. But five o'clock struck, and I had to go and talk to seven selected degree course men on the verandah of the Principal's house.

I found the men waiting, two Basuto, two Zulu, two Xosa and a Fingo. It was really not so different from talking to a group of students at home. It was impossible to remember that most of them were fresh from the mud-hut in the bush and that the brother of one had just been killed in a tribal affray. And that another, when he got back, would have to struggle to turn out a chief who had dispossessed him.

First, they asked me all about Oxford, a rain of eager, detailed questions, the answers received with reverence. (Oh, the responsibilities of Oxford!) India we discussed, and then Somaliland and the League of Nations. Then they began to ask me for detailed information about the exact constitutional relations between South Africa and England. It was pathetic to see in what a hopeless direction their minds were working. Soon they came into the open. They asked me terrible questions.

'What does England think of the situation out here?'

I explained that we were quite detached, that we were more liberal than South Africans but that it was easy for us to be so as our interests were not involved.

'Can England do *nothing*, then?'

I explained how, even with the recent South African-German trade treaty which so closely affected us, we had not so much as protested.

'But South Africa is a possession of England.'

I tried hard to explain.

'But the *King!* He is King of South Africa. What does he think? Will *he* do nothing?'

More constitutional history. Then:

'But, Miss, what do you yourself think of the way we are treated?'

Now for it! I had already asked the Principal if he objected to my talking politics in the College, and he made the very proper reply, *'Magna est veritas et praevalet'*.

I said I thought the policy was wrong: that every consideration, religious, social, economic, directed us to put all our energies into raising the black people; that so long as the reward of effort was a share in the best we had to offer, so long would they be attached to our civilization, would feel a stake in it. But then, it was easy for me, coming in from outside, to be impartial. Could they not make the effort, great though it was, to understand what the whites felt about it. Did they not realize, now they were educated, how great was still the gulf between their people and ours; and how the whites, one to four, feared to be swamped by a race so different from their own.

'Are they *afraid* of us?' It seemed a new idea. They were spellbound. I began to get a cold feeling. I had before me the first of Africa's university men, all about to take their degrees and go out, marked men and leaders of these masses, the still backward masses. I felt I had got into a position into which I must go further because I could not retreat.

'You are going out into the world highly educated, feeling and thinking almost as we do and yet you will be treated—well, you know far better than I how that will be. You will have every temptation to become embittered, to become agitators and to take short cuts. Your lives cannot be altogether happy; you have had this great privilege of education and it is going to cut you off and mark you out among your own people and among the whites. But if you do try to take short cuts the results could be disastrous. If you do all you can to make relations worse instead of better, do you know what will happen? Supposing it leads to outbreaks of violence, do you imagine for a moment you can succeed? I want you to look up and answer me. Even if there were a temporary success? England would have to back law and order in South Africa—as the whites see it. It is *your* people who would suffer, not the whites. They would crush you easily, in spite of numbers. You know that?' They all said 'Yes'. 'A very heavy responsibility rests upon you. All your effort should go back into your people to raise them. They are not ready yet to claim and make effective use of political power. What your race is capable of will be judged largely by what you, the first few highly educated members of it, do with your leadership. Where you have now a dozen you will need hundreds, then thousands, educated and united, to win and use your rights. And remember, too, that all the white people who are working for you will be defeated unless you work with them. If you make mistakes they may become helpless.'

That is the gist of what I felt driven to say and from that we went on and spoke with the greatest frankness of the whole situation. I do not know if they felt the same sense of solemnity that I did because the subject was so heavy with dread. I felt it was almost unfair of me to talk or let them talk of it. It was like talking of the hills and sea to a man chained hand and foot in a dungeon. I think I shall have hard work to keep my emotions in order while in this country. What I had felt for American Negroes, Samoans, Maoris, was nothing to what must be felt for these people, especially for these few to whom we have given this terrible gift of intellectual training. Was it fair to talk to them like this, in full social and intellectual equality, when outside of the charmed circle of Fort Hare, they may not sit in the same railway carriage, or eat at the same table, but must live under a different law, in a semi-servile state? Hertzog and even Smuts refer to the blacks as barbarians.

They seemed to me intelligent, patient, earnest people; perhaps patience and a sense of humour may save them from the envenomed hostility shown by some Indian leaders towards whites which would have made such a conversation as this impossible. (I have often tried it in Geneva and elsewhere.) Yet one trembles to think how little the Indian has to accuse us with, in comparison with these people.

I was already late for an appointment at the Presbyterian Hostel, Iona, where the Warden had asked me to dinner to meet the students. They were all working in the common room. I peeped over one tufted head. *Undirectional Reflexes. The Thorndike Theory.* Over another, a larger tome, Lowel's *Primitive Society.* Some had sat their exams that day in social anthropology. They produced the papers, with questions ticked, explained what they had done, and complained about the unfairness of the paper. At the Warden's request I made an appeal to them to rest before exams and not to work late. Evidently human nature, however different racially, makes the same reactions to examinations. I saw their shower-baths and went up to their dormitories. Some have rooms for three. There were books on or by every bed.

The hostel is a pleasant new building. Two sides of a quadrangle, with Moorish arches, have been built. The rest is to come. Through the arches was seen the open country under the clear night sky, ridge upon ridge of dusty blue veld. It will be a great pity when they build up that quadrangle. Why should people live in a box on the veld?

I now had to motor over three-quarters of a mile away to Lovedale, the most famous of all South African missionary institutions, a Presbyterian foundation begun in 1840. Here I again met Dr. Henderson, who took me up to the big hall, which can seat about 800 of the 1,000 pupils of all ages who fill Lovedale.

I found myself, all unprepared, addressing the Lovedale Literary Society. . . .

The next morning I was up early in order that I might call upon two native members of the staff before I transferred myself completely to Lovedale. First we went to see Professor Jabavu, perhaps the most famous living South African native. His father was famous, too, for the production of a South African newspaper, and both were educated at Lovedale. Jabavu is very black and rather squat-faced. I have found both here and in America that the highly intelligent and refined-looking African is not necessarily the one we should pick out for intelligence when we judge their faces by our standards. . . .

## *Basutoland*

I don't think I have explained what I was doing alighting in the Orange Free State capital. I had always hoped that on this journey I would somehow get to Basutoland. I had read the romantic history of this mountain kingdom, now surrounded by white South Africa. But to understand the drama of Basutoland's position I must insert a little history.

Early in the nineteenth century a very remarkable African, Moshesh, had gathered together the tribes broken by the bloody Zulu tyranny and had welded them together into a miniature nation backing upon these mountains. He had later been driven off his rich lowlands by the encroaching Boers but from his dramatic table-shaped stronghold of Thaba Bosiu he had called a halt to Boer invasion. Hearing that other tribes had been helped by white people called 'missionaries', he sent an agent with 200 cows to buy some of these valuable beings. This man fell in with some French evangelical missionaries and so began a most useful relationship and the process of the early conversion and Western education of this rugged people.

Moshesh was a diplomat as well as a fighter. When he defeated an English force, which left forty dead Lancers on the field, he characteristically sent a message: 'You have shown your power, you have chastened. Let it be enough!' What he most wanted, indeed, was British annexation to save him from the Boers and in 1868 he got his way. He said: 'I am glad that my people should be allowed to rest and lie under the large folds of the flag of England before I am no more.' And, in a letter to Queen Victoria: 'My country is your blanket, and my people the lice in it.' But would the Queen and her successors hold on to that rather distant blanket? The lice proved restive and in 1883 Britain handed over the difficult little state to Cape Colony. This Government, in turn, found the Basuto difficult to govern and, after failing to disarm them in the so-called Gun War, they handed the state back to Britain.

At the making of the South African Union in 1910 there was strong pressure from both British and Boer leaders to take over the three British-ruled native territories. Basutoland was wholly, and the others, Bechuanaland and Swaziland, mainly, surrounded by South African territory. A compromise was worked out laying down the conditions under which the three territories *might* be handed over to the Union. In 1924 the first fully nationalist Afrikaner Government won the election and began to impose its repressive policies on its Africans. It also made increasingly strong demands for the three territories. Although the poverty of Basutoland drove some half of their active males at any one time to work long stints in South Africa, the people were passionately against being handed over. Naturally I was keen to see these sturdy people and their dramatic scenery and also to find out how Britain ruled them.

In Capetown, while riding with the Imperial Secretary, I had confessed my desire to see Basutoland and, if possible, one other of these so-called British Protectorates. He had passed on my wish to Lord Athlone as Governor-General and so here I was alighting at the little terminus of Maseru a few miles into Basutoland.

I always have a sinking feeling when I first encounter a new enterprise, never knowing what sort of reception I shall get and what personalities I shall have to encounter and from whom I shall have to elicit help. I therefore looked anxiously along the modest platform at which I had alighted. There was only one occupant, a fair, slender man, over six feet high, dressed in an immaculate whipcord suit of rather military cut. He introduced himself as the Assistant Commissioner of Maseru district (that is Assistant to his chief, the Resident Commissioner of Basutoland), and therefore in charge of me. He drove me in his car to the local hotel. It was not at all attractive but he explained that his own house was full of his family and guests.

The day was still young after my morning run in from Bloemfontein. So I asked if I could start work in the afternoon. He put me in the court, a large, simple structure, with the bare requisites of justice, a platform, a table, a dock and a witness box. It led out of his office so that from the magisterial table where I am now sitting as I write up my diary-letter, I can call across to him for information and papers. I can already report that among all officials I have met he excels in unselfishness and courtesy. In fact, writing later, I can report that he has almost played the part of my secretary. . . . As, in addition, he is very tall, over 6 foot, handsome and elegant, I find him rather formidable. This kind of fact is an integral part of my narrative because the whole success of each enterprise depended upon my reception at the hands of the responsible official. It was the personal factor at Fiji that made my visit there partially a failure; here in Basutoland it looks like making it a success—or I hope so, for I am only at the beginning of it.

At four o'clock on the first day, the A.C. (as I shall now call him) dashed me back to the hotel to change for tennis at the Residency and then took me there. As it poured with rain I played bridge with the Resident Commissioner, his wife and the A.C.

The R.C. is a good man. That is the first impression he gives and, I must confess, it is a surprising one. One does not expect, nor generally find, saints at the head of an administration and the R.C. seems to be almost that. Quiet, modest, simple, earnest, sympathetic, thoughtful—I have chosen all the adjectives carefully and they ought all to be superlatives. To be beloved and respected, as he seems to be, by the whole of a small society like this in Maseru is a rare tribute when one remembers how these official groups are often beset by jealousies and the friction of personalities. He was charming to me. He said the A.C., who had been there much longer than himself, knew far more about the working of the administration and the Basuto than he did himself. He would therefore hand me over entirely to him. Yet he would see me at any time and do all he could to help. He would not think of allowing me to leave after a week. I *must* stay at least a fortnight. He apologized for not entertaining me at the Residency: his wife had just had a motor accident and was still rather badly shaken. And the A.C.'s house was full of visitors. So I went back to my hotel and a good evening's work on the official literature. I feel that I am in for a very satisfactory visit.

I spent most of this morning with the R.C. He was Secretary in Uganda and after twenty years in that country he finds he has left his heart there and that it is difficult in four years to get to understand such different people and circumstances as he finds in Basutoland.

I can now see why Basutoland, high up in its mountains, is called the Switzerland of Africa. The boundaries of the Orange Free State, Natal and the Cape radiate from Basutoland like spokes from a hub. So Moshesh held a very important strategic position. I can see vividly how the Dutch stole all the flats, some of the best farming land in South Africa, and why the Basuto thought themselves justified in cattle-lifting from this *terra irridenta*. They have been so indulgently handled by the British that they forget what they owe to us and in their famous national Council, ignoring later events, they always refer back to Moshesh's original agreement by which the chieftainship and customs were to be kept intact. The Paramount Chief and the lesser chiefs have a great deal of power and a wide jurisdiction and the exact powers of the Government are rather hard to define. The Union, and especially the Dutch, resent this island within their boundaries and itch to take it over from the British. Hence a stream of protesting Basuto delegations to Britain.

The Basuto border is an obvious economic border. Outside it are wide European farms, railways, natives in their serf-like position, working for their masters, governed by a hundred restrictions. Inside the railways stop, the mountains begin, and in Maseru, only just within the country, the natives fill the town, strolling around with their heads held high, every look and movement proclaiming that they are in their own country. They wear great flopping hats and are robed, toga-fashion, in blankets of striking designs and glowing colours. Maseru is the city of galloping hoofs. As I sit now writing in the Court House I can hear the rapid, light tattoo of the little ponies and past the windows I can see the Basuto dashing full-tilt up and down the town. There is no etiquette about speed; here, you ride quietly across country, but in the town you ride like cowboys in a wild west film. Rows of ponies, fifty deep, are tethered to rails. By contrast the bowed oxen plod, step by step, four, seven, even nine pairs, with the great waggons, which are so much a part of South African history, moving climsily after them. They bring in grain, but mostly wool and bales of the long, silky, curly Angora hair which grows so well in the mountains.

In the evening I went a long ride on one of the A.C.'s ponies which, my being very out of condition, I had a great battle to hold. A girl staying at the A.C.'s house and another official came with us and we wound up a precipitous pass on to one of the stone tables that the Basuto made impregnable. It was down this very pass that they tumbled a body of British Lancers, not one of whom escaped alive. From the top we could see inland magnificent ranges of mountains, not flat-topped but rising ever higher to jagged peaks. I felt how glorious it would be to penetrate them and leave the flat borderland far behind.

I dined at night at the A.C.'s house and found his wife a most charming woman, though very delicate. The terms for the Basutoland service are hard; leave is rare and passages to Britain are not paid so that those who enter the Service and have families are almost compelled to become South Africans. They have the further disadvantage of the high altitude which does not suit everyone and they live in a small white community. But they have great advantages which made me compare their lot with that of my sister's family in the Colonial Service. Here they can have their children with them, sending them to school in the Union; they have, at most times, I understand, a glorious climate, hot, sunny days and cold or cool nights. And plenty of ponies. And the country itself is most beautiful, though very few penetrate it as the stations are all on the border, and there are practically no interior roads, so that the whole mountainous interior was practically uninhabited until recent years when pressure of population has driven a growing number of natives to live where there used to be only summer cattle posts. As administration is indirect [ruling is through local chiefs] there is really little need for officials to go much into the interior.

This morning the A.C. held his Court under the pine trees outside the Court House. It was rather a striking scene. A few benches for the public were filled with natives lolling in their vivid blankets and big hats. Beyond them were many more all lining up to sign on for work at the mines in South Africa. I sat beside the A.C. A guarded prisoner stood in front of us, a fine, fiery individual, whose face looked quite impassive though on close inspection the movement of his neck muscles showed him less impassive than he seemed. On one side stood a white man, a slim, rather swagger young trader who was accusing the man of theft with violence at his store twenty miles out. On a bench in front were arranged the stolen goods which had been found hidden under rocks in the mountain. A goodly selection he had made—fifteen blankets, five pairs of trousers, pants and vests in bundles, bags of tobacco, cardigans, tea, candles and soap. It was all very informal: at the adjournment for morning tea the A.C. asked the trader into his office. I began to ask about the case but stopped myself, apologizing, as the matter was still *sub judice*. But that did not seem to matter and they talked it over together. Afterwards it transpired that the big crowds of natives who had rolled up, seeing a white woman there for the first time, thought a divorce case was coming on.

Today the A.C. motored me out to see Morija, the big mission institution which was begun nearly a hundred years ago by the Paris Evangelical Society, and which, but for a temporary expulsion by the Boers in the last century, has worked in Basutoland ever since. The missionaries were very hard hit by the war and the decline of the franc. Now, though they are still by far the biggest mission, they are losing every year to the Roman Catholics who have won over the Paramount Chief, at present a woman. It seems strange to find Latin Protestants and also to find them in a British colony. The head of this Paris mission is an Italian: his walls were hung with pictures of Mussolini. He was a little man, with a little wife and seven very diminutive children. The natives are being turned in considerable numbers into Paris Evangelical catechists and teachers to staff their village stations. One excellent thing they are doing is encouraging the Bastuto to write stories and legends in their own language and they print them, having the biggest printing press of any mission I have seen. They seem on excellent terms with the Government as represented by the A.C. But they are in a state of gloom—because of lack of workers, and of funds, and they have lately been struck by a terrible scandal.

I spent the next few days meeting the various officials and working hard at education, police, health and agriculture. I thought that on the whole this Government has an able staff, working with a very good spirit. I did an all-day circular tour as far as the road runs and gazed longingly beyond this terminus towards the mountains. We had a Father White (Kenelm Order, Anglican) with us and he was very much against my taking a picture of a Mosuto lady bathing in the stream, but she did not mind. I was then taken to Roma, the Roman Catholic Mission, which is being handed over, rather surprisingly, to the French Canadians. (Is this because they will find it easier to understand—and surpass—the French Protestants?)

This is indeed a red-letter day entry in this diary-letter. Before I arrived here the A.C. had planned a two-week trek into the mountainous interior of his district. There are no roads so it means riding with pack animals. The Resident Commissioner has now decided that I am to go with him. It is an unbelievable opportunity and a very surprising offer. The only trouble is that I am very much out of condition after all this travelling around with no exercise and I can only hope that I shall be able to stand it and not be a drag on the A.C. Those blue ranges going up and up in height look pretty formidable.

I am writing my diary on the first night of the trek. Yesterday was a great struggle to get ready. I had to pack off the few things I should need on trek: these are to go off ahead with the horses in pigskin saddle-bags. Then, last night, the Resident Commissioner gave a big dinner-party at the Residency to give me a send-off. The whole small official world, including the Assistant Commissioner's wife, was there. We played bridge and danced. Everyone was much interested in the coming trek. To me the evening was radiant with anticipation of the adventure.

I write in haste. I must get this letter off at once. I will try to keep some kind of a diary on trek. You can imagine how excited I am.

The A.C. called at 8:30 a.m. and we went off in his car as far as the road would take us, a terrible road in which we bumped over boulders, leaped spruits or churned through streams. We reached a store and there found our fourteen ponies all waiting for us. We had lunch under a cherry tree, loaded with fruit, and watched the natives bringing their wool and grain on pack-oxen to sell to the trader.

Then we said good-bye to the car which was driven back by a Mosuto, and set out at 12:30 p.m. on the first part of the trek. I chose Stumpy to ride as one of my two horses and the one selected for the Earl of Athlone, the Governor-General, when he was up here the other day. My second mount is a grey, smaller, but more spirited. To my surprise the pack-animals are all left running loose, the four mounted police keeping them in order. It seemed so strange to see six horses loaded with tents, beds and one's own personal luggage careering off, sometimes making a detour up a slope or strolling into a mealie field to eat forbidden fruit from which the police chase them off with long whips. But the horses seem to know their business and more or less keep with you. They could not, however, be induced to form up and pose for a picture of the start which was taken by the man who was to drive back the car.

We set off at a trekking jog which reminded me of similar expeditions in Somaliland. I had been warned not to talk to the A.C. on trek, as he hated talking when riding, and had, so far, always trekked alone, making a positive rule of it. So when he made conversation I answered in mono-syllables. In the end I had to explain why. But he said he would waive his rule as it was only 'babbling' that he could not stand. This means, I suppose, that I shall have to try to talk intelligently but not too intel-ligently.

I stopped once at the sound of singing and saw a line of men all hoeing in a field, raising their hoes in time with their song and very gay about it. I got a picture of them and they roared with laughter at me. 'Are you a man or a woman,' they yelled, so the interpreter said.

We rode steadily uphill all afternoon, until we suddenly found ourselves on the brink of a great fall of ground, with a valley cut by a tortuous stream at the foot. It was a most precipitous descent, with no proper path, and it was almost terrifying to see right below us our pack animals finding their own way down the rocks. I can't say I enjoyed it, sometimes scrambling and slipping down a rocky shelf with a long, sheer drop on one side. I got into trouble for holding my horse up; apparently, when mountaineering on horse-back, you have to give them all their head and let them make their own way. I was very thankful when we emerged on a grassy ledge and dismounted for a long rest. The valley still seemed far below but the mountains were a little nearer. Right underneath, wrapped in almost a circle of river, was the roof of the last trader's store on our route, shining out of a clump of trees. Here we were to spend two nights.

We dropped down, forded the river and climbed up to the store. The people who kept it were very nice and made us most welcome. The A.C. had arranged to introduce me everywhere to the natives as his sister but of course he did not attempt this with these people.

I spent a long time examining the store. Whereas in the old days nearly everything came from Britain, now only about 30 or 40 per cent does. The rest is from Germany, France, Japan, Czechoslovakia and America. Small ironmongery and prints (cloth) from Germany; cheap blankets from Aus-tria and France; silk handkerchiefs and stockings from Japan; glass and jewellery from the Czechs; small ploughs from America. Things of the very best quality come from Britain, a sturdy £4 Paisley blanket as against thinner foreign ones, far better coloured, from 10s to 30s. The trader showed me a big spade which is delivered to him right away in the mountains for 3s 6d. German. I noticed its price-mark was 7s 6d. Not a bad profit? I saw a highly coloured, highly scented pomade in a glass jar roughly copying the white woman's cream jar, with gold label and screw-top. This is actually sold to the native women for 6d. It comes from France. The English do not seem to study their market, do not produce cheaply or push their goods when made. And Africa is going to be a huge, ever-growing market with a vast appetite for cheap ploughs and agricultural instruments and, ultimately, for sewing machines, gramophones and cheap motor cars.

I spent about an hour this evening working through this store. It is a most illuminating aspect from which to study the contact of black and white. For at the store you find out not only what the native needs, an index of his Europeanization, but what he produces, for he brings to the trader his produce—hides, wool, mohair and grain. The trader complains of the quality of the produce, grain dirty and broken by threshing on the earthen floor with oxen; mohair cut too short because the owners dared not wait lest thieves should cut it in the night; bad quality too because, in a land without fences, the angora has sometimes crossed with inferior goat. So the tale goes on. We say, 'Let the native develop on his own lines.' But if he does, and at his own pace, he cannot compete in the world's market. We may ask 'Why should he? He never used to.' He must because of the rising cost of the government and education we give him—and he now demands—and because, with the increasing pressure of population, the land as he uses it cannot support him. The agricultural and veterinary offices try to nag and regulate him into greater efficiency but the word is hardly yet in his vocabulary and theirs is uphill work. The indirect rule spells patience with abuse and inefficiency; and patience these days is a rare virtue in public administration and business. We might be a *little* patient. But the paces are so different, as if a motor car were to be hitched to an ox-waggon. To detribalize a native and then Europeanize him is easy; it has only taken about two hundred years in America and it is going on fairly quickly in the South African towns. But to raise a whole community in its own setting is a different matter: a little quicker in the towns and perhaps by more direct rule as in the Transkei, but still very slow. In Basutoland it will be slowest of all, as far as South Africa is concerned, as the state is largely cut off by mountains, by indulgent British rule, and by a long policy of crystallizing the power of the chiefs.

In the afternoon we went to see the natives dipping their sheep and goats in the very simple tanks that have been constructed all through the country. This is because the Union won't stand contact with the scabby sheep of Basutoland and threatens to retaliate all ways, including shooting them across the border fence. The operation has been reduced to its simplest terms; it is also rather amusing, except for the sheep. Eight sheep are caught with the help of tiny boys who struggle and drag at one leg to haul the terrified creature to the stinking green vat in which it will be submerged to its eyes and nose. The sheep are all held sitting up like a row of grannies, with the most varied expressions of misery and resignation. A little sand-glass is turned to mark the five minutes, and the sheep are flung in, to splash wildly in the dip, held under part of the time by long prongs.

At night I interviewed some local worthies in the stifling shed behind the store where the store-guard sleeps. There was one Frederic who told me some reasons why he considered the morality of the Basuto had degenerated. I will spare you, though he did not spare me and the inadequacy of the store-hand as an interpreter made it worse. We sat on store goods, crouched together, the three of us, the old man talking Sesuto, and his meaning flickering vividly over his keen, black face while, with a great range of intonation and apt gesture, he discoursed upon the old sex-discipline of the tribe, and how with clothes and school the old, strong, rigid fabric has collapsed.

Then came a chief, Mojela, dashing up on his gasping and beaten pony, much as the Somalis used to dash. A bad man, I thought at first sight, and was not surprised to learn he had just been concerned in a ritual murder, when he and one or two others (including the brother of my Basuto friend at Fort Hare) dashed an old man from the precipice, having a ritual use for parts of his flesh. But evidence against a chief is hard to obtain. . . .

We visited a leper settlement. We went in pouring rain, and splashed about in muddy yards, with the lepers all huddled in wet blankets or lying in their rooms.

Leprosy is terrible in Basutoland, though old missionaries say there was not a case sixty years ago. It is hard to believe that it has spread contagiously in that time. It is maintained that clothing has had much to do with it. Nakedness in sunlight is hygienic but when women, having had the toilette of Queen Victoria once vividly impressed upon their minds, emulate her contour by strata of petticoats and count wealth and importance by their number, leprosy, a disease of dirt, has every chance to spread. (We saw one woman strip six skirts from her body to cross a stream, and she still had a few left.)

There were about five hundred people in the settlement, in all stages of the disease, from those whose extremities were dropping away from them, or who had the repulsive nodular type, to comely young people who showed no visible signs of rottenness and yet who were doomed in spite of their youth. It was a shock to learn this. The children looked so jolly compared with the older patients that I could hardly believe it when, in response to my cheerful comment, the matron said 'Hardly one of those will be alive in a few years.'

I must not lacerate your feelings by describing the horrors of the advanced cases nor of the children born into the doomed place. It is the custom in this country, when a child is born, to draw out one of the reeds in the thatch, so that it extends over the door. For a time no man may enter that hut except the husband. Here, having corrugated iron, they had extended a piece of rope on a rod, to mark this unhappy event.

They think little here of the new oil which is injected, and about which I had heard so much that was hopeful. 'I think it helps,' was all I could get from the matron. They do not even make the injections compulsory—they can come or not for it as they like. The process is painful and they do not want to harass the people. They discharge a few every year, some as hopeless but no longer contagious, a few who are cured, or are hoped to be. These last are not necessarily ones who have had injections. They believe that cleanliness and good food are the only cure, and these the leper can seldom get in the village, where semi-starvation, if not brutality, is the treatment for the useless member of society.

The A.C. was evidently a popular visitor. He talked to them all very cheerily. And reproved me for my silence. 'Have you forgotten your Sesuto?' I realized that I was not even greeting the lepers: I was looking at them as at things—cases—not people, absorbed in my own horror, rather than giving real sympathy. I tried my best after this and the attempts to respond through those dulled eyes and perished faces showed that humanity was still alight in them. The A.C. made his little set speech explaining me; some of them asked questions and made complimentary speeches though speech was sometimes distorted and almost unrecognizable.

The settlement is a terrible drain on a small country, costing £20,000 a year, and with no hope, it seems, of diminution. . . .

This is my last day in Basutoland. . . .

## *Durban*

I arrived in Durban very tired, rather late and with no idea where to go and spend the night. Then I remembered a hotel-keeper I had met on the Perth-Durban boat who had once treated me to champagne. So I went to his hotel. He was out but they gave me a room. When he came he made a great fuss. He had me moved out of my room and gave me a suite looking over the sea. He proudly showed me round it. It led out of his own suite in a separate block from the hotel and I began to wonder if I was in for trouble. However, when, with much pride, he showed me his own suite I was relieved to see that it showed all the signs of his being married.

After dinner on the verandah, word having gone round that I was studying native affairs from England, I was attacked by the Natalians, and listened while I was told that (1) I had no business there; (2) I was quite incapable of judging until I had been ten years in the country; (3) the natives were spoiled; (4) education was at the root of all the trouble.

Having been on the go since five in the morning I put up a very poor defence and retreated to bed.

A long and exciting day today, 1 February. A stifling night made sleep difficult so I got up early and worked and dashed up the town to buy a dress and get money from the bank.

Back at 9:30 to find Durban's Superintendent of Native Locations and his car waiting for me. He took me first—very honestly—to see one of the bad parts, a long row of single-room hovels, with mixed Indian and native families bulging out of the dark doorways. Then we went to see the compounds, where he can hold 3,000 natives and is always needing space for double that number. (Where do the unaccommodated live and sleep?) Here are endless boards on iron bars for 3d a night: there are boards with fairly clean bedclothes for 6d: here is the disinfectant well in which the boards are dipped every week: here is the more permanent quarter, with a few possessions hanging over each bed, the sort of aimless variety you find in any boy's pocket, string, whistles, mouth organ, but also paper flowers, and here and there a rosary or a text. Each aperture is closed and all cracks covered by newspaper. African labourers never seem to want fresh air in their sleeping quarters.

We then went down to the headquarters of the native trade union, the Industrial and Commercial Union. It is in a very low part of the town reached through crowded slums of mixed races. We found it hard to discover as the last I.C.U. premises were wrecked by the whites in the recent serious anti-native riots, when there were deaths on both sides. The Natal I.C.U. is the most militant of all and, under its Zulu leader, Champion, has broken away from the main stem. . . . But just because it is violent it attracts more support and has a large income. The I.C.U. premises, which are masked behind a warehouse door, are enormous, an old sweet factory, dark and inclined to rot, but with several huge rooms.

Champion is the arch agitator of the Union. . . . He is responsible for the present boycott of the municipal beer-halls. The City Council made many thousands a year out of them: now they do not make as many pence. It was his activities that a few weeks ago led to the Minister for Justice, Pirow, flying to Durban and leading a raid of armed police to overawe the Durban Zulus. In June this year the white mob tried to storm these I.C.U. headquarters of Champion's and there was loss of life upon both sides. In September the Zulu women attacked the beer-halls. It appears that the authorities would like to see Champion's arrest and deportation. That seems sure to come. One question for the police must be how to get him out of this rabbit warren in the underworld without serious bloodshed.

We found Champion in an office blocked off from an upper room in the factory. We went through crowds of natives to get there. It was an act of great courage on the part of Mr. X, my guide, and an official, to bring me here. I am afraid, if it should get out, he will in for trouble, for of course, to white Durban, there is only one opinion about Champion and that is that he should be put up against a wall and shot.

Champion is a big Zulu. He greeted us with some ceremony, more especially directed to me and made a little speech. When I held out my hand he put his behind him on the grounds that I was breaking the rule of the whites in offering mine to a black man. He is very clever. That impression is immediate. He has all the African's command of words, tones and facial expression, added to the alertness and cunning engendered by adversity. He is so embittered and reckless that he did not try to placate Mr. X, my official guide. He looked him straight in the eye and accused his department of various serious faults, mainly of refusing him any place to live in spite of repeated applications. I felt hot for my companion and hoped he would be able to stick it, for any sort of explosion under these circumstances would be most unfortunate. He kept his head, however, and disclaimed any idea of penalizing Champion for political reasons. He had no room for him in the married quarters.

'And so I, a married man, am divorced from my wife by the municipality. That's very moral!' said Champion, who has great command of English.

Perhaps my readers, not having spent the last three months in South Africa, will not realize the extraordinary nature of this visit and this scene in which a senior white official was put through it by a native agitator in the latter's own office.

I intervened, before worse could occur, and asked Champion a series of questions. He proclaimed it as his main object to raise the wages of the workers. One Commission has accused him of 'poisoning the minds of his people against the Europeans.' 'That day I glory in,' he said. 'Up till now, though they were oppressed, they did not understand how or by whom. Now, thanks to me, every native in Durban knows. The only hope lies in discontent, because discontent produces organization.'

'But do you not want to co-operate with the whites?' I asked.

'Miss, I do. But *they* will not co-operate; they will not even speak to a native. From first to last in all our troubles here, has any official ever thought of asking the natives their opinion? Do we ever go near their Native Department except to stand about for hours until we can get a pass or get fined for not having one? The Native Affairs officials in this city are absolutely unapproachable and unsympathetic. *Of course* I would co-operate. I know we cannot do without the whites in this country. But the white will do nothing for us until we can organize and speak up for ourselves. It is sympathy and understanding we want. We get it from you. Do you know that your coming has achieved something that has never happened before: that the Superintendent has come down to the I.C.U. It was worth while your coming to Africa just for that achievement.' Here my companion hastily disclaimed any official significance in his visit. 'I know, I know,' Champion said, 'but all the most important things in the world are done unofficially.'

I then sat back while the two went at it and discussed the whole range of differences and the possible formation of a new joint advisory committee of town councillors and natives that is on the cards at present.

Watching, I could not *like* Champion. I suppose it would be hard for any white person to like a native agitator. His position must be too much for his character in this generation. He breaks into stump oratory, shouting and banging with his fist at the least provocation. His head is swimming with self-esteem and his outlook distorted by egotism. . . .

Champion, at the end, turned to me and said there would be a huge gathering on Saturday night of natives of every sort and kind. Had I the courage to come? To the native population of Durban it would be a great event that a white woman, and one from England, should come down to their gathering. I did not know what to say. I was attracted and frightened. And I could feel the horror of the official at my side. I hedged and said I would let him know and I saw he feared this was a refusal. Outside we saw rows of clients waiting for Champion. He escorted us through the great, mouldering, dark, barrack-like place and into the sordid street.

I need hardly say that my official guide said that *of course* I was not to accept Champion's challenge. He said it would be quite impossible even for him to go to such a place at night.

We went on and visited the married quarters area and poked into houses. I won't describe them, though I have made careful comparisons and mean to write something on the housing of natives. He admitted that he had only a hundred houses and that he had thousands of applications. He charges them £1 a month, and they cost him £2 7s. Now he cannot build any more, because without the help of the profits from the beer-halls the Council will not face the capital expenditure. Those profits must have been enormous for out of them night-schools were run, and welfare work and even a hospital were financed. In other words, the native pays out of his wretched wages. The whole economic-financial situation strikes one as being unsound. But if you say that it amounts to subsidizing the employer and allowing him to pay inadequate wages, the answer is that all whites are directly or indirectly employers and that the present arrangements are better for the white community than a general rise of wages which, it is *said,* would cripple South Africa. I have looked into wages a bit here. The Zulu 'boy' who does my hotel room gets £2 a month, the docker £2 to £2 10s. Indian waiters in this hotel get about £5 a month. The manager admits that they have not risen since he first went into business many years ago although the cost of living has risen so enormously and the needs of the natives, with education and urban life, have also increased. . . .

In the evening I trammed around Durban, having another look at it and calling on people. I was thinking all the time, however, of the night, and being torn between fear and attraction. I have no doubt that Champion, from a white man's point of view, is an unprincipled and dangerous man. Having brooded on ways and means and not liking the idea of going down into those parts with an Indian taxidriver I decided to get hold of a reliable white driver who would take me and fetch me away. So I rang up Champion, who said he was already making preparations, counting on my coming, and that he would see to my being fetched and taken back. That cut out my plan for possible retreat. So I fell back on another. I left for the hotelkeeper a note giving the name and whereabouts of the place to which I was going and saying that if I were not back in the hotel by 11 p.m. then arrangements would have gone wrong and I must be fetched. It was all rather an Edgar Wallace novel but I had to be mysterious as I did not want to be stopped from going.

It was a stifling night, loaded with wet heat, and all the hotel people were sitting out along the *stoep.* A woman who heard I was interested in natives came up and sat beside me, and proceeded to blackguard them and, by inference, me, in the most outrageous manner. She was a handsome,

white-haired woman, in a beautiful evening dress, and loaded with jewels.
I really felt quite sick as I listened to the usual flow of words—spoiled—
lazy—animals—keep them down. She knew nothing—nothing. She
boasted a life-time in the country, and knew not the first fact of the
situation. And the unprovoked vindictiveness with which she attacked me
for daring to study the question! 'You wait until you have been ten years in
the country before *you* advance an opinion.' I don't know whether I was a
bit tired and therefore nervy, but I could not stand it. Argument was
useless, and I did not want a scene on the *stoep,* especially as Champion
would shortly arrive and run the gauntlet. So I got up and said it was
useless to answer her, so wide apart were we in outlook. Then I went to
another seat. Presently a smart new Buick swung up to the doorway with
some natives in it and Champion came out. Fortunately no one recognized
him and I hurried into the car before people had time to realize what was
happening.

The Africans drove off at most furious speed. Not even in Paris have I
been driven so fast through a town. The streets in the Asiatic and Indian
quarters were crowded and when at last we drew up at the I.C.U. there was
a dense crowd of natives round the door and along the pavements. Champion shouted and swung his arms to make a lane and they parted, staring
in silence. The building, a large disused factory, was like a hive of bees,
every part of it packed. There must have been several thousands of natives
there and the heat and smell were overwhelming. Champion took me to an
upper room where several hundred natives were already sitting on
benches and many more standing and squatting all round. He sat me at a
table in front of them and got up to make a speech. For my benefit he
spoke in English and had it interpreted. He said that already they all knew
about me as he had addressed them earlier about my visit. He paid various
compliments to me and my country and the idea that I should 'tell
England' of their wrongs roused, alas!, a cheer.

'Our visitor has come tonight to learn about us and we want to teach her
all we can. But most of all, let us show her that, in spite of having black
skins, we are human beings, with the desires, the faults and virtues of our
species. General Smuts, in one of the extraordinary series of addresses he
has lately been giving in England and America, said that we are as patient
as donkeys. Has he read his Bible? Does he remember that the time came
when a donkey opened his mouth and spoke, and, yes, even refused to go
any further? Well, we are beginning to speak and we mean to be heard, or
we shall refuse to go any furhter, and what will happen then?

'We want our capacities recognized. There is nothing an African cannot
do if he is given a chance. You, Miss, were driven down here by a black

man: that man is also a skilled mechanic and he can take that whole car to little pieces and put it together again. We have started an all-black clothing factory here, and this suit I am wearing, and Mr. London's (the man beside him) were made there.' (Quite well cut navy suits.) 'I have yet to learn that any of our men who have been to London or Edinburgh or even Oxford have failed to pass their examinations in the usual time.'

But I lost half the speech as I was gazing at the audience. It comprised every type, young bucks in short-cut double-breasted waistcoats and Oxford trousers (these *very* popular with the Bantu) through all possible grades and shades of shirts and collars to the collarless and the coatless, to men with hair plaited in porcupine spikes and women in nothing much but brass wire and beads. They sat or stood, shining with sweat, staring at me with their big black-brown eyes and absolutely dumb. Then the choir, probably from some secessionist church, and looking highly respectable, appeared and at Champion's order, since they were to sing to *me* and not to the audience, stood right on top of me and sang an anthem about the captivity of Sion. Champion, evidently deeply moved, or acting, rose to say that for Sion he read Africa and asked when God would turn *her* captivity.

The whole audience now stood up and, singing in harmony, roared out the Bantu national anthem, 'Africa'. It was most inspiring, the word itself kept recurring in different tones, mournful or defiant. I must try to get the words.

It was now my turn to speak. I got up, fully aware how careful I must be in what I said. I was greeted with stimulating applause and Champion came forward to interpret. The pause, for interpreting, checks the flow, but enables you to keep them waiting for the point in a way that with practice, I imagine, could be made very effective. This was my speech as far as I can remember.

"Tell your people not to be afraid that I am going to make a long speech. I only want to tell them why I am here. I should not dare make a speech. Africans are so much better at speech-making than white people.' ('I don't agree with that,' said Champion.)

'Why am I here tonight? It is not because I agree with Mr. Champion. I don't agree with him, with much of what he is doing, and much of what he has said. But I have come because I want to learn. I want to see all sides of this problem of South Africa and it is a great pleasure for me to be able to spend an evening here among you, in your own place, and see how you enjoy yourselves." Then I told them something of my travels and of my hope, when I returned to England, of lecturing and perhaps writing on what I had learned. I finished up by telling them about Fort Hare and

warning them about the difficulties of education, and the danger of thinking it was a cheap or easy thing to gain but that, in the long run, it was the
only salvation.

The next thing on the programme was a European dance. I was made to
sit in the middle while the couples circled round me. They dance very well
though the women's bad figures show up in their scanty, thin dresses. They
all moved slowly and decorously and exactly on European lines though
they certainly grapple together with a completeness unusual in our ball-
rooms and cheek to cheek is the rule rather than the exception. A row
three or four deep sits round the hall and I was told that is always so and
that the spectators are content to pay their entrance and sit all night long
just gazing at the dancers. I suppose anything is better than lying in
congested heaps in their minute houses and hovels. But no wonder so
many are accused of being stupid and sleepy next day.

But the big event was preparing below. Soon a muffled noise I had been
hearing began to grow and grow, and Champion came and asked me if I
were prepared to see what they had got up for me. "It is the real thing, you
know," he explained, half apologetic. I went down and found the huge hall
that is the entire ground-floor of the factory filled literally to suffocation.
They must have run into hundreds, though it was difficult to see them all in
the big, half-lit space. They were all men, and all naked but for a thong
round the loins and metal armlets and anklets and on their heads a few
trimmings of metal and fur such as suited each man's fancy.

The great bulk of them were squatting at the back in ranks, each armed
with a heavy stick, with which he struck the floor as he shouted his song.
There was hardly room between my chair and these men for the first dance
team to come in, especially as they must dash in at a gallop, and whirl their
sticks round their heads. "Don't be frightened," said Champion. "However near they come to you, they won't hit you." But I remembered this
from Somaliland and how men, frenzied with the dance and apparently
quite unseeing, will, with quite reliable accuracy, miss you with their
spears by a few inches.

Well, the dance was really splendid. One after another the teams, each
about two or three hundred strong, replaced each other. They got more
worked up as the night wore on. It was impressive, almost beyond bearing,
to have a row of a hundred or more naked brown men, leaping and yelling
within a few inches of you, their faces drawn into terrific grimaces, their
eyes glassy with excitement, their mouths wide open to shout and scream
and their whole bodies contorted with movements that demanded their
whole strength to perform. I thought the rickety old floor would give way
under the crash of their feet, especially as each crash was accompanied
with the pounding of hundreds of sticks, and a simultaneous shout so that

the rhythm was deafening. One team did a dance founded on the British Tommy, and evolved, I suppose, by a native labour corps in France. It was a priceless burlesque. They marched in ranks, formed fours, saluted, bringing their hands down with a resounding smack on their bare thighs, carrying their sticks like rifles, whistling famous half-remembered tunes of the war, and trying to imitate the stiff march of the white man, so unlike their own gazelle-walk.

But their own war-dance was the best of all. There were about three hundred dancers, all wearing white fur rings round knees, ankles and wrists, and carrying sticks festooned with white feathers. The joints of their arms were bound with gold and silver wire; some wore baldrics of leopard or catskin or embroidery of white and scarlet beads. The Zulu physique can be magnificent; many were slim and tall and some looked more Hamitic than Negro. Certainly this dance showed the Zulu off in all his glory.

The impressiveness became almost overwhelming. I was surrounded by these flashing brown bodies with muscles running up and down skins glossy with sweat. Yet it was beautiful, this living frieze of dark bronze bodies. Now they advanced, singing with sticks levelled at me like spears. Champion shouted the translation in my ear:

> Who has taken our country from us?
> Who has taken it?
> Come out! Let us fight!
> The land was ours. Now it is taken.
> We have no more freedom left in it.
> Come out and fight!
> The land is ours, now it is taken.
> Fight! Fight!
> Shame on the man who is burned in his hut!
> Come out and fight.

I was relieved when, with one great final roar, the dancers all fell flat on the floor, their bodies nearly dovetailed into each other and the sticks laid out in a long straight line. Champion said that the dancers were mostly men who had lately come in from the kraals, the majority of them working as house-boys. I could see another line of young men in the red-bordered calico of domestic service filing in, each carrying a little bundle containing the precious trappings of tribalism.

As I looked it suddenly struck me that these splendid young men could be the grandsons of the Zulu warriors who inflicted such a terrible defeat upon British regular troops at the battle of Isandhlawana in 1879, killing with assegai and rifle 800 regular British soldiers and as many native levies. Did they ever recall those days of their great military power as they stooped to menial tasks under their white masters or were nagged in the kitchen by white housewives? How those Durban matrons would have stared to see how their docile house-boys spent their Saturday night!

I had lost all sense of time. I looked at my watch. It was well after eleven! It was a terrible moment—I had far more to fear than Cinderella. I remembered my note on the manager's desk which told him where I had gone. Suppose they sent police to fetch me out of here—if police dared to come. 'Take me to a telephone,' I shouted in Champion's ear. He read my face: he asked no questions. We rushed up to his office. I found the number but in the continuing din from below I could neither hear nor be heard. Champion guessed the danger: in a few minutes I was in the car with him being raced through the docks and slums—now mercifully empty—until I jumped out of the car and ran into the hotel. I rushed to the manager's room. There on his desk lay my note—unopened! Clearly he was having a night out! I felt faint with the realization of what might have been. My only defence was that I had not realized the extent of recent disorders, of how police and unofficial white men had lately used their revolvers on Zulu strikers with loss of life on both sides, nor had I any idea of the kind of entertainment Champion had prepared for me. . . .

# KATHERINE FANNIN*
# (Ethiopia and Kenya, 1934)

The following selections from articles written by Katherine Fannin are unique for the reportage they contain on Ethiopia. In 1935 the Italians conquered the country. Although they never completely subdued the indigenous people, the Italians installed a colonial government headed by the Duke d'Aosta. By 1939 Italy had joined Germany as part of the Axis pact, and the British in Kenya were concerned about the apparent arms buildup on their northern border. The Foreign Office in England was also worried about the Italian threat to their colonial territories bordering Ethiopia.

As a woman "traveler" Fannin was the ideal spy. She had met the Duke d'Aosta in 1934 when he was in Mombasa. Furthermore, she was the distant relative of a British counsel, Henry Salt, who had been posted to that country early in the nineteenth century. Armed with a copy of his book, *Voyage to Abyssinia,* published in London in 1814, and a small medal that Salt had been awarded by the Ethiopian government, Fannin set off for Addis. In early 1939, the Duke D'Aosta welcomed her with enthusiasm. He provided her with passes for open travel throughout the country—her stated aim was to retrace the steps of Henry Salt—and a car and a driver.

For three months Fannin toured what was then referred to as Abyssinia, noting the increasing arrival of mostly poor Italians from the south of Italy, carefully recording where they were settling and what agricultural pursuits they were carrying out. Her major interest, however, was the road system that the Italians built throughout the country; the buildup of troops; and the military operations in progress.

Only a woman would have been able to make a circuit of Ethiopia as Italy prepared for war. Fannin was brave in the extreme. When she returned to Kenya, Fannin reported her adventures and her findings to the British government and to the Kenya authorities. "She had the eye of an eagle and noted everything she saw." As a blooming reporter, Fannin also published her travel accounts in the *Sunday Post,* some of which are

---

*Katherine Fannin in the *Sunday Post* (Kenya) March 26, 1939.

NAIROBI, MARCH 26th, 1939.     Price: 10

## Some of the Contents

# KENYA LADY'S ABYSSINIAN JOURNEY

### 7,000 Miles on New Roads Across Italy's Colony.

About three months ago Mrs. C. G. Fannin, wife of Kenya's Surveyor-General, broadcast from Daventry a brief account of her safari from Mogadiscio through Addis Ababa to Djibuti. Since then Mrs. Fannin has spent more than two months in Abyssinia on her way back from Europe.

To a representative of the Sunday Post this intrepid lady gave a brief account of her unique journey. The main impression in Italy's new colony was one of successful pacification and astounding progress. Mrs. Fannin travelled over seven thousand miles by road in Abyssinia, and practically the whole of that distance was on newly constructed roads, either of tar macadam or well-made stone surface.

"Did you see any signs of the dissatisfaction that we read about so often?" I asked Mrs. Fannin.

"None whatever. The fact that over nearly seven thousand miles I travelled with one native driver and no escort, and had no adventure of any kind, shows how the natives have settled down under Italian rule."

"And these thousands of miles of roads—how have they been constructed in this short space of time?"

"Of course there are about 200,000 Italian workmen in the country. The natives themselves have never been accustomed to manual labour, and practically all the making of roads is done by the Italians."

**A Pioneer Journey**

"Which was the most strenuous part of the journey?"

Mrs. Fannin had no hesitation. "The trip across the Denkali desert from the Red Sea was a real adventure. No English woman has been across that way before, and I think only one Englishman. When I tell you the thermometer showed 180° in the shade, you will understand why. It is a desolate country of black rocks and lava, like the Rift Valley gone mad."

**Progress in Colonization**

Mrs. Fannin stayed for three weeks at Addis Ababa as the guest of the Governor, the Duke d'Aosta, and travelled from the capitals as a centre in all directions to see the work being done by way of colonisation.

She was much impressed by the magnificent country south-west of Addis Ababa, land so rich and with magnificent forests and grasslands and a fine climate. "Here the Italians plan to settle a million of their people."

"The natives are rapidly coming to appreciate the value of civilised rule. Red Cross work and new hospitals in all parts of the colony are being pushed on with praiseworthy speed. In agriculture experimental crops of tea, coffee, wheat, and all European produce are being planted and good results are being obtained. Under the tolerant rule of Duke d'Aosta the more recalcitrant tribesmen are beginning to settle down as law-abiding subjects."

Altogether this journey has given Mrs. Fannin an impression of steady progress and successful, well-organised colonisation.

# 23 Warships £20,00,000 Fo...

Singapore, Thursday. three British warship East Indies and China... £20,000,000 ...

---

## It's an Ill Wind

With the occupation of Czech territory by Germany the remaining portion of the textile industry which was not in Sudetenland passes into German hands. Czecho-Slovakia has exported considerable quantities of yarn and also cloth to European countries, especially Holland, at prices below Lancashire rates.

...that they are under the German financial system these Czecho-Slovakia manufacturers are expected to do yarns, especially to Holland.

*The Sunday Post with the article by Katherine Fannin*

excerpted below. Her interest was in the Italian community, in the modernization schemes, and in military matters. Thus we receive a view of the colonizers more than the colonized in reading excerpts from Fannin's travelogue. In terms of public consumption for the Kenya press, Fannin denied guerilla warfare persisted. "I travelled nearly seven thousand miles with a lone native driver and no escort, and had no adventures of any kind, [showing] how the natives have settled down under Italian rule." "The natives are rapidly coming to appreciate the value of civilised rule, Red Cross work and new hospitals in all parts of the colony are being pushed on with praiseworthy speed. . . . Under the tolerant Duke d'Aosta the more recalcitrant tribesmen are beginning to settle down as law abiding subjects."

On the Danikil desert, which she crossed, "that was an adventure. No Englishwoman has been across that way before and I think only one Englishman. When I tell you the thermometer showed 180 [degrees Fahrenheit] in the shade, you will understand why. It is a desolate country of black rocks and lava. . . ."

Fannin has been described as "loyal as could be. British before anything; utterly incorruptible." She had migrated to Kenya in the early 1930s, intending to marry a civil servant in Tanganyika but fell in love instead with Henry Fannin, who was then Commissioner of Lands in Kenya. When young, Fannin was a "handsome woman," which is how she appeared when she met the Duke D'Aosta in Mombasa, and later in Addis. She wrote well and was regarded as a good journalist. However, by the 1950's Fannin's life took a downward turn. First, having gained too much weight, she had difficulty walking, which limited her activities in Mombasa. Then she lost control over her mind. She died in the mid–1960s surrounded by more than sixty cats ("she loved cats"), and admired still by acquaintances for her spunk in deceiving the Italians back in 1939.

# Englishwoman in Abyssinia

I have just read in a paper printed in England an article on what the Editor imagines is the life of the Italian community now resident in Abyssinia. I say "imagines" because it is quite obvious from the rubbish he has written that he cannot, at any rate recently, have been in that country. Amongst other things he says "Even in big towns like Addis Ababa it is wiser not to stir out of your house after dark." As he has specifically mentioned Addis, perhaps a brief account of present conditions there will be of interest.

The town itself reminded me a little of Nairobi [Kenya]. It is widely scattered over rising ground, and backed by an attractive range of hills. From practically any part of it there are extensive and lovely views of plains, and distant extinct volcanoes. As most people are aware, the town is only about fifty years old. It is an incredible jumble of native huts, brand new stone buildings, wood and iron and shenzi plaster Abyssinian houses, Coptic churches—some in the picturesque octagonal form, one Copt cathedral in more conventional shape; cinemas, hotels, shops, banks, churches, a few excellent stone houses which previously belonged to foreign nationals such as the Legations which are now Consulates; various hospitals and schools, and a few new factories. The most striking feature of the actual town part of Addis is the central hill on which is the fortified Grande Ghebbie—the Emperor's (Menelik's) rambling wood and iron palace, a collection of rather indifferent smaller buildings, a Coptic chapel, barracks, arsenal, and a few mud huts all contained in a fairly high stone wall loopholed and barred with massive spiked gateways. Menelik's tomb is there, and the whole place is now sort of a museum which one can visit by asking permission of the Italians. . . . The Little Ghebbie is on another hill about a couple of miles away. This too is in a walled enclosure, and is the small modern and rather uninspired straight up and down two storey palace the Negus [Haile Selassie I] built himself. It is now the official house of the Governor General (the Duke d'Aosta) and two flags are flown there. One on the house itself is the picturesque blue white and gold Royal Standard of the House of Savoy; and the other, flown from a flagstaff in the grounds immediately before the main entrance is the green, white, and red national flag of Italy which of course (like our Union Jack) is flown on all public offices and Government buildings, and at all centres of Italian administration, even if the D. C's [District Commissioner] office is a tent or a small mud hut.

## THE NEW TOWN OF ADDIS ABABA

But the Italians are not going to do much to the present Addis—it is not worth it. Instead, they have made a magnificent plan of the new town, which is to arise a few miles south, and at a lower altitude. The present one is very nearly 9000 feet up, and quite definitely too high for real comfort. I do wish I could give illustrations of their town building proposals, of which I have four different plans all based on detailed topographical surveys. When these schemes have been completed the new Addis should be one of the most dignified and intelligently planned cities in Africa. . . . Native layouts are in this plan too, and have garden and open space amenities. . . .

## LIFE IN ADDIS

In the first place there are about thirty thousand Italian men, women and children now resident there. They represent practically every class and walk in life and follow much the same customs they do at home. People get up early, shops and offices open at about 8 a.m., work is until one o'clock when the majority eat their main meal of the day (chiefly mountains of spaghetti washed down with very good Chianti red or white). This is slept off until about 8:30 p.m., after which people return to their jobs. . . . At night they eat a small meal, and then the social part of the day seems to begin. It is quite extraordinary. People there then start off for the cinemas when most people here would be asleep. Lights are blazing everywhere, people sitting in cafes or at pavement tables, wireless and gramophones going, dozens of men and women walking cheerfully about taking the air. I used to ask my friends if they ever go to bed at all. . . . For three solid months I couldn't have averaged more than five hours sleep a night; I was having all the time to compete with total strangers (and foreigners at that) to speak a mixture of foreign languages, and to undertake really arduous journeys, and yet I loved every minute; was thoroughly happy and had the time of my life. So I have come back with another theory, and that is, if you are really enjoying yourself you can do with an incredibly small amount of sleep and feel no ill effects at all.

## WHAT SOME PEOPLE DO

I started to give a list of the different professions represented in Addis, both of men and women; but it developed into a catalogue so I am leaving it out. One post I feel I must mention though and a woman's job at that.

The Italian Government has appointed one very able and charming woman whom I got to know and to like immensely to a special office of the Native Political Affairs Department. Her work deals with every conceivable matter affecting the administration and welfare of native women and children, and she is the official liaison between them and the Government. I thought this an excellent idea; because being a woman herself she naturally has a much more just appreciation of women's problems brought to her for advice than any man could possibly have. On the various occasions I visited her in her office at Addis I always found her surrounded by bevies of Abyssinian women to whose requests, difficulties or complaints she listened with understanding and impartiality. It was obvious to anyone that she was both liked and trusted. I was told that her work is proving a valuable experiment; especially in gaining for the Italian administration the confidence of all classes of native women who now feel they have some one directly interested in their welfare. . . .

## A CONCERT AT THE VILLAGGIO SAVOIA

. . . I am going to enjoy myself (even if nobody else does!) by talking about various Italian social occasions in which I found myself involved during my wanderings in Abyssinia. The first entertainment was a Concert at Addis; a typical "in aid of" attended by the rank and fashion, so to speak, of Italian East Africa; with all the women in very grand and lovely gowns, long gloves and the contents of the family jewel cases. I blessed with a sixth sense which made me include my best dress and suitable garnishings in the most solid of my modest two and a half bits of luggage. . . .

The Concert was held in the large recreation hall of the 19th Regiment of Grenadiers at Villaggio Savoia and we were all in our places before the semi-State arrival of the Viceroy and H.R.H. the Duchessa. I was taken by friends, and found myself in a front-row side seat about 6 feet off the stage and with a fine view of the whole house. There were a couple of dozen very grand gilded and tapestried chairs, almost minor thrones, with ball and claw legs and high floral backs for the Governor-General and his entourage. [The chairs] looked too elaborate to be comfortable, but undoubtedly added to the elegance of the scene. Lovely flowers banked the stage, and someone with imagination had contrived faintly pink general lighting so we all felt we looked our best. The Consular Corps had the whole row of seats immediately behind the Royal party, and I observed with interest the dignified entry of the diplomats: those honest men sent abroad to lie for their countries; ours amongst them. The hall was brilliant with jewels and orders sparkling, and the whole place stiff with glittering uniforms. . . .

I sat, in silver gown and long white gloves. . . . After the concert we left in a crowd of brightly lit cars and I found myself being taken on to a succession of parties where people I didn't even know by name were perfectly charming to me. . . . It was all the greatest fun, with dancing to gramophones, midnight snacks of red hot chicken and a savoury spaghetti, and finally an exhilerating drive at 4 a.m. up an alarming road to see a famous view.

## THE OFFICERS' GYMKHANA

Another festive occasion was a daytime affair on the Racecourse. It was an invitation meeting. Similar to those held elsewhere it was very much a social occasion with everyone in their best, horses groomed and shining, native syces [grooms] proud of themselves and their charges representing everything from satin-coated race horses to sturdy pie-bald Abyssinian country-breds. It being a military show all officers were in uniform. There was a band, a grandstand bedecked with flags opposite the hardest jumps, and some of the gilded arm chairs that were used for the Concert for the Governor-General's party.

## A PRIVATE PARTY

A third occasion was a dinner party at a private house to which I was bidden at 8 p.m. My Italian hostess, both tallish, fair-haired and blue-eyed, had converted an Abyssinian house in Addis into a charming home with pale walls, lovely rugs, old pictures from Italy, and a collection of ancient weapons and shields. Upon arrival we guests were given largish glasses of very sweet vermouth and handed silver dishes of chocolate cream. After we had chatted a bit a very spick and span Eritrean native butler dressed in high-necked starched white jacket with brass buttons and white cotton gloves, announced dinner and we filed into a softly lit room with a long table decorated with Venetian glass fish and trails of flowers. Other native servants in white livery were standing behind the chairs. . . .

## THE ARTERIAL ROADS

When I am asked "What impressed you most in Abyssinia" I have one answer: the ROADS—first, last, and all the time. In the Italian view the cheapest and quickest method of opening up and settling a country is to establish as soon as possible a series of superbly built tarmac arterial roads capable of standing up to unlimited heavy traffic; to build a network of stone-ballasted all weather district roads to link up the arterial system, and from the start to construct on all routes bridges capable of supporting a minimum of twenty six tons, so they do not have to be rebuilt when districts develop.

The tarmac roads cost the equivalent of ten thousand pounds [fifty thousand dollars] a mile, and the Italian Public Works Director has carte blanche and direct orders from the home Government to complete the arterial system in the shortest possible time. . . .

These tarmac highways are about thirty feet wide, have solid stone foundations, sometimes as much as two meters in depth; are, then built up with a centre spine, and side buttresses of squared stone blocks, fitted in with graduated stone chips and rubble, finished off on top with a hand-laid mosaic of small flattish stones, sealed and waterproofed with a five inch coat of heat and wear-resisting bitumen, and finally re-inforced along the sides with solid earth banks. When all is ready they are practically inde-structible, and nothing short of an earthquake or a direct hit by a bomb, could make much impression on them. . . .

## THE UALCHEFIT PASS

Driving south-west on a tarmac racing track from Asmara in Eritrea to the River Taccazze that winds along the foot of the stupendous Tigre escarpment of the Semien, I passed through that Abyssinian "Canter-bury" the sacred village of Axum where a much revered Coptic Abuna— High Priest—has his little sixteenth century church; and where in the courtyard of the latter (women are not allowed in Copt holy of holies) I had the rare privilege of seeing the church's treasures. The grave and dignified "Chapter," a collection of polite and friendly Abyssinian priests, brought out for my inspection their wonderful God Book of Amhara, a parchment tome about the size of a bank ledger with massive gold covers, full of brightly coloured paintings of the lives of saints, martyrs, and of the Queen of Sheba, who is supposed to have come from Shoa. Ethiopian painting is curiously Byzantine in effect, and very childish in execution. But it has one delightful characteristic. All good people are drawn full or three-quarter face and look you in the eye with both of theirs. But un-desirables, Satan, dragons and such are always in profile; for you see, it is well known in Abyssinia that only the honest man can look the world in the face. (So now you know!)

I was also shown the elaborate gold and jewelled three-decker crowns worn on state occasions; a perfectly marvellous solid gold triptych ikon of the Virgin; a number of lovely gold and silver eight-pointed ceremonial crosses; and masses of beautiful embroideries, not local work, but gifts from Egypt and elsewhere. Abyssinians are devout Copts, and it is very interesting on Sundays to see the big picturesque congregations at their curious octagonal churches. All natives in Italian East Africa are of course absolutely free to worship as they please; and while the enormous majority are Mohammedan or pagan, well-known Copt monasteries such as Debra Tabor, Debra Libanos and others have a big following and are well supported.

Before I left Axum I took films of the Abuna and his "Chapter" grouped on the odd collection of stones known as the Coronation Chair. It put me in mind of some druidical relic; as did the hundred or so disordered monoliths standing in a nearby field. The Commissario told me that these and other Axum antiquities such as pillars with unidentifiable inspections had roused such interest amongst this country's archaeologists that already learned old beavers in Rome and Padua and other university towns are conducting spirited paper warfare in support of their own pet theories. . . .

After driving through plains and cultivation, and across the River Taccazze on the Gondar road, one suddenly comes to the fantastic upflung jumble of needle peaks and precipices of the Semien. Imagine chain after chain of violently eroded wild red sandstone mountains twelve to fourteen thousand feet high; sunless gloomy valleys covered in dense undergrowth; five thousand foot crumbling precipices and tables, and so far as one can see no way of reaching the top except by scrambling on hands and knees, or by flying. Two and a half years ago the only way over this formidable barrier which practically isolated Gondar, Lake Tana, and northwest Abyssinia was a dangerous and difficult mule track where one false step meant the end of one's earthly troubles, to say the least of it.

This February I drove up and over that ten thousand foot barrier on a wide superb roadway that is blasted out of a sheer precipice for some thousands of feet and is carried to the top on walls in a series of long zigzags and hairpin bends. Along the edge is a good wide stone balustrade, and I can tell you I felt extremely grateful for its presence! Half way up I sat on it (to un-dizzy myself) and swung my heels over eternity while I listened to the silvery whisper of a little Florentine fountain beside me. For there in that savage and pitiless country some Italian thinking of home has persuaded a tiny mountain steam to throw a feathery jet high into the clear air, and to tinkle into a little stone basin all garlanded and set about with terracotta flowers and dolphins beautifully carved and fashioned: a labour of love if there ever was one. . . .

Fifteen thousand Italian soldier road-builders made this military road, and made it in the face of enemy opposition; for when work began Abyssinians held all the surrounding heights. Even now for greater security civilian cars and lorries travel through this perfect ambush country in guarded convoys. I had to do so too. But beyond the top of the Pass is a lovely fertile plain stretching away to Lake Tana, and thirty miles or so along there is already a big settlement of Roman peasants ploughing the land, growing grain of various kinds, and building small houses; for this year they expect to be joined by their wives and children.

## THE DANAKIL ROAD

By no stretch of the imagination could this be called a military road, for it crosses an area where the Italians have never had any native trouble, and it is being constructed to connect the Red Sea port of Assab with Addis Ababa. As such it is one of great commercial importance and is one of the chief arterial roads.

In Dankalia another desolate, savage, and wildly difficult country has had to be traversed. . . . Nesbitt, the only English person besides myself who has so far crossed this extraordinary country, aptly describes it as resembling nothing but telescopic photographs off the moon. He is quite right: a veritable Abomination of Desolation but oddly fascinating. . . .

On my trip across Dankalia, I encountered a delighted and (to me) welcome illustration that when it comes down to brass tacks we are all— whatever our nationality—pretty much alike; as this example may show.

Driving along the tarmac in the middle of the wildly lonely desolate hell of lava boulders, what should I come upon but a struggling mass of lorries, some going right and some left like an elephantine set of lancers, and all in a thorough state of blasphemy while, from behind a barrier of empty petrol drums a cheerful gang took their ease in the shade of a steam-roller and passed the time in quip and jest. A very large and unnecessary board said ROAD CLOSED; and equally large and officious red arrows pointed one down truly discouraging deviations. There were tarmac sprayers about, but so far as I could see the road itself continued its lovely smooth blue way. So while the congested lorries sorted themselves out and bumped away to right and left, I stopped for a "tell" as we say in my native Devon, and to drink (in cold coffee) the healths of their respective majesties of Italy and England. All was friendliness and great goodwill, and when I was ready to leave, barrier and boards were moved aside, and I was politely waved through.

Before I left on my way to the road camp where I was to spend the night, I said to the cheerful foreman, "Between ourselves, why is this road closed?" and got the delicious answer: "Signora, do you think I am going to have people making horrible marks on my beautiful new asphalt! What do you think roads are FOR? I won't have my lovely tarmac ruined by their clumsy great lorries. They can go round."

I referred [earlier] to a settlement of Roman peasants who are cultivating the land on the high plateau beyond the Ualchefit Pass in northwest Abyssinia. They are married ex-soldiers, and as soon as their small houses are built, will be joined by their wives and families from Italy. At present the men live in sort of long communal barracks, and spend the day ploughing wide fields, breaking new land, planting grain, and experimenting with vegetables. . . . This particular settlement is at Kilomero 63 miles from Gondar, and is therefore a good long way from any big centre. It is also the so-called bandit country but nobody seems to worry about that. All work is done by the Italians themselves. . . .

In Italy a family is reckoned as a man, wife, and three children, and family settlement is being worked out on this basis. At present such settlement is being confined to married ex-service men with good records. They are drawn very largely from over-crowded agricultural districts in Italy, and therefore have a tradition of work on the land in their blood. Families are carefully picked so that only hardworking self-respecting folk are chosen for this scheme, and settlement is by districts; that is: all peasants settled in one area in Abyssinia will be from Apulia; and other from Venetia, and so on. This is being done deliberately so that settlers will not feel too strange or lonely in their new lives in Africa for they will hear their own country dialects spoken and have as neighbors those from their own parts of Italy. . . .

The Italians hope in time to settle very large numbers of their people in their Empire—perhaps millions. This, they contend, can be achieved only by the people themselves working. So in this Government scheme there is (and will be) absolutely no place for what might be called the "employer class of farmer." Italian peasant settlers are now their own farm labour, their own shamba boys, tractor drivers, ploughmen and everything else; while their women-folk look after the children, cook, and run the household generally. In other walks of life, too, work will have to be found for all, so I imagine you will get, on a large scale, conditions which obtain at present amongst the 800,000 men and women already in Italian East Africa. Italians themselves are doing every sort of job—farm hands, waiters and maids in hotels, and private houses; mechanics, builders and masons, road gangs, shop assistants, children's nurses, soldiers, cooks, little store and restaurant keepers, car and lorry drivers and a host more.

Who can say what problems, natives and otherwise, the Italian Government will have to face as have all white Administrations in Africa? And who can foresee the future of a big white population set down in this incalculable continent?. . . .

But to return to the present: I happen to come from a remote but lovely country district in England, and like most country-folk, have an affection for the land and for the people who live and work on it—whatever their nationality. Perhaps it was this reason that made me feel when I saw the sturdy friendly peasant families working so willingly on their little holdings, that I would like to wish them happy and peaceful lives in the new Empire of which all Italians are so proud, and for which (a fact often overlooked) all classes are having to make very real sacrifices.

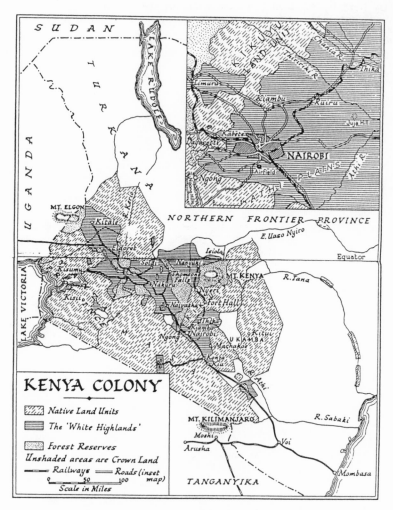

*Map of the Kenya Colony in the 1950s*

# JOCELYN MURRAY*
# (Kenya, 1954)

The last missionary we encounter was born in New Zealand. Jocelyn
Murray was originally trained as a teacher, not as a missionary who was
then placed in the classroom. Her early goal had been to study anthropology; thus her choice of Kenya was a natural one, since it brought
Murray into contact with a culture different from her own.

An entire century had passed between Hinderer's mission to Nigeria
and that of Murray in Kenya. Beginning in the late nineteenth century,
colonialism had wound its tentacles around almost the whole of the
continent. By the 1950s Africans everywhere were festering in rebellion, if
not yet in open resistance. Nigeria was teetering on the brink of independence. Kenya, however, was in the midst of a rising that was variously
referred to as "the Emergency," or "Mau Mau." This became a prelude to
a blood bath for especially the Christian Kikuyu, had not first an unsatisfactory military solution been imposed; and, more fortunately, later a
political one. Kenya gained her independence in 1962–63 while Murray
was still based in Kahuhia.

The roles of missionaries had changed, too. Africans were in charge of
their own churches. Some of the paternalism associated with the early
missionaries had been replaced with a modicum of equality between the
races. African teachers joined outsiders. Classes were segregated by gender, as were the teaching staff.

Hinderer was used up by her years in Africa, repeatedly succumbing to
the fevers. Advanced medical knowledge and a healthier upcountry climate made it possible for the youthful Murray to end her career as
missionary and begin a second life in America, where she studied for a
Ph.D. and wrote a history of the CMS *(Proclaim the Good News)*.

Perhaps the most dramatic change was psychological. Can one imagine
an Anna Hinderer distancing herself from the doctrinnaire approach of her
calling and questioning her role as missionary? In one of the final selections of her memoir, Murray looks back over her years among the Kikuyu

---

*Jocelyn Murray, "From Wellington to Kahuhia"—a memoir especially written for inclu-
sion in this volume, June, 1990.

and asks to what extent was she a missionary? Noting that she was part of a movement away from "missionary societies" to "mission partners," Murray concludes that, after twenty years, "understanding what I did, and why, is a process in which I am still involved."

Beyond her status as missionary teacher, Murray was an astute on-the-scene observer of one of the most complex indigenous uprisings in the late colonial period. In the memoir that follows, she recounts her memories of "The Emergency" from the mission station where she was posted.

# From Wellington to Kahuhia

It was a long way, in 1954, from Wellington, New Zealand, to Kahuhia, an educational mission station in the centre of Kenya.

It was a long way for me intellectually. I was twenty-four, an elementary school teacher with an arts degree in English and Philosophy. I had been brought up in a strict and rather narrow but happy home, with parents whose chief interest was their church. In 1953, when I decided to go to Kenya, there was then a "state of emergency" because of the "Mau Mau" rising, but little of that news reached New Zealand newspapers. I had never met or spoken to an African, or even a black American. I imagined myself to be without race prejudice but it had not yet been tested. I was not given training in a missionary institution, because women teachers were needed urgently for the expanding girls' intermediate boarding schools. Before I left New Zealand, the extent of my reading about Kenya were Negley Farson's travel book, *Last Chance in Africa,* and Jomo Kenyatta's *Facing Mount Kenya.* I was naive, idealistic, and ignorant; I had never before been out of New Zealand; I was also friendly, practical and curious. I had always wished to study anthropology but at that time in New Zealand the subject was not taught in any university (although the country had produced several outstanding anthropologists).

It was also, in terms of distances, a long way from New Zealand to Kenya. At the beginning of February 1954 I started my journey. One ship to Sydney, and a week's wait; a P. & O. steamer to Bombay, calling at every port around Australia's southern coasts, and Columbo; ten days in Bombay, and finally the old B.I. *Kampala* from Bombay to Mombasa, calling at Goa and the Seychelles. It took six weeks. On the last ship I met my first example of brutal and unconcealed racial prejudice (a settler from Southern Rhodesia). The last leg of my journey was the magic overnight train from Mombasa to Nairobi—getting into one's bunk just away from the palms of Mombasa, and waking up next morning to see the gazelle and giraffe on the plains east of Nairobi. After a night in Nairobi, seeing but barely comprehending the armed police and the white women wearing revolvers at their waists, it was north to Kahuhia, an early CMS mission station in Fort Hall (now Murang'a) in the Central Province, home of the groups involved in "Mau Mau"—the Kikuyu, Embu and Meru. When I woke up in my new home, I was truly and literally "facing Mount Kenya."

Kahuhia had been founded by British Anglican missionaries of the Church Missionary Society (CMS) in 1905. After a slow start the church had grown rapidly, and there were now dozens of churches with African clergy in several parishes, with a missionary Archdeacon and an African

Rural Dean at Weithaga, our neighbouring mission station, which was the pastoral centre. At Kahuhia there were three missionary women, all teachers, who lived together in the "Ladies'" house, and two missionary couples—the men ran a teacher training school for men. There was a day intermediate school for boys, two primary schools, and the girls' intermediate boarding school where I was to teach. The large stone church had an African clergyman, and he with his family and a number of teachers—all Kikuyu—lived on the station. And because of "the emergency" there were also a number of "refugees", both at Weithaga and Kahuhia. These were Kikuyu Christian men and women, with their families, who had refused to take the Mau Mau oath, and were therefore believed to be safer living at the mission station than in their individual homesteads. This was not an imaginary danger; a number of Kikuyu Christians had already been killed because they refused to demonstrate their solidarity with their fellow Kikuyu by drinking the blood of what they saw as a "pagan" oath.

I started teaching almost immediately, since the upper classes were taught in dormitories, well built with cement floors, but there was no electricity and no running water. Tanks collected rain water for drinking, and other water was pumped up from the creek in the valley by a ram. At that time the girls had only hurricane lamps to use after the swift African night came down without twilight just after 6 pm. We had pressure lamps as well, which gave good light but were a lot of work.

Our own house was also built of the local stone, with polished cement floors. We had an elderly man as cook, a housegirl, and a part-time laundry girl. There was also Kamau, the old gardener, who spent much of his time cutting the wood for the range and the fire which heated bath water. I was not, as a New Zealander, used to any servants, let alone four, but it did not take long to see that we could not have run the school without their help. Milk had to be boiled, food bought at local markets (for the school as well as for ourselves), clothes were ironed with a charcoal heated iron, lamps had to be cleaned, cement floors polished. The teacher on duty had to be down at the school by 7 am, and did not finish the evening rounds till 9 pm, and that was in addition to classroom work, administration, and all the extra bureaucracy of the "Emergency." At the beginning and end of term every girl in the school (since they were all Kikuyu) had to have a pass, signed by the district officer, so that she could go home and return. The district hospital was ten miles away and no vehicles—buses or lorries—were allowed on the roads, so any patients for the hospital had to be driven there in the mission car. We had no firearms on the station, and no armed guards, but there were watchmen who escorted us at night, with torches and spears (!) and we slept with whistles under our pillows. In the case of an attack on the station the church bell would have rung. We also had a Very pistol to call the local police in case of an alarm (since we had no radio or telephone), but the only time we tried to use it it would not fire. What we would have done if we had been attacked I do not know.

We never were attacked. Nor were any other missionaries, whether Catholic or Protestant (although I think a Catholic convent was once taken over, although nobody was hurt at all). We always believed that our lack of firearms was a protection, since settlers seemed sometimes to be attacked for their weapons. There was certainly nothing whatever to stop a gang coming in to the station, and although we had no guns, we had lots of food. One of our missionaries, the Schools supervisor, travelled constantly around the district visiting schools, and letting the teachers know in advance when he was coming. Once a month he carried quite large amounts of cash to pay the teachers, again giving notice. He was never attacked either, not even when he raised the alarm after an ambush in which the local District Officer was killed.

What does a missionary do? In my case, it was quite clear; my first and primary work was to teach in the Girls' School. I taught English, and History, and Scripture, and Home Economics, to the girls in the two upper classes. The girls were in their seventh and eighth years of schooling, and could have been as young as thirteen, but in fact were mostly seventeen or eighteen. In class I used English, but I was also directed to learn Kikuyu, and it was soon clear that to get to know the local people one needed to speak their language. The Sunday services at the parish church were all in Kikuyu. So my teaching load was reduced to give me time for study, and I spent time with an English-speaking teacher from the boys' school and an old retired Kikuyu clergyman who helped me with pronunciation. Kikuyu had been well studied by early missionaries, and by 1954 the whole Bible and a number of other books were published and available. During vacations we sometimes had lessons from the Anglican bishop in Kenya, Rt. Rev. Leonard Beecher, and his wife, Gladys Leakey, who had been born in Kikuyu country and spoke Kikuyu as her first language.

As well as teaching, and learning Kikuyu, I had two separate cultural adaptations to make. The first was to the upper middle-class life of the English missionaries; the second was to the culture of the Kikuyu Christians. Because of the Emergency it was not really possible to get to know the Kikuyu who were not within the mission orbit.

I am not sure if the missionaries I was with would have admitted that they lived as upper middle-class English, and at the time I hardly recognised it myself (I had never visited England then). Most of the men had a "public school/Oxbridge" background; some of the women had been to Girls' Public Day Schools—that is, they had been educated at private, not state schools. Our meals and mealtimes were those of English society of a

generation earlier. Later I had more Australian and New Zealand colleagues, and also English missionaries who came from different back-
grounds and saw no need to change their ways in Kenya, and life became a
little more informal. We did not, needless to say, live like the European
settlers, but a three-course meal served by the cook at 7 pm was very
different from what I had been used to in New Zealand.

In one way I was more fortunate than I knew. There was never a time
when African guests were not welcome in our house and at our table;
English-speaking teachers came to the "missionary" Bible study group. I
did not then know that on many mission stations this was not yet the case.
Although Kenya had no legal "apartheid" there was an accepted social
segregation which newcomers found it difficult to ignore.

My real introduction to the Kikuyu Christians came through the "fellowship meeting." The Christians who were part of the "East African
Revival movement" met weekly for hymn-singing, spiritual sharing, Bible
study and prayer, held at the church and in the vernacular. When I was first
taken by my colleagues, it was suggested that I should "give my testimony" which, through translation, I did. Afterwards one of the Kikuyu
men present, a leading Christian who was a *fundi*—a stone-mason, not a
teacher—told me that, like most of the missionaries, I was not a Christian!
This was a considerable shock. I had, without really knowing it, been
introduced to the East African Revival Fellowship, and was about to be put
through the "trial by testimony" which has happened to so many young
missionaries.

I had grown up in a Christian home, and had accepted my parents' faith
in a natural way. They were Baptists, and in my mid-teens I had been
baptised as a believer and become a church member. At university I had
gone through periods of intellectual doubt, but there had been no great
crises of faith or life. This was the case with very many missionaries. So
our testimonies were straightforward and rather dull. In the Revival something more was expected—guilt, struggle, brokenness—and a testimony
expressed almost as a formula. This was foreign to me, and it was many
years before I was "accepted."

But I soon grew to like, appreciate and then to love the men and women
whom I met through the Fellowship. As well as the weekly meetings,
every month or so there would be a "District meeting" when we would
spend a whole day, usually at a church/school site, with singing, testimonies, preaching, and communal meals outside on the grass, where I
learned to eat *njenga* and *ngima* and the delicious bean stews. As I
literally sat at the feet of the old Kikuyu women, and listened to what I
could understand, I began to learn about a kind of faith and love which
owed little to books, but which had been tested in living.

I met also the "confessors"—men and women who had refused to take the oath of allegiance to the nationalist movement the government called "Mau Mau", and who had been beaten and tortured and in risk of death because they refused. In our school dormitories was Teresa, whose father Andrew had died, and Apufia, whose uncle and aunt had been killed together. Our laundry girl, Esther, had been beaten and become deaf in one ear after being beaten. Rufus and Marian and their large family came from another mission at the far south of the district, near the forest, and they too had been beaten. Then there was Mwangi, the travelling evangelist, a former teacher, and Samueli, a pastor, who had been badly cut about and left for dead on the same night that Andrew died. The bishop had transferred him to a church in Mombasa, where he could recover himself in peace.

What was the conflict about? That was more difficult to find out. It was certainly about land. It did not take a long residence in Kenya to understand the resentment which the Kikuyu felt towards the white settlers who farmed the land they saw as their inheritance. It was about self-government, and reaction against racial prejudice, and the right to determine, themselves, what kind of country they lived in. But because I encountered the movement through Kikuyu Christians who rejected the traditional "pagan" oaths which the resistance movement asked them to swear, and also the violence to which the oath would have committed them, I saw the pagan aspects, and the violence, rather than the struggle against injustice and prejudice. The Revival Christians also refused to join the Home Guard and carry arms against the gangs, and were in thus consistent in their peace stand, although Christians already involved in the administration (like Chief Paulo of Njumbe) carried arms. On the lines of "those who are not for us are against us," this refusal to join the Home Guard and carry arms meant that the Revival Christians suffered from both sides—the Administrative forces and the gangs.

They later suffered, like most Kikuyu, from being forced to live in large fortified "villages," under the villagization programme which was aimed at controlling the people and especially preventing them from carrying food and supplies to the gangs in the forests. (Kikuyu traditionally lived in homesteads on their own land.) Christians who had "taken the oath," for whatever reason, were as liable as any other Kikuyu to be detained under the Emergency regulations. Since the Administration used informers, often former gang members, it was very easy for such men to get their own back on the Christians. Feuds within or between families, often over land, were fought out in this way, and the conflict which divided the Kikuyu from the rest of Kenya was also dividing them among themselves.

With the other missionaries, I was aware of this, but there was not on the whole a great deal of discussion about the larger aspects of the conflict. Individual missionaries, especially the Archdeacon and the Rural Dean in our area, and the Bishop and others in Nairobi, were much involved in securing justice for individual Kikuyu. The secretary of the Christian Council of Kenya, who had previous experience of conflict in the Middle East, made an important contribution, and a number of missionaries and African evangelists worked in the detention camps, and gave humanitarian and spiritual aid. But there seemed to be little *political* interest in what was going on.

Therefore we scarcely realised—I know I did not—that although the Kikuyu Christians were against the methods of the Mau Mau rebels, they were not against the aims of the movement. They too wanted self-government, the return of alienated land, the right to live under an independent government headed by one of their own people and not in a colony. It was only after Mzee Jomo Kenyatta, released from prison and then from detention, had gone home to Gatundu, that this began to dawn on us.

I have often thought about this in the years following, and especially after knowing more of what happened in a fairly similar situation much later, in Southern Rhodesia (Zimbabwe). There some missionaries became very much involved with the "freedom fighters"; some missionaries were also killed, whether because "caught in the cross-fire" or by intention is not always clear. Some missionaries also were neutral or opposed to political change. In Kenya missionaries were opposed to the violence of "Mau Mau", and were on the whole without sympathy towards its aims, although they defended the rights of the Kikuyu in general and were not against political independence when it came.

I feel now that we missed very real opportunities of discussing political issues with our students and Kikuyu friends, at a time when it would have been possible to do so. But what has that to do with being a Christian missionary? Surely teaching leading to conversion was what was required of us?

Yes. That was required of us, and as far as we could we co-operated with the church, which by the time I arrived in Kenya was already able to do such things itself. But I think the church—at any rate that part of it with which I was involved—had lost a vision of the wholeness of the Christian message, which it had once had. In the 1920s a missionary at Kahuhia, Handley Hooper, had helped and encouraged young local Christian men in their founding of the Kikuyu Central Association. At much the same time Archdeacon Owen, in the west of Kenya, became well-known (even notorious) among white settlers for his encouragement of young African politicians.

In fact, as I realised later, Christians in Britain were really more aware of the larger issues than we were—although we were the people "on the spot." There was something almost amounting to a conspiracy of silence on the part of Kenyan church leaders (mostly members of missionary societies) about the sometimes brutal treatment meted out by the government forces to the Kikuyu people, and about conditions in the internment camps. Protests were made in individual cases, but it was left to those in Britain to take up issues with the Colonial Office. This was more so in the earlier days of the Emergency; later on missionaries were more ready to protest.

One of the most memorable and difficult incidents came at the period in the Emergency when a number of so-called "terrorists" had surrendered. Some of the young European administrators (who seemed to have a fairly free hand) decided to use some of these men to identify others—as informers, in fact. But they added a macabre touch of theatre by dressing the "informers" in long hooded robes, and having the suspects pass in front of them. By rattling a tin containing beans the informers signalled suspects. This ceremony was known as "screening." One day we received a message that the next day our mission station was to be screened. We could not warn anyone. On the next morning the station was surrounded by soldiers and Home Guards, and every man, woman and child on the station—students, refugees, teachers, their families, domestic servants— were taken to the football field and made to pass before a group of white draped figures, who never spoke but rattled the tins under their robes. So the sheep were separated from the goats, and at the end of the day a group of men and women from the station, including several leading teachers, were taken away to the local police post for further questioning. Since capital offences included such acts as feeding a gang member (even if he was a close relative) we had plenty of reason for apprehension. In fact all those detained, except for one, were released after a few days, but it was an example to me of the rough justice which exists in conflict situations.

In early 1958, after I completed four years at the school, I was due for leave in New Zealand. Although I had visited a good deal in Kikuyu homes I had never been able to stay overnight anywhere, largely because of the Emergency regulations. I felt I could not return to New Zealand, where I would be asked to talk about my life in Kenya, without this experience, and I was finally given permission by the local Administrative Officer to stay at the home of a village headman whose daughter was a pupil in the school. That was a memorable visit, and it led to a friendship with the whole family which continues to the present day. By this time I could speak enough Kikuyu to be able to communicate even with the old grandmother, and I soon found (with my pupil and her friends) that one of the most enjoyable things to do was to sit around the grandmother's fire, eating roasted grain, and listening to her songs and stories.

When I came back from leave the Emergency was in effect over, and great changes were beginning. Within a couple of years Jomo Kenyatta had completed his prison sentence, but he was kept in detention, and agitation for his release began. It was at that time, and during the rejoicings which went on at the time of his release and return to his home at Gatundu, that I really felt isolated as a European. For during the Emergency the Kikuyu Christians had formed a group with us missionaries; we stood between the mass of Kikuyu on the one hand, and the administration and the white settlers on the other. Now the Christians had in many senses rejoined their people; once the violence was over they were free to express their wish for independence. This took me (and I think other missionaries also) by surprise; we could not totally share their aspirations, but nor could we identify with the whites who opposed them. I supposed observers would say that we felt threatened, and certainly it was clear that our future role was going to be very different.

In thinking back over this first period in Kenya (I worked there until 1967, with two further breaks) I ask myself in what sense I was a missionary. I was certainly sent by one church to work with another church. My official work was purely educational, allowing for the fact that we were a Christian school and I led prayers and taught Scripture classes. The church was already established, and preparation for baptism and church membership, when it involved our pupils, was done by the church and not by us as missionaries. I was in fact, though I did not understand it until much later, part of the movement away from "missionary societies" and toward "mission partners" or "fraternal workers", as such people are now often called. In my first years in Kenya there was an annual missionary conference. Almost all the CMS missionaries in the country, with a few invited African church leaders as visitors, met together for several days. There was a mission secretary, whose role seemed parallel to and sometimes more important than the bishop's role. Our welfare, physically and in other ways, was considered when postings were made.

Before I left Kenya all this was a thing of the past. The "mission secretary" had become a minor figure, and all real power in posting missionaries and in their welfare lay with the diocesan bishops—all nationals. In theory this was what we had been working towards; in practice it did not always work out so well.

I have now lived away from Kenya for over twenty years. It is no longer my home. But I will always be grateful that I was able to spend eleven years there. I received much more than I gave; understanding what I did, and why, is a process in which I am still involved.

# BIBLIOGRAPHY

Alexander, Caroline. *One Dry Season: In the Footsteps of Mary Kingsley.* New York: Knopf, 1989.

Baker, Anne. *Morning Star: Florence Baker's diary of the expedition to put down the slave trade on the Nile, 1870–73.* London: Kimder, 1972.

Baker, Samuel White. *Albert Nyanza Great Basin of the Nile.* London: Sedgwick & Jackson, reprinted 1962.

Barker, Lippino (Lady). "Letters from Africa." *Eclectic Review* 17:226–255.

Caddick, Helen. *A White Woman in Central Africa.* London: T. Fisher Unwin, 1900.

Callaway, Helen. *Gender, Culture and Empire: European Women in Colonial Nigeria.* Urbana: University of Illinois Press, 1987.

Cater, W. F. (ed). *Love Among the Butterflies: The Travels and Adventures of a Victorian Lady.* London: Collins, 1980.

Cecil, E. "Women Emigrants to Africa." *Nineteenth Century London* 51–71:1905.

Colenso, Frances Ellen. "Zululand," in *British Empire Series II.* London: Kegan, Paul, Trench, Truber & Co., Ltd., 1899.

Cushman, Mary Floyd. *Missionary Doctor: The Story of Twenty Years in Africa.* New York: Harper & Brothers, 1944.

Dinesen, Isak. *Out of Africa.* London: Putnam, 1937.

Dundas, Anne. *Beneath African Glaciers.* London: H. F. & G. Witherby, 1924.

Fannin, Katherine. *The Sunday Post,* March–April, 1939.

Forbes, Rosita. *From Red Sea to Blue Nile: Abyssinian Adventure.* New York: Macaulay Company, 1925.

———. *The Secret of the Sahara: Kufara.* New York: George M. Doran Company, 1921.

Gaunt, Mary E. B. *Alone in West Africa.* London: T. W. Lowrie, 1912.

Hall, Mary. *A Woman's Trek from the Cape to Cairo.* London: Methuen & Company, 1907.

Hewitt, Gordon. *The Problems of Success: A History of the Christian Missionary Society 1910–1942.* London: Hodder Christian Paperbacks, 1971.

Hone, Richard A., (ed). *Seventeen Years in the Yoruba Country: Memorials of Anna Hinderer gathered from her Journals and Letters.* London: Seeley, Jackson & Halliday, 1883.

Huxley, Elspeth. *Four Guineas: A Journey Through West Africa.* London: Chatto & Windus, 1954.

———. *Flame Trees of Thika.* London: Chatto & Windus, 1957.

Kingsley, Mary. *Travels in West Africa.* London: MacMillan & Company, Ltd., 1897.

———. "Life in West Africa." in *British Empire Series II.* London: Kegan, Paul, Trench, Truber & Co., Ltd., 1899.

Lugard, Flora Shaw (Lady). *A Tropical Dependency.* New York: Barnes and Noble, 1906.

Markham, Beryl. *West with the Night.* Boston: Houghton Mifflin, 1942.

Moir, Jane F. *A Lady's Letters from Central Africa.* Glasgow: James Maclehose & Sons, 1881.

Mott-Smith, May. *Africa from Port to Port.* New York: D. Van Nostrand Company, 1930.

Murray, Jocelyn. *Proclaim the Good News.* London: Hodder Christian Paperbacks, 1985.

Paulme, Denise, (ed.) *Women of Tropical Africa.* Translated by H. M. Wright. Berkeley: University of California Press, 1960.

Perham, Margery. *African Apprenticeship: An Autobiographical Journey in Southern Africa in 1929.* New York: Africana Publishers, 1974.

Rodwell, Edward. "The Way It Was." *Standard* (Kenya), March 20, 1983.

Romero, Patricia W. *E. Sylvia Pankhurst: Portrait of a Radical.* New Haven: Yale University Press, 1990.

Shreiner, Olive. *Thoughts on South Africa.* London: T. Fisher Unwin Ltd., 1923.

Stevenson, Catherine Barnes. *Victorian Women Travel Writers in Africa.* Boston: Twayne Publishers, 1982.

Strobel, Margaret. "Gender and Race in the Nineteenth- and Twentieth-Century British Empire." In *Becoming Visible: Women in European History,* edited by Renate Bridenthal, Claudia Koonz, and Susan Stuard. Boston: Little Brown, 1987.

———. *European Women and the Second British Empire.* Bloomington: Indiana University Press, 1991.

Summers, Carol, "Intimate Colonialism: The Imperial Production of Reproduction in Uganda, 1907–1930." Paper presented at the Johns Hopkins University Atlantic Seminar, April 26, 1988.

Warner, A. "British Central Africa," in *British Empire Series II.* London: Kegan, Paul, Trench, Truber & Co., Ltd., 1899.

(Windsor) Marie-Louise, H. H. *Letters from the Gold Coast.* London: Methuen & Company, 1925.

Winternitz, Helen. *East Along the Equator.* New York: Ballantine Books, 1987.